TORONTO
REBORN

TORONTO REBORN

DESIGN SUCCESSES AND CHALLENGES

KEN GREENBERG

FOREWORD BY DAVID CROMBIE

DUNDURN
TORONTO

Cover image: Sophie Paas-Lang
Printer: Marquis

Library and Archives Canada Cataloguing in Publication

Title: Toronto reborn : design successes and challenges / Ken Greenberg ; foreword by David Crombie ; afterword by Zahra Ebrahim.
Names: Greenberg, Ken, author. | Crombie, David, 1936- writer of foreword. | Ebrahim, Zahra, writer of afterword.
Description: Includes bibliographical references and index.
Identifiers: Canadiana (print) 20190053240 | Canadiana (ebook) 20190053291 | ISBN 9781459743076 (softcover) | ISBN 9781459743083 (PDF) | ISBN 9781459743090 (EPUB)
Subjects: LCSH: City planning—Ontario—Toronto—History. | LCSH: Toronto (Ont.)—Buildings, structures, etc. | LCSH: Land use—Ontario—Toronto. | LCSH: Urban renewal—Ontario—Toronto —History. | LCSH: Cities and towns—Growth.
Classification: LCC HT169.C22 T584 2019 | DDC 307.1/1609713541—dc23

1   2   3   4   5   23   22   21   20   19

Conseil des Arts du Canada   Canada Council for the Arts

Canadä

ONTARIO ARTS COUNCIL
CONSEIL DES ARTS DE L'ONTARIO
an Ontario government agency
un organisme du gouvernement de l'Ontario

We acknowledge the support of the **Canada Council for the Arts**, which last year invested $153 million to bring the arts to Canadians throughout the country, and the **Ontario Arts Council** for our publishing program. We also acknowledge the financial support of the Government of Ontario, through the **Ontario Book Publishing Tax Credit** and **Ontario Creates**, and the **Government of Canada**.

Nous remercions le **Conseil des arts du Canada** de son soutien. L'an dernier, le Conseil a investi 153 millions de dollars pour mettre de l'art dans la vie des Canadiennes et des Canadiens de tout le pays.

VISIT US AT

dundurn.com | @dundurnpress | dundurnpress | dundurnpress

Dundurn
3 Church Street, Suite 500
Toronto, Ontario, Canada
M5E 1M2

For my grandchildren, Martin, Isaac, Hana, and Sara, and for all the children who will inherit this extraordinary city

The best plans are those that liberate other people's plans.

— Jane Jacobs

As we navigate the complex heterogeneous city, we experience the indissoluble layering of different times and places and the simultaneous juxtaposition of elements from disparate worlds. Linear chronology and spatial separation are fractured. There is no clear before and after or here and there. The fusion and contrast of different elements underlines the uniqueness of each moment, overcoming preconceived dichotomies and incompatibilities. The combination of coincidences bears witness to ever-evolving life.

— Adapted from Meret Meyer, "'Total Art' and the Notion of Modernism in the Work of Chagall"

Contents

MAPS

DOWNTOWN

1. St. Lawrence Historic District
2. Wellington Place
3. Regent Park
4. Queens Quay
5. Bentway
6. Leslie Street Spit
7. Lower Don River
8. John H. Daniels Faculty of Architecture, Landscape, and Design, University of Toronto
9. Ryerson University
10. Quayside
11. Corktown Common
12. Trillium Park
13. Berczy Park
14. Sugar Beach
15. Sherbourne Common
16. George Brown College
17. Ontario Place/Exhibition Place
18. Allan Gardens
19. Nicholson Lane
20. Stackt
21. King Street Pilot

SUBURBAN CONTEXT

a. Mississauga City Centre
b. York University
c. Thorncliffe Park
d. North York City Centre
e. St. Clair and Old Weston Road
f. Main and Danforth
g. Eglinton Avenue plazaPOPS
h. Meadoway

Foreword

There can be little doubt that Toronto is going through an extraordinary, perhaps even revolutionary, time and experiencing profound change. The city is in the midst of a long period of massive growth. The population of Toronto is increasing at a rapid pace, and with the astonishing development of a huge number of condominiums and other forms of housing, the city is becoming denser and more crowded. While these changes have helped to make the city richer, economically and culturally, they have also put stresses on Toronto's infrastructure, physical and social.

Along with the growth and changes in the city's population, there has been a dramatic shift in the working world in Toronto. The old industrial backbone of the city's economy is largely gone. Technological innovation has ushered in a mesmerizing digital universe and a new age of artificial intelligence — and the jobs that go with them. A greatly expanded service economy is also part of this mix. The changing nature of work, accompanied by growing economic inequality, is placing new demands on the city's shared assets and commitment to fairness and opportunity.

Globalization of markets continues, while the great challenge of climate change re-enforces the rise of a greener economy. In line with this, Toronto has, over the past half century, had a sea change in its attitude toward nature and its natural heritage. While still committed to a path of progress rooted in the exploitation of nature for its raw material wealth, Torontonians have begun to embrace the notion that humans are part of nature and not separate from it. And that it follows that economic and ecological issues and policies are not mutually exclusive but are connected and interdependent.

Our understanding of community and its potential has undergone a similar renaissance. We live today in a global movement of peoples — from continent to continent, from country to country and countryside to city. Nowhere has this phenomenon had greater impact than in Toronto. Waves of migration, especially since the Second World War, have recast the demographic basis of the city, requiring Torontonians to broaden their comprehension of human diversity and search for new ways to widen the circles of social inclusion.

These historic challenges to the city's economy, ecology, and sense of community, and its responses to them, are reshaping the idea of Toronto and its place in the world. While change is never easy, for Toronto it has arguably been its lifeblood, the secret sauce if you will, forging our own unique strengths and character.

Throughout Toronto's history, times of great change have brought out the city's best as Torontonian's reimagined themselves. Indeed, the city has been this way before: industrialization that came with the arrival of the railroad in the mid-nineteenth century collapsed time and space in a way formerly unknown, fundamentally altering the city and spurring new thinking on the design and function of an urban Toronto. Later innovations in transportation and communication — the car, radio, television, and industrial production and distribution — have continued the transformation, also reminding citizens that economic opportunity is most often why people come to Toronto and why they stay. All of this has driven new generations to devise how best to hold on to the essential habits of mind of the old world order, while tooling up for a new one.

Toronto's history has similarly been helpful in fostering the potential to engage profitably with the new age of ecological sustainability. Today's always-evolving understanding of nature in our lives did not come full-blown from some institute of learning. We have been able to benefit from an exceptional legacy of thinking and doing by earlier Torontonians.

From the First Peoples to the preservationists of the nineteenth century and the conservationists of the twentieth century, these deep and rich perspectives continue to inform the environmental and sustainability movements of our own time, and influence public debate on Toronto's ecological future.

Toronto, of course, has always been a gathering place for people, and, consequently, it has an extraordinary tradition of understanding the crucial importance of community life. Torontonians have learned that communities are not only physical places; they are the psychological spaces that help people fashion answers to the most fundamental and personal questions throughout their lives: Who am I? Where do I belong? How do I behave? Human diversity has become the defining characteristic of Toronto. Not only as it absorbs thousands of newcomers every year, but as it charts new courses in embracing the gamut of human experience and personal expression.

Change and our response to it, in turn, impacts the development of our public realm — that compendium of public institutions and services that serve citizens both individually and collectively. Though often simply taken for granted, the determined investment in this connective tissue between the private worlds of Torontonians and the greater community is integral to defining the city. It is the glue that holds Toronto together, creating the sinews of civic community day and night, 365 days a year. It is an essential platform for the city's economic growth, environmental sustainability, and socially cohesive communities. And most importantly, it roots Torontonians in a commitment to equality of opportunity and social peace as the city moves forward. The constant shaping and reshaping of the public realm in Toronto requires each generation to reimagine, reinvent and reinvest in it. As William Thorsell, former editor of the *Globe and Mail* recognized, "the public realm in Toronto strengthens the definition of the possible and deepens the sense of the human. Toronto's strength has been — the value of its neighbourhoods, the appreciation of its cultures, the requirements of social justice, the quality of its infrastructure, the wealth of its ethnicities, the power of community, the depth of education and the complexity of its social life."

The unfolding story of Toronto is much like the history of Toronto: it is about change and the persistence of things and the magic created when

Preface

I wrote most of this book prior to June 7, 2018, the date that Ontario elected a Progressive Conservative government led by Doug Ford, giving it a resounding majority. Since the Ford government took over, there has been a dizzying succession of "shock and awe" moves that will have direct and indirect consequences for Toronto, and that are impossible to ignore.

Most dramatically, and without warning, the Ford government decided that it would slash the size of the Toronto City Council in half, rejecting the city's decision, based on years of study, to add more councillors in order to better balance voter representation in the city's wards. The decision undermined the city's presumption of a certain right of self-determination — one enshrined in custom, if not in law. A generally understood respect for local government and civic democracy, largely if not always respected in practice by the provincial government, had been frontally assaulted. It was the brutality of the process that most shocked Torontonians.

There was an underlying antiurban tone in Conservative messaging leading up to the election, with the PCs employing wedge politics and playing on negative stereotypes to exaggerate perceived differences between city and rural dwellers. Myths were perpetuated and divisions fostered, leaving a deeply polarized electorate. The Ontario political landscape was skewed along geographic lines. Indeed, a map showing which ridings elected which parties is instructive — the significant urban-rural divide is clearly evident. Not only Toronto, but cities across the province tended to elect "progressive" candidates, whereas rural ridings, some suburban ones, and small-town Ontario favoured Conservatives.

While the PC margin of victory was strong in terms of seats won, it was not so convincing in terms of the popular vote. The PCs won only 40 percent of the popular vote (there was a 58-percent voter turnout), and so a mere 23 percent of the electorate actually voted for them. However, because of the "first past the post by riding" rules governing elections in Ontario, the Conservatives were able to elect a solid majority of seventy-six of the 124 MPPs.

Many of the underlying tensions I will describe in this book were brought to the fore and exploited in the election. Appeals to "family values" expressed a coded desire to turn back the clock to an imagined simpler time, when many of the complexities of contemporary life could be ignored. Many of the ways in which society is evolving (often most evident in cities) — greater acceptance of gender differences, increasing acknowledgement of environmental challenges and of the need (and desirability) to move from car dependency to new forms of mobility — were painted as threatening, and city dwellers were demonized as "out-of-touch downtown elites."

In the winner-take-all situation, the provincial government seems to have come away with a belief that it has a mandate to put the City of Toronto in its place, both with direct actions (such as reducing Council) and by pulling Toronto back from many of the progressive initiatives it has been pursuing. If the forced amalgamation of Toronto with its postwar suburbs in 1998 (which will be returned to later) was Act One in that provincial government's effort to contain and constrain Toronto, then the seemingly punitive cutting of Toronto City Council from forty-seven to twenty-five councillors — an action that was never mentioned by the Conservatives during the provincial election campaign — was Act Two.

What this election did, among other things, was return to sharp focus a particular piece of nineteenth-century history that haunts Canadians still. The British North America Act was passed by the British Parliament on March 29, 1867, to create Canada as a new, self-governing federation, consisting of the provinces of New Brunswick, Nova Scotia, Ontario, and

Quebec. At that time, 80 percent of the population in those provinces was rural. Cities were relatively small and were not considered to be politically competent. Reflecting that perception, Section 92(8) of the Act states: "In each Province the Legislature may exclusively make Laws in relation to … Municipal Institutions in the Province." Local governments from that point on have been referred to as "creatures of the provinces." This was not a radical departure; it simply enshrined what had been generally accepted up to that point. (The BNA Act was superseded by the Canada Act of 1982; however, the status of municipalities vis-à-vis provinces was not changed.)

Today, of course, the urban-rural proportions are reversed. As the fourth largest city in North America, with 2.6 million residents, the City of Toronto is more populous than six of the provinces — Manitoba, New Brunswick, Newfoundland and Labrador, Nova Scotia, Prince Edward Island, and Saskatchewan. Yet, in law, Toronto's city government still functions without much status, existing at the pleasure of and subject to the will of Queen's Park.

In its May 16, 2016, report, the Toronto Ward Boundary Review recommended an increase in the number of wards, from forty-four to forty-seven, a decision stemming from the recognition of the growing size and complexity of the city. Some city wards had grown 30 to 45 percent above the average ward population since the previous review in 2000. Approved in November 2016 by City Council after public consultations held over a two-and-a-half-year period, the decision to implement the report's recommendations was an important step in the city's ongoing commitment to local democracy. Many new candidates began campaigns, leaving their jobs, raising funds, and beginning to canvas. Most importantly, perhaps, the change in boundaries would probably have resulted in a Council more reflective of the city's growing diversity.

Then, out of the blue, came the bombshell news that the PC government planned to cut the size of the council, leaked on Thursday, July 26, 2018. The following day, Doug Ford made it official. He announced that Bill 5 — the plan to reduce Toronto Council ahead of the October 22, 2018, vote — would align municipal wards with federal and provincial ridings to "streamline the decision-making process at city hall and save $25 million." The move immediately drew outrage from Council members and would-be councillors who had put their hats in the ring, and was condemned by citizens at many town hall meetings. Most disturbing was the timing — made mid-election, without any prior consultation or warning.

This was a particular attack on Toronto, as it turned out that the reduction in the size of Toronto's council would not be mirrored in any of the other municipalities in the province. As a result of the decision, well over one hundred thousand Toronto residents would be represented by a single councillor, whereas in other municipalities councillors generally represent significantly fewer constituents. An extreme example: in the riding of Leeds-Grenville, represented by the PC minister of municipal affairs Steve Clark, there are ninety-six councillors for a population of seventy thousand people, or one councillor for every 729 residents.

It was hard to miss the personal animosity the premier displayed toward the city, where he had served one term as a councillor from 2010 to 2014 when his late brother, Rob, was mayor, and where he had run unsuccessfully for mayor in 2014. In language that was harsh, partisan, and hyperbolic, he called Toronto the "most *dysfunctional* political arena in the country," and said the only people fighting his ruling were special interest groups and left-wing councillors hoping for a "free ride" on the backs of taxpayers. "They're just worried about a job," he claimed.

Leaving aside the heated rhetoric, there remains a critical question, one that flows from the BNA Act: Who should decide on a fundamental issue like the size of a city's council? The province, or the city itself and its elected representatives? The answer should be clear. And in almost any other jurisdiction, it would be. Try to imagine, for example, this scenario: a New York State governor suddenly announces that he is going to slash in half the number of elected representatives in New York City, the country's largest metropolis. To do so (as Ford later revealed he was willing to do), the governor declares that he or she is prepared to override the U.S. Constitution. Inconceivable? A bad movie plot? But this was exactly what happened in Ontario.

A roller coaster of uncertainty and chaos followed Ford's announcement. On August 20, City Council voted to proceed with a legal challenge to Bill 5 in Ontario Superior Court, on the grounds that the provincial government's decision to introduce sweeping reforms to Toronto ward boundaries during the campaign violated constitutional freedoms. It was argued that Premier Ford's action represented a capricious and arbitrary action in the middle of an ongoing election that violated the Canadian Charter of Rights and Freedoms.

An initial court ruling on September 10, by Judge Edward Belobaba, confirmed this position, deeming Premier Doug Ford's council-cutting Bill 5 unconstitutional. In his written decision, he stated that "passing a law that changes the city's electoral districts in the middle of its election and undermines the overall fairness of the election is antithetical to the core principles of our democracy." This momentary victory was short lived, however. Almost immediately, Premier Ford condemned the ruling and said that his government would reintroduce Bill 5, invoking the notwithstanding clause of the Charter of Rights and Freedoms in order to get around it.

This determination to use the notwithstanding clause was potentially even more threatening to the city than the legislation itself. The dramatic step would make Ford the first Ontario premier to use the clause, which allows government, in the most extraordinary circumstances, to create laws that operate in spite of certain Charter rights that those laws appear to violate. Premier Ford threatened to use the clause again in the future. Toronto's impotence in the face of this and other future issues was truly revealed.

Ultimately, on September 18, with a little over a month to go before the election, a panel of three Ontario Court of Appeal justices rejected Justice Belobaba's ruling against Bill 5. Their ruling acknowledged that the bill introduced in mid-election disrupted the campaigns that were already underway, that it was undoubtedly frustrating for candidates who had started campaigning with a reasonable expectation that they would be operating under a forty-seven-ward platform, but ultimately concluded that "unfairness alone does not establish a Charter breach." In other words, fair or not, reasonable or not, the 1867 legislation that makes cities the "creatures of the provinces" is the law.

So, following two months of uncertainty and considerable animosity between Queen's Park and Toronto City Hall, Toronto headed to the polls to elect a Council slashed by twenty-two seats.

This was a rude awakening for the city. In dramatic fashion, this struggle revealed that there is a serious piece of unfinished business. Canada is a modern, urban nation, in which 80 percent of its citizens live in a handful of big-city regions such as Toronto, and yet these urban areas are still governed by legislation passed over 150 years ago that undermines their legal status and their citizens' capacity for self-determination.

While, as of this writing, it's still unclear why Ford believed reducing the number of Toronto city councillors to be so important that he was willing to use the parliamentary "nuclear option" — the notwithstanding clause — to ensure passage of a bill to effect that change, what seems to have motivated his decision is his vision of the role of cities and city government — a vision that is vastly different from the consensus amongst Torontonians themselves. The provincial government is operating from a core conviction that less government is better, and that the least is best. By shrinking Council, Doug Ford's Conservatives were not only reducing the number of civic representatives available to serve Torontonians, they were also attempting to shrink the services that the government could provide.

This desire to decrease government provision of services is buttressed by the Ford government's view that as many of these services as possible should be privatized. In addition, the government doesn't place a high value on extensive citizen engagement; reducing the size of the "dysfunctional council" (too much debate) and centralizing power is seen as more efficient. According to this view, a Toronto hallmark — the close and personal relationship that constituents have with local councillors that helps to ensure, at neighbourhood level, citizen input on issues such as development and the delivery of local services — becomes expendable.

While most often justified as budget-cutting measures in aid of deficit reduction, the impetus for cutting services runs much deeper. Ultimately, the PCs' belief system values self-reliance over a system that sustains a collectivity of mutually supporting individuals and families, all of whom benefit from their combined human potential. These different core values drive entirely different kinds of accounting: one focuses on short-term, individual bottom lines (ten cents less per litre at the gas pump, a buck a beer); the other takes a longer view, seeing the benefit of improving life for all citizens, emphasizing solidarity, equal rights, access to services, and the importance of shared life in public spaces — values stressed elsewhere in this book.

This divergence in goals and perspectives raises profound questions for Toronto. Can the most diverse city in the world continue to be a place of upward mobility and self-actualization for new arrivals — and those already here — if we take away the supports that open paths to success for those who are struggling? Do we have any responsibility for our fellow citizens, or do we become an atomized society with little sense of social adhesion beyond family and clans? And how does this shift in values manifest itself on the ground?

This tension is now being played out across a number of fault lines. And these substantive issues must be the focus of close scrutiny and attention. A first may be the goal of social inclusion, resisting the global tidal pull of economic polarization. In the summer of 2018, Doug Ford commissioned financial consultants Ernst & Young to prepare a report on how his government could achieve "efficiencies" to fulfill his oft-repeated vow to cut $6 billion from the provincial budget. This report provided no easy fixes. In fact, it confirmed that the bulk of provincial spending goes to services that Torontonians care deeply about: public health care and education. The options that were presented, however, could dramatically alter how those services are delivered. These two essential (and provincially funded) services are crucial underpinnings for social equity in a large and increasingly diverse city that is already wrestling with economic disparities.

As events unfold, a troubling pattern is appearing, one with significant consequences for the city. The PCs have declared that Ontario is "open for business," and they have backed up this claim with actions designed to keep wages and benefits low while introducing tax cuts that disproportionately benefit corporations and wealthier individuals. An initial blitz of provincial initiatives includes the cancellation, midstream, of the three-year basic-income pilot, which had been helping four thousand Ontarians; axing the scheduled move to a $15-an-hour minimum wage; and "getting rid" of the previous government's labour reforms, which increased sick day benefits and paid vacation entitlements, and offered protection for temp agency workers. Needless to say, these actions will increase poverty rates in the province and exacerbate income polarization.

Addressing housing affordability, one of the most serious challenges the city is facing, will require significant involvement from all three levels of government. While the federal government has made affordable housing a top priority, it is not yet clear how the Ford government will respond to this urgent need for provincial funding and support.

Eliminating independent review of its actions in many key areas, the provincial government has scrapped the Environmental Commissioner of Ontario and the Ontario Child and Youth Advocate, moving these critical roles into the office of the Auditor General. Initially it attempted to do the same with the French Language Services Commissioner (although a hasty retreat was forced regarding the latter by major backlash).

In an editorial in the *Toronto Star*, columnist Martin Regg Cohn has persuasively argued that the Ford government also seems to be mounting an attack on the young. In addition to opportunities for sustainable employment, education itself is on the chopping block. The Conservatives have withdrawn previously promised funding for three new post-secondary satellite campuses, which were to be located in Markham, Milton, and Brampton, some of the region's fastest-growing suburban communities, as well as funding for the Universtiy of Windsor and the Ryerson law school.

Shortly thereafter, the Conservative government also cancelled plans for a new French language university in the province, undermining a basic national commitment to bilingualism for the large Franco-Ontarian population. At the other end of the age spectrum, early childhood education was also dealt a blow when moves to enlarge publicly funded daycare in licensed and supervised facilities were replaced with grants to individuals — a practice that often results in families in need foregoing licensed child care and having to resort to non-professional babysitting.

The city's drive to foster social inclusion, gender equality, and awareness of the dangers of the digital landscape amongst the young is being thwarted by government moves like the scrapping of the updated 2015 sex education curriculum and reversion to the 1998 syllabus, which predates legalized same-sex marriage, LGBT human-rights protections, and social media. The provincial government's move is now facing court and human-rights challenges and is stirring a backlash among students themselves; in the meantime, Toronto schools are having to negotiate a very unsettled educational environment.

The natural environment is also under threat. Toronto had set itself the goal of being one of the world's most sustainable cities, launching a variety of initiatives related to energy consumption, carbon emissions, and climate change readiness. Doug Ford, however, campaigned to end carbon pricing, calling it a "government cash grab" that does "nothing for the environment," and the province has gutted most of its climate change programs. By extricating Ontario from its cap-and-trade environmental alliance with Quebec and California, the Conservatives have destroyed an arrangement that brought in $1.9 billion annually to bankroll greenhouse-gas-reduction initiatives, with an enormous cost penalty, and replaced it with a dubious Climate Change Action Plan that does not put a price on carbon emissions and will impede Ontario's embrace of the green economy.

The majority of this cap-and-trade money was funding energy-efficiency programs in communities like Toronto — in schools, public housing, transit, and hospitals — and it was working. Ontario's greenhouse gas emissions in 2016 were the lowest since reporting began in 1990, and by 2014 the province had met its emissions-reduction target of 6 percent below 1990 levels. And all while the economy and population grew. This achievement enhanced Toronto's reputation for environmental initiatives and drew in foreign investment.

Another major challenge for the city is the need to move away from auto dependence and deal with our major deficit in transit investment and active transportation. The province is pursuing a plan to upload the TTC (Toronto Transit Commission) to the provincial transit agency, Metrolinx, which could have ominous implications. Scarce resources needed for expansion of the transit system within the city may instead be allocated to fund subways in far-flung, low-ridership areas — areas, not coincidentally, where the PCs enjoy substantial political support. Another threat to public transit is the provincial government's irrational aversion to light rail technology, an aversion that is based on the mistaken belief that light rail impedes automobile traffic. This privileging of cars is also at the root of the PCs' resistance to expanding Toronto's network of protected bike lanes.

Initially, it even seemed the PCs were preparing to open the Greenbelt to allow for low-density sprawl. That idea was seemingly shelved in response to serious pushback from a broad coalition of environmental groups, but then Bill 47, the "Open for Business Act," was abruptly introduced, allowing companies to override important environmental protections, without consultation or public notice, including the Clean Water Act, the Great Lakes Protection Act, the Greenbelt Act, the Lake

Simcoe Protection Act, the Oak Ridges Moraine Conservation Act, and the provincial regional land use Places to Grow Act.

The Toronto waterfront, and in particular Ontario Place, are in the government's sights. Local residents may be excluded from the decision-making process about the future of those lands, and there is worry that local needs will be ignored. Renewed musings about the government's openness to a casino resort have also caused alarm. A sudden and bizarre fire sale by Ontario Power Generation (OPG) of the monumental Hearn Generating Station and its strategic sixteen-hectare site in the Port Lands to a major Conservative party donor for a paltry $16 million has raised additional alarms about the government's commitment to long established revitalization plans for the waterfront. Threats to "fix" Waterfront Toronto, seizing on some damaging and in many cases inaccurate conclusions in the provincial Auditor General's report and the firing of a number of board members, have put that agency and its ongoing work in the Port Lands in some jeopardy.

As this provincial government's plans unfold, they will undoubtedly influence the shape of the city, its ability to thrive and prosper, and ultimately, the quality of life it can offer its citizens. These are serious headwinds the city is battling, and it remains to be seen how far Toronto will be pushed off course in its attempts to become a successful, prosperous, sustainable, and equitable city for all.

But for reasons I will elaborate later, I remain persuaded that the city's forward momentum, its strength in human capital, its entrepreneurial and social energy, and its desire to move in progressive directions will prevail.

Toronto may be temporarily hobbled by all these troubling moves (and there will certainly be more), but it is hard to imagine that it will spiral into decline or lose its drive. It is too important, too dynamic, and too resourceful to be repressed. Toronto's critical mass and bench strength will enable it to continue to move forward on all of these fronts; perhaps with setbacks and lost opportunities, but forward nonetheless.

The stakes were already high and have now grown higher, but I believe there are workarounds that will enable the city to advance in key areas, addressing such things as inclusion and social equity, environment, mobility, and housing affordability. In fact, this set of challenges may push the city into action in new ways, forcing it to forge new alliances and find new modes of operation. Necessity, as they say, is the mother of invention.

The current friction with the provincial governments should not, however, cause the city to see itself as an island. In the long run, the city needs productive relations with senior levels of government, given the roles and responsibilities they share. This same pattern is also true at the regional level. In some respects, Toronto had become disconnected from the city region surrounding it, and ironically that may be partly a consequence of the "too big, too small boundary" enshrined by the forced amalgamation in 1998 (more on this later), but these relationships have become even more critical as the Greater Toronto and Hamilton Area grows and urbanizes.

The truth is, it is rare to have all levels of government perfectly aligned. Tension is more the norm. Reaction and retrenchment in one area can motivate action in another. When there was a hostile federal government, resistant to investing in clean energy, it was the Province of Ontario and the private sector that drove the renewable energy agenda. Now the situation is reversed. Perhaps the emerging tech sector, which plays a strong role in the city's economy and has a mobile, educated workforce, will demand a Toronto that is walkable, bikeable, transit-friendly, and offers creative affordable housing options. Clearly more onus will be placed on the city itself to advance its progressive agenda, with or without provincial support, in this period, but its efforts may be bolstered by new forms of federal-municipal alliance.

The fight over the size of Toronto City Council may lead the city to revisit the internal workings of City Hall, and to pursue innovations that can be made by drawing on citizens to play more roles within the political structure that has been imposed. It may also be that Torontonians will finally have the motivation to develop a possible antidote to the forced amalgamation that created the current megacity of Toronto. Subdividing the twenty-five new "mega-wards" into smaller areas, with a finer grain of empowered community boards or strengthened community councils, may now be a timely and useful strategy.

Finally, Canada may now have sufficient incentive to address the flaw in its governmental structure, which dates back to the 1867 disenfranchisement of cities. Not only Toronto's municipal government, but also big city mayors across the country are now acutely aware of their vulnerability and have taken up the cause. It isn't clear how they can effect this change, however. Amending the Constitution seems to be out of reach. Still, some movement on this would be a logical step in the evolution of the relationship between the Government of Canada, its provinces, and its cities, which are not only home to most of its people, but also drivers of the economy.

There is a powerful cautionary tale here about the potential crippling effects of deep and enduring social divisions. Canada does not want to end up in a place where ideological and tribal divisions become the gaping chasms we see in the United States. This is not the first or only time that geographic differences have manifested themselves in Canadian politics. Where and how people live shapes how they see the world. The problem is that the "politics of demography" can erode any sense of common purpose or shared identity based on mutual respect for difference. There is now a special onus on political leaders to avoid exploiting and exacerbating such divides, instead reaching across them to make our form of politics more attentive and responsive to the diverse set of needs of an enlarged body politic. This is not a zero-sum game. Strong and vital cities like Toronto and city regions like the GTHA, empowered to fulfill their destinies, will ultimately make a stronger Ontario and Canada.

INTRODUCTION
Toronto as Crucible

I arrived in Toronto in 1968, immigrating from the United States in the period of great turmoil caused by the war in Vietnam.

Although I relocated under duress, I immediately felt welcomed. The city felt remarkably malleable, not fully formed. It seemed to be still evolving, open to new ideas and desires, receptive to reshaping by me and other new arrivals. I had the sense that this was a place where I could contribute and most fully be myself. Toronto was on the cusp of a great change, and I was quickly caught up in the unfolding story of my adopted city. After completing my studies, I worked as a young architect, and then founded the Division of Architecture and Urban Design at the City of Toronto, running it for ten years under the direction of three mayors: David Crombie, John Sewell, and Art Eggleton.

Through this stint at city hall and later work as a professional (and engagement as a citizen), I have had a front-row seat as a participant and observer during decades of remarkable, often inspiring — and at times frustrating — change in this extraordinary city. I shared some of this experience in my earlier book, *Walking Home*, published in 2011, in which Toronto had a role among many cities. This book gives me a chance to come back to what is happening in Toronto almost a decade later in a more focused way.

Each of us has some stressful formative experiences that motivate (and sometimes obsess or even traumatize) us. One of my own subterranean drivers comes from my childhood peregrinations. Moving from place to place, often abruptly, changing cities, countries, neighbourhoods, schools (sometimes in mid-year), and friends was disruptive to say the least, even if sometimes it felt exciting. In hindsight, I realize that this constant disloca-tion has led to an intense compensating homing instinct, and, though cou-pled with a taste for travel, a need to be rooted in a place. This, in part, is what steered me to my career in urban design and to my intense love affair with Toronto. Like an attentive lover, I have been sensitive to its changes and moods ever since.

I am convinced that something out of the ordinary, if not truly unique, is occurring in Toronto. It feels like the city is emerging from a chrysalis. The processes of continual redefinition and renewal have ever been in play in our city, and there have been other periods of enormous upheaval and growth spurts; but in the last fifteen years or so, the direction has altered while the pace of change has intensified and accelerated. Fuelled by a pow-erful vortex of market forces and demographic pressures, Toronto has be-come a locus for immigration, investment, and development, and our cur-rent spectacular growth shows no sign of abating.

Toronto is being transformed by the simultaneous pressures of enor-mous and sustained growth; an unparalleled increase in the city's diversity, bringing an expansion of the talent pool and new ideas; an imperative to achieve greater environmental sustainability; and relentless, often disrupt-ive technological innovation. The city is very rapidly becoming more verti-cal, denser, and more mixed.

All of these factors are present to some degree in other places, but in Toronto the first and second — radical growth and an increase in the eth-nic diversity in the population — are at unusually high levels. These forces are converging to form a crucible in which radical change and innovation are being galvanized. It is rocking the status quo of previous assumptions, familiar ways, rules, and practices, and pushing us out of our comfort zone. The city is at the tipping point, in the throes of a rebirth.

I have come to believe that Toronto has moved to a new level and is at a decisive moment of transformation into a new type of city: changing as much in kind as in scale. The contours of this new city are becoming visible, emerging from the old established roots — literally arising on the frame, the traces, the memories, and the structures (physical, social, economic, cultural) of an older Toronto. The city is being pushed into this new territory by an infusion of new, boundary-stretching ideas and forces.

I believe that much of what has led to the remarkable transformational shift underway in Toronto can be traced back to a critical turning point in the late 1960s and 1970s, which I described briefly in *Walking Home*. At that time, my introduction to the city and the launch of my career coincided with a dramatic series of events that set the stage for what was to come. Toronto was a city on the verge of massive change in line with the anticity polemic of that era. But then, a dramatic series of events occurred, setting the stage for a major course correction.

Toronto's guide to its future in 1969, its Official Plan (like that found in many other cities at that time), called for a kind of progress inspired by the principles of what was then the modern movement in city planning. Among other things, it was based on a full embrace of the private automobile, including massive highway construction (with a complete interwoven network including the Spadina, Scarborough, and Crosstown Expressways); ripping up streetcar tracks; separating places of living from places of work as much as possible; replacing traditional main streets with shopping malls — the Dufferin, Pape and Gerrard Malls were, in fact, built as prototypes; demolition of major civic buildings — Union Station, Old City Hall, and the St. Lawrence Market were all considered for demolition — to make way for the new; and a call for widespread "urban renewal." A vast boomerang shape indicating proposed demolition appeared on a city document, hovering ominously over the whole downtown and adjacent inner city neighbourhoods. In other words, a gutting of the city was in the offing, preparing it to be remade in the name of a then widely held view of "modernity."

To many, these were frightening prospects. A citizen resistance grew out of a unique amalgam of the city's traditional small *c* conservatism and a new, left-of-centre coalition, motivated by a sense of civic empowerment and led by an engaged civic leadership. The resistance grew like a snowball, gaining momentum as new champions emerged. In a series of hotly contested municipal elections, an increasing number of progressive city councillors were elected, supported by grassroots activism and community backlash.

Once they had a majority, the new "reform council," led by beloved mayor David Crombie, used their mandate to reverse course, rejecting the dominant postwar modernist template. With the unlikely intervention of then premier William Davis, they famously put a highly symbolic nail in the coffin of the Spadina Expressway, which would have eviscerated a series of downtown neighbourhoods, and cancelled a whole network of other city-damaging highways in its wake.

It is hard to overstate the importance of the change. This was a complete about-face for the city, one that would have far-reaching consequences, setting Toronto on a very different trajectory. The car was significantly dethroned as the primary mode of transportation; plans to rip up streetcar lines were thwarted, making Toronto one of the few cities on the continent to retain this form of transit. Urban renewal and "block-busting" of long-established neighbourhoods to make way for tower-in-the-park style redevelopment was halted. Heritage preservation was embraced, saving a number of cherished structures from demolition — including the St. Lawrence Market, now the throbbing heart of a revitalized neighbourhood; the glorious 1898 Richardsonian Old City Hall; and the magnificent beaux arts Union Station.

The middle class stayed or returned to inner-city neighbourhoods. Population attrition was reversed. The city's traditional neighbourhood main streets, which had also been scheduled for transformation into car-centric arterial roads, were seen with fresh eyes and received new support from strengthened and decentralized neighbourhood planning site offices and the widely imitated Toronto invention of BIAs (Business Improvement Areas co-funded by the city and local businesses), of which Toronto now has more than any other city.

The separation of land uses (dividing where people lived from where they worked, with an onerous commute by car to bridge the gap) had been exposed as a failed model for urban living; it was not delivering what it promised. The vision of contented citizens able to live in quiet, pastoral suburban neighbourhoods and then make their way quickly to work via wide highways was belied by the reality of the growing inconvenience of congestion, negative impacts on health caused by a sedentary, car-dependent lifestyle, unanticipated social isolation, and mounting environmental impacts.

The reform council pushed back against the "suburbanization" of the downtown core, fighting to prevent the spread of widened roads, a profusion of surface parking lots, and segregated land use. A new Central Area Plan was formulated that introduced mixed-use zoning to the city's downtown core, and that would eventually bring hundreds of thousands of new residents into the heart of the city to enliven the previously sterile nine-to-five central business (only) district.

The big planning and design challenge: how to actually implement the course correction. This was the challenge that drew me to city hall as a young architect with a growing interest in urban design.

David Crombie recruited me in 1977, along with a whole corps of young, motivated change agents. Working with the newly elected politicians, we formed a think tank, a kind of collegial brain trust. We came from many backgrounds, and not all were formally educated as "planners," but we shared a mission.

We played different roles on a team dedicated to stopping the speeding freight train of "modernization" and shifting to another paradigm for the city's future. I headed the newly minted Urban Design Group, which became the city's Division of Architecture and Design, and my team and I were called upon to play a central role in this transformative moment. It was exhilarating.

We were trying to articulate a competing vision for the city, and we were working in a pressure cooker. Our vision was based on faith in the existing city. Its basic tenets were to move away from land use separations, car dependence, and urban renewal, instead aiming to protect the city's existing neighbourhoods and architectural heritage, halting the expansion of urban expressways, promoting public transit and pedestrian environments, and encouraging downtown living, with lively main streets as vital neighbourhood spines.

We had a sense of tremendous transformational potential, applying new ideas and concepts that connected all the way from the city street to the city region and expanding the array of available tools and strategies. We aimed to make big moves, pivoting from defence to offence, from stopping the Spadina Expressway to creating the mixed-use Central Area Plan, launching the mixed-income St. Lawrence Neighbourhood for ten thousand new downtown residents on a stretch of obsolescent industrial sites and anchoring it with a linear park on an abandoned rail corridor, and expanding the role of Business Improvement Associations to support local shopping streets.

Combining strategies and tactics, we changed the way planning and urban design were done in Toronto on the fly. Mayor Crombie controversially introduced a forty-five-foot "holding bylaw" to buy time to prepare the Central Area Plan. We pursued a policy of "de-concentration," linking development and diversification of land use to transit capacity, exporting office space to emerging downtown centres in Scarborough, North York, and Etobicoke.

With my newly formed Urban Design Group, and inspired by a similar effort in New York City under Mayor John Lindsay, I had a chance to play a key role. We were inventing theory, policy, and practice all at the same time. The city needed new kinds of buildings, and guidelines were rapidly formulated to shift the emphasis away from free-standing towers in the park or plaza. This urban design precept, which called for tall buildings separated by wide open spaces, was intended to provide more light, better views, and privacy, and to promote healthy conditions. In practice, however, it was hostile to the city fabric, undermining the social qualities of neighbourhood street life. What we needed was a new generation of buildings with good street manners and animated frontages to bring new life to the city's sidewalks.

As well as making decisions involving private development, we wanted to bring new attention to the public realm — the civic infrastructure of streets, parks, and squares that comprise almost half of the land area of the city — which needed periodic renewal. We needed to integrate these two sides of the equation in order to create more welcoming spaces supporting pedestrian-oriented urban life.

The first test bed for my group was in what was called the St. Lawrence Historic District, a.k.a. East Downtown. At the time, it exhibited all the results of scorched earth planning — ubiquitous surface parking lots created by demolitions. The area was lifeless, forlorn, and gap-toothed. There were a few surviving architectural treasures: the St. Lawrence Market, St. Lawrence Hall, the iconic Flatiron Building, and some surviving structures on Front Street with unique cast-iron facades.

Resurrecting this neighbourhood was going to take a lot of work. Fortunately, we had tremendous support from the mayor and City Council, and a handful of enlightened owners in the area became allies.

The Central Area Plan set the stage, providing legislation and a vision for new mixed-use development compatible with the district's historic shape and feel. These new buildings were to be inserted on vacant parcels. Two development streams came together: these new buildings (mixed-use, combining living and working), and the public realm. The objective was to get both private development and public realm improvements on the same plan, which we dubbed the "unofficial plan" because although it was not a legislative requirement it was still a powerful instrument for coordination and persuasion.

When looking through the lenses of traditional bureaucratic silos, the opportunities for change were hard to see. But they were revealed in brainstorming sessions that brought all the parties around the same table to examine the issues together. We were encouraged by local stakeholders to explore future development opportunities, to see physical and land-use relationships between groupings of buildings and public spaces, and to identify synergies that had been obscured when individual interests in the area were working in isolation. We were practising a kind of planning that was tangible, physical, and experiential, putting theory into practice through example. The city's legacy of artefacts on the ground — heritage buildings and landscapes — was a valuable resource, adding richness and depth.

Take Market Square on Front Street, a prime example of the kind of infill we wanted to create. The building occupies what was formerly a large surface parking lot. We proposed a dramatic new four-metre-wide mid-block pedestrian route through the site on axis with the spire of St. James Cathedral. Architect Jerome Markson and his developer clients embraced the idea. Working closely with colleagues in other departments, including Parks, Public Works, and the Toronto Historical Board, an area-wide Public Improvement Plan identified transformational opportunities such as widened sidewalks on Front Street, the insertion of Sculpture Garden on King Street, improvements to St. James Park, and the creation of Berczy Park behind the Flatiron Building on a former parking lot. On the strength of these projects, in 1986 the Urban Design Group received the Governor General's Medal in Architecture for our work on the "Architecture of the City."

The Urban Design Group had its own annual capital budget. We collaborated with other departments so that when streets had to be torn up anyway, we were there to enhance the work of the line departments like Public Works and make improvements at the same time, avoiding extra annoyance for the public.

Our approach to this area became a kind of template for other neighbourhoods — existing, emerging, and new. In each area, we aimed to develop a fine-grained pedestrian network combining public and private spaces and initiatives. From these initial examples we drew key lessons about interdepartmental and public-private collaborations — and about the great value of modelling, revealing hidden potential through a close reading of context.

Eventually, we exported these ideas about reshaping the city right across the city, into the downtown core, and throughout the neighbourhoods. We collaborated on introducing the new, large-scale infrastructure into the two hundred acres of obsolescent railway lands between downtown and the harbour. We expanded the public realm for pedestrians (and, over time, cyclists), transforming wastelands that had been abandoned by industry into common ground for the city's new, increasingly dense and diverse version of itself. And as we rediscovered and linked these areas, and the city filled in, we also developed a new sense of ourselves as Torontonians. This time of ferment was eventually to have far greater impact than we imagined.

Fast-forward to the present. Today, we feel the reverberations and dividends from that period, compounded by radical growth and unprecedented diversity in the ensuing decades, as Torontonians repopulate the downtown core, near neighbourhoods and transit corridors, in unprecedented numbers. Citizens are on a quest for shorter commutes and greater convenience, and many are opting into a new urban version of the North American dream. It looks and feels different — not the single-family dwelling set back in the landscape with a sweeping drive and fleet of cars, nor its scaled-down townhouse cousin in a new subdivision — but living in a more modest multi-storey unit in a neighbourhood where it's possible to walk to buy groceries and take transit to work.

This change in citizens' lifestyle has brought a significant change in outlook for the city, as more and more Torontonians weigh personal priorities like getting rid of the second car and even the first, biking or walking to work, living in a smaller space, trading a yard for a balcony or rooftop garden, using smaller appliances, and generally living with less stuff. Toronto is rapidly becoming a much more densely populated city, and this reality is compelling people, whether they like it or not, to try out new ways of living together, of sharing collective space. It is also becoming a city with a higher proportion of renters. A recent report by the Urban Institute in the United States suggests that the preference among millennials for *where* to live is stronger than their focus on homeownership, which is declining relative to previous generations as they seek out big city environments.

In Toronto, there has been extraordinary growth in a relatively short time in the downtown and surrounding neighbourhoods. And as the number of residents increases, the core of the city is becoming palpably different — more life on the streets and in the parks, and multi-generational neighbourhoods with a wide variety of residents. Singles, couples, and families of every generation increasingly live in high-rise buildings. People live and work in new ways, move around the city differently, and use public spaces more. One might say Toronto is picking up a thread that was abandoned three generations ago, when denser North American cities had apartment buildings, streetcars, and active shops on main streets. It's reviving an urban culture that had receded, on this continent, to just sections of a few cities like New York, Boston, San Francisco, and Montreal.

The shift is not occurring in a vacuum, and it is important to place it in the global context of technological and economic factors and political and social trends. In this same period other cities have also experienced their own versions of this radical shift in gears, challenging and stopping highway projects and urban renewal, attempting to chart a new course. In the end, as each city experiences these pressures and trends in its own way — a combination of culture, conditions on the ground, and local circumstance — distinct patterns appear. Nature and nurture combine, forcing each city to evolve, giving rise to a new urban DNA. It is those particularities that make each city unique.

In *Walking Home*, I explored these themes broadly, using examples from a number of cities. This account, written eight years later, has allowed me to look more closely at what makes Toronto special right now. One of the factors that distinguishes the city's metamorphosis and, I would argue, makes the shift more impactful than in many other American and Canadian cities, is the population's inherent conservatism, which meant that through the 1950s and 1960s Toronto lagged behind other cities in implementing the dominant postwar auto-oriented paradigm. Many of the city's neighbourhoods survived relatively intact; it still had streetcars, and a significant population still lived downtown. Toronto's citizens are now reaping the rewards of a time lag at that pivotal moment of redirection that followed in the 1960s and 1970s when the city capitalized on its slowness and reversed course.

At the same time, Toronto is also constantly learning from other places. This process is accelerating as the city becomes more open to the world, absorbing ideas, reinterpreting them, and making them its own, inviting the best and brightest from elsewhere, both new Canadians and visiting professionals, to contribute to the city's evolution. For example, change in Toronto has been inspired by many of the compelling sustainability and mobility innovations of the Nordic countries. The city has also drawn on ideas from the developing world, like the Ciclovía from Bogotá, Colombia, where 120 kilometres of streets are blocked off to cars for runners, skaters, and cyclists, and temporary stages are set up in city parks for a whole range of outdoor activities every Sunday (attracting 30 percent of the population). Bold civic actions like this have inspired our own more modest version of Open Streets and other new uses of public space. The people and government of Toronto have come to realize that they are partners in a collective learning curve, and these innovations become grist for city reshaping.

I am convinced that a remarkable fate is in store for Toronto. The city has a magnificent opportunity to become something other, something better — a new version of itself, of which it is as yet only dimly aware. I want to chronicle the way the city's reality and sense of itself is changing. I believe that this is Toronto's moment.

Toronto is taking its place in the world's panoply of important and interesting cities for a variety of reasons. Amongst the most important of these is the fact that Toronto is managing relatively well as a multicultural city. It is succeeding as the most diverse city on the planet. People are understandably curious about how and why that is happening, who is involved, and how it plays out on the ground.

Cities have their moments, celebrated transformations when they change not just in size but in kind. We might consider as examples the mass migrations to early twentieth-century New York that sparked the creative ferment of the Lower East Side; Montreal's stunning invitation to the world with Expo 67; the liberating "opening up" of Barcelona after Franco's death in 1975; Berlin's euphoria when the wall came down in 1989; and, more recently, innovations in addressing the informal sector in Bogotá and Medellín, Copenhagen's expanding pedestrian network, the Strøget, and Vancouver's repopulating of the downtown peninsula.

We even coin terms from cities' names — *Manhattanize, Vancouverism,* and *Copenhagenize* — to describe these transformations. City planners and others make pilgrimages to these places to admire, and in some cases to emulate, the change. These cities' stories have each contributed to a collective learning curve.

It may be Toronto's turn for an eponymous term. However, "Torontoisms" will be harder to define, more subtle and geographically diffuse. The rebirth I hope to capture may seem messy and disorganized, but I believe some underlying patterns can be detected as the city becomes denser, more diverse, and greener. Like the cities cited above, Toronto, too, may be expanding the realm of the achievable in significant new ways.

Toronto possesses a crucial ingredient, not engineered intentionally, but there nonetheless. From a mid-size, unprepossessing, majority-Anglo-Saxon city, Toronto has become, almost in spite of itself, a burgeoning, heterogeneous metropolis. The city is growing at an annual rate of 0.86 percent, attracting new residents every year from around the world, including many from Asia, Africa, and Latin America, and as a result it is becoming less white. According to the latest census, over 50 percent of

Toronto's residents were born in another country and over 50 percent of the population identify as members of a visible minority. With these recent immigrants and the many more internal migrants that have made Toronto their home, it has truly become an "arrival city." In fact, Toronto can now be described as a city with no majority population, a city where the term *minority* has become moot.

In other cities, such diversity has been problematic for some residents, a source of great consternation, but this diversity has become, for now, a source of great pride for Toronto. This clearly wasn't always so. The city was once known as the Belfast of the north, and some citizens contemptuously referred to new arrivals as "DPs" (displaced persons). Why and how that changed is a critical question that needs to be studied and better understood, since racial and ethnic tensions still exist in the city, and Toronto's relative success in this area cannot be taken for granted. Still, the city's push toward multi-hued, multi-dimensional inclusion, while clearly not without challenges, does not appear to be forced and seems to be gaining momentum.

This transformation isn't always smooth, but it is inexorable, as Toronto moves way beyond the perceived tenets of multiculturalism laid out several decades ago by Prime Minister Pierre Trudeau and his cabinet around identifiable ethnocultural populations then in Canada. The city has extended the definition to include a multiplicity of other identities, including gender, sexual orientation, and the growing number of mixed ethnicities. It is embracing people of all ages and physical abilities.

These changes have led to a vastly expanded understanding of why the places people live must be designed to support that astonishing diversity — because it is 2019! But also because inclusive design makes everyone stronger, not weaker; more able, not less; more equipped to deal with a world that is itself increasingly diverse and complex.

Through striving to recognize the immense variety of people that make up Toronto's population, the city has become a more humane, more compassionate place. Citizens of all kinds have pushed each other to recognize the worth and rights of all, and to therefore acknowledge and confront inequities: the terrible lack of affordable housing and services, to put real faces and voices to the ravages of job loss and dislocation, the forces of polarization and inequality.

Remarkably, however, despite the very real stresses — economic, social, political — felt by many in the city, Torontonians of today are not turning against each other, not seeking easy targets to blame for perceived failings. This fact is all the more compelling as so many areas of the world have seen a turn toward ethnic and religious purity, xenophobia, the loathing of otherness, and the politics of fear. In some ways, Canada, and Toronto in particular, is the unassuming voice that challenges the roar of the angry mobs elsewhere. The fact is, the city seems to enjoy its diverse state, and while far from perfect, it is clearly on a different tack.

It is interesting to see how differently Canada and its neighbour, the United States, are reacting to similar changes in the world — social, economic, and environmental. Canada is, by and large (it is all relative), embracing change, moving in more progressive directions, seeking greater social inclusion, shifting to the new economy (albeit with some difficulty), and increasingly acknowledging environmental imperatives and their potential for positive change. The country has experienced relatively less mainstream or overt racist and nativist politics and fewer open expressions of hate and deep divisiveness. The United States in the age of Trumpism, by contrast, seems to be seized with polarizing divisions and deep animosities and a lack of capacity for coherent conversation across the divide. The U.S. has also turned its back on progressive economic policy, and has embraced a frightening denial of the facts provided by science, particularly with respect to the realities of climate change.

The 2016 U.S. election and the Brexit vote in the United Kingdom provided dramatic wake-up calls about the allure of right-wing populism, with its embrace of intolerance and division. The American election also demonstrated some harsh realities about the political landscape there. The results were dramatically skewed — Democratic (liberal) cities standing apart from a Republican (conservative) hinterland — showing, again, how cities tend to resist reactionary tendencies. Are there threats on the horizon that could jeopardize the progressivism of Canadian urban centres? Yes, absolutely. There are colliding realities that cities are negotiating in an age of increasing migration and economic stratification. (And as stated in the Preface, while not as extreme, Canadians are certainly not immune to similar divisive tendencies, as evidenced by the recent election of the Doug Ford government in Ontario.)

There is a growing economic divide in Canada, too — the rich are getting richer and the poor and middle class are getting poorer. Obviously, the federal government and the country's provincial governments play the largest role in tackling this issue, but cities, too, have a critical role to play. There are other sources of potential conflict, too — religion, race, sex, gender, ability. The nagging question when the social unrest occurring elsewhere is considered is Could It Happen Here?, which also happens to be the title of a recent book by pollster and social researcher Michael Adams, head of the polling company Environics. After all, Canada has suffered a racially motivated massacre at a Quebec City mosque (along with a great number of individual hate crimes), and at least two conservative leadership candidates tried to shape (as it turned out, unsuccessful) campaigns evoking immigration anxiety and Islamophobia. Canada's vulnerability to xenophobic rhetoric is apparent once again. Breaking from the Conservative Party in September 2018 to form his People's Party of Canada, Maxime Bernier has decried what he called "radical multiculturalism."

Still, drawing on major social values surveys of Canadians and Americans in 2016, as well as decades of tracking data in both countries, Michael Adams concludes that Canada may have more significant defences against the kind of nationalist xenophobia that has arisen elsewhere. This is not cause for smugness or a guarantee of our exceptionalism, he argues, but simply a reflection of the fact that the country may have been somewhat inoculated by its recent political and social history — and that has much to do with the role played by Canada's cities.

A much greater share of the country's population is clustered in a smaller number of cities. Whereas America's ten census metropolitan areas contain just 27 percent of the population, the equivalent figure for Canada is 55 percent. Canadians living in those large urban centres live differently than those living in smaller centres and in rural areas; they inevitably encounter a culturally diverse mix of neighbours and colleagues. This is particularly true in the case of Toronto, which is commonly listed as the most diverse city on earth. This diversity is largely a product of postwar immigration, fostered once Canada retired its explicitly racist immigration policies in the 1960s, and began moving to a points system that has led to huge inflows of talent, energy, and youth from around the world.

Cities have traditionally been places of refuge, protecting difference and minority rights. One historical example is Andalusia, the area of southern Spain in whose cities Muslims, Christians, and Jews flourished together before the region was overtaken by the darkness of the Inquisition. Might there be a parallel in Toronto? Award-winning trumpeter and composer David Buchbinder makes the connection explicit. Teaming up with Cuban pianist Hilario Durán and a crew of top world music and jazz musicians in a project of musical discovery, Buchbinder and the group Odessa/Havana explore the many-faceted, multi-layered, and rich links rooted in their common ancestry in medieval Andalusia, sharing Arabic, Roma, Sephardic, and North African forebearers. Building on the city's extraordinarily diverse musical talent pool, the Royal Conservatory of Music, under David's artistic direction, has sponsored the group KUNÉ (meaning "together" in Esperanto), Canada's Global Orchestra, as a celebration of Toronto's and Canada's cultural diversity and pluralism. Comprising of thirteen virtuoso musicians — twelve from abroad, who had each chosen to start a new life here, and one Métis musician, whose ancestors have been here for centuries — this band looks and sounds like Toronto today, at once global and uniquely local.

This intense intermingling is not just a phenomenon of the past few decades. An earlier precursor occurred in a neighbourhood in central Toronto called The Ward (formally St. John's Ward) bounded by College Street, Queen Street, Yonge Street, and University Avenue. A dense, mixed-use neighbourhood, it hosted extraordinary diversity for several decades of the late nineteenth and early twentieth centuries as successive waves of new immigrants arrived: refugees from the European Revolutions of 1848, the Irish Potato Famine, the Underground Railroad, and then from Russia and Eastern and Southern Europe.

The Ward became the centre of the city's Jewish community from the late nineteenth century until the 1920s, and then, until the late 1950s, became the city's original Chinatown. African-Canadian, Italian, Polish, Ukrainian, Lithuanian, and numerous other non-Anglo-Saxon immigrants also first established themselves in The Ward. It was eventually characterized by disdainful authorities as a slum and demolished to make way for major institutions including New City Hall and Toronto General Hospital, but for a time it offered a taste of what was to come.

As The Ward moved toward its destruction, another neighbourhood slowly developed, slightly to the west, which is now a uniquely Torontonian example of how a culturally layered neighbourhood can thrive. Kensington Market formed in the 1930s as the Jewish market, where the house fronts of garment workers on a few modest streets opened up as market stalls that spilled out onto the sidewalks. Over time, it has grown by welcoming waves of new arrivals, and their food and cultures, to the point where it has become a living demonstration of the city's demographic richness.

But as Torontonians test the limits of their vaunted skill at integration, do they really live up to their reputation? As the barriers have begun to come down for women and visible minorities — interestingly, in the latter case, women have tended to benefit more than men — the evidence is that certain birds of a feather — white males — still do flock together in places like Bay Street law firms and corporate headquarters. Achieving equality is clearly a work in progress and despite many gains, there is a long way to go. But it's clear that for the moment Toronto (and Canada) are outliers, and they have a special responsibility to show how their model works. There is an ethical dimension to the multicultural model, but also enlightened self-interest. Toronto and Canada illustrate the benefits of immigration. It is a clear-cut case of do good to do well.

Large-scale historical, geopolitical, and ethnocultural considerations are ever-present backdrops to the unfolding life of the city. They inform the values and perceptions that shape the way Torontonians approach the choices they make, the politicians they elect, the projects they pursue, and ultimately the ways they modify the city itself. The election of Donald Trump, for example, continues to produce multiple aftershocks in the city. The recently completed and painful renegotiation of NAFTA, rebranded by Trump as the USMCA (United States-Mexico-Canada Agreement) and by Canada as the CUSMA, has significant implications for the city's economy. Likewise, the tightening of the U.S. border, and the redrafting of rules relating to immigration there, are motivating individuals and companies to come and live, work, and invest in Toronto.

In 1970, historian and one-time Toronto city councillor William Kilbourn published an anthology entitled *Canada: A Guide to the Peaceable Kingdom*. The country was described as an underpopulated place in an overpopulated world, a minority democracy lacking a unified mass culture, but one with the possibility of becoming an "international country." In a sense, Toronto may be the embodiment of that vision at a city scale.

Something born of that complex identity does seem to be afoot in Canada, and that something is finding particular expression in the country's cities. Pent-up feelings and ideas are coming to the surface, coalescing, and revealing another side of ourselves. Canada is becoming the "progressive" flag-bearer in a world that is increasingly following an opposite path, showing little acceptance of "the other." Canada is, instead, not uncritically and not resting on its laurels, raising its sights and asking more of itself and its citizens.

Toronto has been an outstanding example of the larger Canadian embrace of progressive values and acceptance of "otherness." The city has a unique potential, should it choose to rise to the occasion, to become a leading example of a progressive, diverse, heterogeneous, and equitable city and those values may define its special place in the panoply of great world cities. Should it continue to reject the division of its citizens into groups defined by ethnicity, religion, et cetera, Toronto has the potential to become that "city for all."

It is fascinating that in a city where not that long ago patrons rose to the strains of "God Save the Queen" before a movie, many public gatherings now open with an acknowledgement that the residents of the city live on traditional Anishinaabe, Haudenosaunee, and Mississaugas of the New Credit territory, an attempt to recognize the debt to the Indigenous Peoples who inhabited the area before Europeans arrived to *tkaronto*, a Mohawk word for the place "where there are trees standing in the water."

The debt Canadians owe to the Indigenous Peoples in the country is finally being acknowledged, along with recognition of the profound impact the residential schools had on their families, languages, and cultures, and a painful but necessary admission of the prejudices and cruelty our society exhibited, which made these earlier crimes possible. Apologies were (and continue to be) necessary, as is restitution and reconciliation.

This new, very powerful understanding is the product of lessons learned from living together in the complex heterogeneous society we have become. It has been argued that the initial acknowledgement of Indigenous Peoples by European explorers and colonists, and then the eventual accommodation reached between Canada's French and English forebears, set the stage for Canadians' broader comfort with differences. Canadians are beginning to understand that Indigenous Peoples (perhaps in an overly trusting way) actually set the stage for the welcoming of the "other" into their midst.

Is there not a link to be drawn to the welcome Canadians have extended to Syrian and other refugees? Have we internalized something? Are we not identifying ourselves with the issues of displacement and otherness in a society where the majority of us were born elsewhere, and are aware that fifty-five million people in the world are now forced to march from their homes?

Canada's acceptance of "others" has shown itself in a variety of ways. It emerged through our experience with slavery and the Underground Railroad, and our progression through the later twentieth century from the often-grudging acceptance or outright rejection of new arrivals before and after the Second World War. In my time, the country has offered a safe haven for American draft dodgers, Hungarians, Czechs, Chileans, and Vietnamese, among many others. The treatment of members of the LGBTQ community has altered significantly. Gone are the days of the notorious bathhouse raids in Toronto; today, it is virtually obligatory for all parties to have representation in the various Pride Parades that take place across the country. Despite this progress, it must be noted, however, that an ongoing struggle by members of the LGBTQ community to overcome stereotyping and inequities in treatment by the police still exists.

In Toronto, this pooling of cultures aggregates as the city grows by the thousands every year, each individual commingling and joining their personal stories to form a larger collective one. Eventually, clusters of shared experience and interests evolve and find expression. Ideas and impulses overlap as the cultural gene pool expands, and individuals' sense of self intertwines with this fused city culture. Notwithstanding Margaret Thatcher's famous quip that "there is no such thing as society," the city is more than an aggregation of autonomous individuals. The population of the city joins together, and an altered form of urban society emerges from this cauldron.

In trying to overcome our historical reliance on the extraction of resources, Canadians are reaching for new roles as stewards of the planet. We are struggling with the difficulty of reconciling our stated goals of meeting climate targets and with the need to create and sustain jobs. Our belief in an endless bounty of fish, lumber, minerals, and fossil fuels has been abandoned; we have had to alter our thinking radically to begin to make the profound shift to an economy based on renewables and to rest more lightly on the earth.

The movement to the city also reflects a shift in employment patterns in the new economy. Canadians have begun to see ourselves as an urban nation, and this is the vital link to this Toronto story, using our brains and not just our muscles, learning when enough is enough, when it may make sense to leave things in the ground, to develop our human resources first and foremost, not just our natural resources. In some new ways, we are drawing on a different world view that has been among us all along: the Indigenous populations teach lessons about stewardship that we have until now paid lip service to, and are finally beginning to fully understand.

Taking these salient facets of Toronto's "genetic" makeup or historic baggage into account, I think it is possible to identify a broader set of inherited Torontonian predispositions or values. Our particular penchant for civility plays a role as a valuable distinguisher, albeit tested at times. There is also an underlying will to make things work even as contradictory impulses and tensions play out, such as our innate conservatism combined with a quest for the new; our boldness and our timidity; our modesty and insecurity; our tendency to procrastinate; our inventiveness and pragmatism; our holdover provincialism and new worldliness and knowledge of what is happening elsewhere.

Through all this, there is, I would contend a direction, a pattern, as our character is revealed; it seems random, but is adding up to something that is for better (in many cases in hindsight) or worse, uniquely us. Toronto's evolution has much to do with a shared sense of the common good, the desire to keep the whole intact and make sure that the city remains livable for the greater number. While our search for solutions may lead to occasional moments of brilliance, there is clearly a low tolerance for risk. Torontonians feel an intense preoccupation with precedent and the implications of change, a desire to want to thoroughly digest everything and not plunge into big mistakes.

Toronto's history is marked by a recurring tension between bold and forward-looking visions and plans, and a much less ambitious reality, resulting from the failure to make big, sustained investments in the future. One might say Torontonians feel an aversion to grandeur, and a tendency toward penny-pinching modesty. This tendency to pull back was part of the fabric of the city right from its founding. Gother Mann's 1788 Plan for what was to be the Town of York (precursor to Toronto) resembled William Penn's grand scheme for Philadelphia or Edward Oglethorpe's famous plan for Savannah with its fifty-two squares. This ambitious, visionary city plan was shelved by Lieutenant Governor Simcoe in favour of a simple ten-block survey, just enough to get settlement started.

Toronto's history offers many more examples of this tendency to reject big visions. The Toronto Harbour Commission's 1912 Waterfront Plan, which included a continuous band of publicly accessible waterfront parks proposed by the Olmsted firm, was value-engineered to remove this "nice to have" element. The Guild of Civic Art's plan for diagonal avenues radiating from Queen and University to the Humber River and Queen and Church to Taylor Creek Park near Woodbine and O'Connor was set aside. John Lyle's 1911 plan for a Federal Avenue, which would have provided an axis linking his new Union Station building and the current site of City Hall, was also ignored. The decision to halt the subway at Front Street in 1949, rather than extend it to the harbour (causing no end of current grief), was another.

There are, of course, notable exceptions, such as the work of visionary city engineer R.C. Harris. Harris built a lower level deck into the Bloor Street Viaduct in anticipation of the arrival of the subway many decades later, and was also responsible for the magnificent water filtration plant named for him in the city's Eastern Beach neighbourhood, both celebrated by Michael Ondaatje in the novel *In the Skin of a Lion*. Or Viljo Revell's startling New City Hall, whose design was the winner of a celebrated international competition. New City Hall was the most iconic early signal of the impending transformation of a city that had survived the war and the Depression without a lot of modern architecture. In general, however, it would not be unfair to say that, for a city of its size and significance, Toronto's architectural history has been short on great civic visionaries or grand gestures of city building. In fact, the city has demonstrated a short attention span when it comes to public works, with an unfortunate tendency to second-guess, start, stop, drop, and then start something else.

Torontonians have a reputation for talking themselves into exhaustion, or of compromising plans beyond recognition. Case in point: Toronto's inability to get serious about cycling infrastructure, even as other Canadian cities are making great advances. Toronto's historically meagre and ad hoc efforts with its waterfront (now ramped up to make up for lost time) is still unfavourably contrasted with Daniel Burnham's bold 1909 waterfront plan in Chicago.

Torontonians tend not to trust or want to give too much power to government entities, or private sector entities, for that matter. They like to split jurisdictions to inhibit overreach. So, Toronto has four or five agencies with overlapping carriage of our waterfront revitalization and sometimes conflicting mandates, reporting to three levels of government. It sounds terrible — dysfunctional, frustrating, and full of lost opportunities. Yet, this caution has produced results both good and bad in hindsight. It spared the city many of the ravages of urban renewal in the sixties and seventies. In fact, Toronto has succeeded as much by what it didn't do as by what it did — demolitions, streetcar removals, and expressways are all bandwagons the city never wholeheartedly boarded.

In fact, Toronto has become expert at muddling through. Its quasi-grid of streets is the perfect example. Made up of bits and pieces of north-south and east-west streets woven together within a larger concession structure instead of an orderly and complete Manhattan-like city grid, it's been gerrymandered to function through periodic "jog alignments" patching disconnected bits together. The burning question going forward is whether Toronto's cautious style will enable the city to deal with the major challenges ahead. A complete rejection of such natural tendencies is unlikely, but it will be interesting to see to what extent Toronto can take on the unprecedented changes required in its own way.

The challenges the city now faces, many of which are problems of its own success, are enormous. We have reached a tipping point where we have outgrown the strictures and supports that sustained a much smaller, more homogeneous city and this is producing significant growing pains. Our growth is occurring at an exhilarating, sometimes scary pace. Our systems and resources are overwhelmed as our institutions struggle to meet demand. Our traditional ways of navigating the city are choked and inadequate; our public services, infrastructure, hard and soft services, and amenities are overburdened. We are literally bursting at the seams, a dynamic metropolis in a too-small suit. From the point of view of many cities these are enviable issues to have, but they come with real and pressing challenges.

We are simultaneously trying to figure out how to shape massive influxes of new development into viable and sustainable neighbourhoods, coping with the impacts of climate change, adapting to the impacts of disruptive technologies, and figuring out how to deal with vast areas of new land opening up on the Lake Ontario waterfront — our new frontier. These are formidable and exciting interrelated challenges, and in many cases, the solutions are at hand. But there is also an overarching need for a new consensus on how to organize ourselves, and how to pay for the solutions to address these big-city needs.

Meeting these new challenges is often controversial, contested, and messy. For example, there is a crippling lack of consensus on how to raise revenues; our politicians rarely dare to say the forbidden *t* word, taxes, let alone introduce them, and as a result the city constantly defers essential maintenance of public infrastructure and expansion of public services. The essential questions are around how we engage and manage the underlying dynamic that has shaped the massive change we are now experiencing. There is still a notable lack of support from senior levels of government for cities, including ours. The "City Agenda" was gaining momentum in the wings at Queen's Park, but that will likely stall with the recent election of Doug Ford's PC government. In Ottawa, however, the fact that 80 percent of us live in big city regions is sinking in.

Toronto also feels growing pains related to how we share space in the city. We had grown used to spreading out in auto-oriented suburbs established in the decades following the Second World War, avoiding friction with our neighbours by using space as a buffer, driving from place to place for specific purposes but rarely overlapping on foot in public spaces. Backyards on leafy neighbourhood streets were the outdoor living rooms for kids to play and dogs to run. As this change to greater density gathers momentum, a combination of urban newcomers — often young people living on their own for the first time and newcomers from a polyglot mix of cultures — find themselves thrown together in close quarters.

Faced with intensifying urban pressures, we need to learn new urban manners to cope with each other. With the switch to denser apartment-style living, chance encounters multiply, and that means becoming more conscious about how we share public space and negotiating a whole new set of relationships as part of city life. We are driving less and walking and cycling more, and competition for the limited space in existing rights-of-way has become intense. As we reach for a more sustainable and fulfilling urban future together, both the allocation of this space and our behaviour within it to meet the competing needs of all users — pedestrians, cyclists and drivers, dogs and children — all need to be renegotiated.

This recalibration applies to a whole array of pressing needs to support city life. In many cases, we are pragmatically exploring new partnerships. We are constantly faced with figuring out how to pay for our shared local and regional needs as a great and growing metropolis across existing municipal boundaries. Not surprisingly, civil society and the public are sometimes leading the changes with government — meant to be the guardian and monitor — inherently less nimble, following and reacting.

There are continued struggles over local governance — both internal and regional. Income disparities, homelessness, housing affordability, and a real and perceived city–suburb divide by geography are realities. Congestion is a huge issue as we struggle to meet our urgent public transit needs — and make the shift to other forms of mobility. Services — hard and soft — are falling behind our levels of need, reflecting an infrastructure deficit and deferred maintenance. The "broken window theory" holds and deterioration breeds neglect, painfully evident in some of our overstressed parks and public spaces.

Underlying all these concerns is the most significant, overarching challenge: the question of equity. Will we truly be a diverse and inclusive city, a city for all? Here is the rub: not everyone is benefitting from our success. Recently, the impetus to develop and invest in the city has been focused on the core of the city and its prewar neighbourhoods, where managing and directing that growth is a major concern. Less investment has been made in the the first ring of postwar suburbs where most new arrivals and low income residents are living, an imbalance that raises significant challenges.

We have only to look around the world to see where "poverty by postal code" can lead. The perfect storm of austerity agendas and increasingly inequitable distribution of wealth produces a vicious circle in which inequality breeds resentment, fuels populism, and fosters corrosive wedge politics. There are, of course, larger forces beyond the city's borders that contribute to this polarizing dynamic, but cities, too, have a role to play.

How do we ensure that the benefits of the city's new vitality are accessible and affordable to its entire population? A related question: Can we sustain and nourish cultural inclusivity against a backdrop of intolerance and tribalism erupting in so many parts of the world? And can we contend with the troubling phenomenon of class segregation by geography in our own city? Torontonians are certainly not immune to these tendencies, and are being forced to acknowledge their consequences.

Living up to an expanded definition of "we" for the citizens of Toronto will be one of our greatest tests as a city. Our success will determine not only what we can do in the face of growing economic inequities, but also what it means to be an open, inclusive city in all senses: income, ethnicity, gender, age, and physical and mental abilities. Who is the city for in the end? Do we grow together as we succeed or grow apart, divided by resources, opportunity, and stereotyping as has happened in so many parts of the world?

Attitudes are changing amid a climate of increasing demands for equal treatment and full consideration. Community members are challenging long-entrenched practices like carding (arbitrary random police checks of racialized young people), "streaming" of visible minority and new immigrant students into non-academic courses, and the prejudicial treatment of members of the LGBTQ community.

We are being forced to ask who can live in this new denser, more integrated city. More compact urban living has become a reality and a necessity; when hidden subsidies to the sprawling regional alternative are stripped away and the true costs are revealed, urban living is inherently more affordable. But that's only true if cities maintain and expand the range of housing options on offer to include different income levels and different needs, including in the newly popular urban neighbourhoods. Is there room for young families attempting to raise children, not only in terms of affordability, but also in units, buildings, and neighbourhoods that are inherently kid-friendly? At the other end of the age spectrum, can we better accommodate an aging population by integrating seniors into complete, multi-generational communities that accommodate a full life cycle to the benefit of all?

Growth is currently unevenly distributed, and the inner suburbs have very different needs and circumstances from the urban core. We need to level the playing field for all parts of the city and make this work with techniques like meaningful inclusionary zoning. This would require a significant portion (usually 20 percent or more) of the dwelling units in all developments of any significant size to meet affordability targets. Other incentives and price supports can address the needs of all ages and conditions, including the growing population of seniors and young families.

Richard Florida's recent book *The New Urban Crisis* takes a hard look at his earlier prescriptions for city success in the *Rise of the Creative Class*. In it he highlights the troubling fact that as the young, educated, and affluent have surged back into cities — reversing decades of suburban flight and urban decline, and putting pressure on the newly desirable parts of cities — this very success has generated vexing new problems of gentrification, unaffordability, segregation, and inequality.

University of Toronto Professor David Hulchanski's illuminating study *The Three Cities Within Toronto* convincingly documents this phenomenon for Toronto, tracking, during the period between 1970 and 2005, the shrinking of the middle class, the export of poverty to Toronto's first ring of postwar suburbs, and the concentration of wealth in the core. This study has now been updated to the present and expanded to include areas beyond the city's borders. On a personal level, while still an architecture student I moved to the Beach neighbourhood in 1969 with my young and growing family. We moved from a flat (sharing a bathroom), to an apartment in a fourplex, to a co-op unit, and finally to a house — all relatively affordable. Obviously, this range of options is no longer available to my young equivalents. Are the negative displacement impacts of gentrification inevitable? If they are, can we at least minimize them? How can we counter the exporting of poverty? And how can this be realized as an explicit goal?

In 1998, these city-versus-inner-suburban tensions were exacerbated by a bombshell that arrived with little warning in the form of a forced shotgun amalgamation of the City of Toronto and its neighbouring suburban municipalities within the former Metropolitan Toronto. Ostensibly positioned as a cost-saving measure, but actually intended to contain and weaken the growing influence of the city, this move was sensibly rejected by over 75 percent of the citizens of Toronto and its neighbour North York in parallel referenda at the time. Yet it was still imposed on the cities by the right-leaning provincial government of Premier Mike Harris.

We had stumbled badly. The amalgamated city was doubly disadvantaged from the start. It was too small to deal with regional issues in an exploding GTA. At the same time, it was too big, too monolithic to address the complex needs of a diverse collection of communities with very different characteristics. (The Golden Task Force solution in 1997 had anticipated this problem and would have created a Greater Toronto Area Federation of thirty autonomous cities.)

The amalgamated megacity still often feels divided against itself. It ushered in an era of "them and us" wedge politics, fuelling animosities and resentment between city and suburb within our expanded city, our own mini precursor to the red state–blue state Trump phenomenon in the U.S. The impacts on the evolving urban agenda have been far reaching, and many advances on key issues have been stalled.

Economically there were none of the promised savings. The province downloaded many provincial responsibilities to the megacity without supplying the resources needed to address them. The idea that bigger bureaucracies are more efficient and that savings would be realized was revealed to be an illusion. What it did bring about was the bugbear of standardization, the obsession with one size fits all that ended up fitting no one, from standard garbage containers, to zoning "harmonization," to uniform (often postwar suburban) street standards that are frustrating for all. It led to an inability to experiment, to let many flowers bloom locally, to bring government closer to people in very different environments.

Amalgamation alienated many citizens from their municipal government. Many feel that city hall has become remote and inaccessible — and for many citizens, it is. Before amalgamation, Toronto, North York, Scarborough, and Etobicoke were developing their own distinctive places, cultural identities, and plans for transformation of their city centres. Paradoxically, amalgamation actually exaggerated the tensions between the prewar city and the postwar first ring suburbs and damaged effective coordination on truly regional issues, such as transit and fare integration beyond the old Metro Toronto of 1953.

Forced uncomfortably into the same mould, struggling for diminishing resources, a sense of a zero-sum game emerged among the megacity's diverse districts, with the electoral majority in the suburbs often feeling like they were on the losing end and the citizens of the old city of Toronto feeling like their identity has been compromised.

Amalgamation occurred over twenty years ago, but the negative consequences of that ill-considered move still haunt us. We are struggling to absorb the strain on our traditional form of municipal governance, and it's still an open question whether we really are one city.

One could argue that amalgamation led directly to the election of our notorious mayor Rob Ford in 2010, riding a wave of populist resentment. It is hard to exaggerate the disruptive impact of his tumultuous reign, which saw a number of personal and work-related controversies and legal proceedings, including a substance abuse scandal that was widely reported in the national and international media. Eventually, City Council handed over certain mayoral powers and office staff to his deputy mayor, Norm Kelly, for the remainder of his term. John Tory has been mayor since 2014, recently winning re-election in 2017, and has been a calming influence, restoring some semblance of order to city hall. Nevertheless, the Ford years introduced a host of civic confrontations that have stayed with us, like scattered buckshot disrupting the urban agenda. The "war on cars," really a war on the bicycle and pedestrians; the attempt to abolish Waterfront Toronto and unseat its CEO; the push to replace long-standing plans for the Lower

Don Lands with a megamall and Ferris Wheel; the attempt to derail the creation of a mixed-income neighbourhood at Regent Park; the demonizing of the umbrellas at Sugar Beach, and the attack on public washrooms at Cherry Beach for soccer players; the refusal to participate in Pride; and the rejection of Open Streets: all stem from a basic visceral uneasiness about the city as an inclusive idea and an ideal worth pursuing with care and an eye for quality. No act of public generosity was too small to attract the attention of his malevolent radar.

The accumulation of these retrenchments and sniping attacks, both large and small, through those years prevented Toronto from fully taking its place among the roster of top progressive cities making rapid and significant advances in city-building on the public side of the ledger. In a sense, we are still in the aftermath of that chaotic period and seeking answers to two key questions: How did we get to that impasse, and what can we do to get beyond it?

This shift to a different kind of urban future is unavoidable. But massive change is complex and challenging. It requires skillful leadership to make it a project of the entire community with shared rewards and outcomes. What we experienced when Toronto City Hall was led by Rob Ford was an ideology of denial and rejection — a futile wish to turn back the clock, akin to the denial of climate change. While we may now be comforted by the fact that the mayor has relatively limited powers in our Canadian system, the capacity for damage has been great — through the bully pulpit and the ability to appoint committee members and chairs (notwithstanding the heroic efforts of other councillors to pick up the pieces and soldier on).

The most basic attack was a challenge to the legitimate roles of government and civil society in guiding and managing the city. Toronto was gearing up for one of the most important political debates in its history when City Council squared off over the budget in the fall of 2011. To meet Mayor Ford's stated goal of cutting $700 million, deep and broad cuts were proposed, ranging from less plowing and cleaning of streets; to sending more trash to landfills; to cutting public health programs, school breakfasts, crossing guards, grants to arts and culture, parks maintenance, planning, public art, and drug prevention programs; eliminating bus routes; and closing library branches, among many other things. Although the combination of these core service cuts, user fees, staff reductions, and dismantling and sell-offs was never presented as a totality but was fired out like random scattershot, the big picture was of an unprecedented assault on the idea of municipal government itself. Had these recommendations all been followed, the result would have been a huge, self-inflicted wound.

Here is the paradox. While cities like Toronto are huge net generators of wealth and the key to national prosperity, their tax revenues are exported to federal and provincial coffers and not equitably returned. This problem was aggravated in Toronto by the forced and unpopular amalgamation in 1998 and the downloading of many responsibilities without revenues to support them. But facing this funding gap, rather than attacking the revenue side of the equation, Mayor Ford's response was that "Toronto does not have a revenue problem but a spending problem." He argued that a "Gravy Train" — a wasteful, inefficient, and bloated city government — could be cut back to balance the budget with no tax increases and no major service cuts.

The Gravy Train became a handy electoral slogan, but as the scope of the proposed cuts was revealed, that Gravy Train was revealed to be the cover for an ideology that would reduce municipal government to a skeleton crew performing minimal functions. According to the mayor, "cops, garbage and smooth streets" were the essentials; the rest was "nice to have" but "unaffordable." If this sounds familiar, it was the full embrace of the well-rehearsed rhetoric that we hear every day from south of the border, but being applied in a radical way to Canada's largest city, arguing that little or no government is the best government; that if we could just cut taxes, let the free market function, and let people fend for themselves, the world would be a better place.

Toronto undoubtedly had a serious budgetary problem, although Ford's $700 million was a grossly inflated figure. To genuinely solve this problem, however, in municipal government a combination of strategies and tools is required, not just an axe. Clearly some efficiencies were in order; there was no doubt the city could get more for its money and work smarter. This drive for real efficiency and search for innovation should be built into any governing process. But it was not just on the spending side: there was also a serious revenue problem. Toronto needs greater support from the provincial and federal governments, but it also needs to make full use of the powers it does have to tax itself and appropriately use other financial tools recommended by such diverse groups as the Board of Trade and the CivicAction. Polls suggested that citizens were willing to support such increases if it were clear that monies would be wisely spent.

A clear example of the courage to make the hard choice to opt for the promise of the future over the fears of the present was Mayor Michael Bloomberg's leadership of New York City. Bloomberg brought a businessman's commitment to strategic investment to municipal management, yielding impressive returns. As a citizen of the city and an entrepreneur who built a major business empire, he viscerally understood the need to maintain basic services such as police, fire, libraries, education, and parks. If those services were allowed to decline, faith in city government would be shattered, leading to the inevitable outflow of more talent and more jobs, not to mention the nicks and gashes inflicted on those most vulnerable.

The minimalist, private-sector-does-it-all ideology creates vastly bigger problems than it proposes to solve. It fails to grasp the importance of the critical balance between public and private roles that is at the heart of what makes cities tick: that a city with competent governance attracts and retains entrepreneurial energy (not the cheapest city); that providing resources, services, and a "helping hand" to those in need, or incentives to local enterprises or activities, especially in an city of new arrivals, is good economics; and that the failure to provide these produces vastly larger expenditures when serious problems arise (and indeed can bring on those serious problems). Quality of life, the key asset in the contemporary global economy, takes a severe hit when public space, cleanliness, public health, public transit, housing, the integration of new arrivals, and arts and culture are starved. By hampering cities' ability to do what they and only they can do as problem solvers, we fail to make the essential move into the new green, knowledge-based economy. A sense of "no, we can't," an overreliance on the private sector, a loss of balance: all cause a vicious downward spiral. It is like sitting down on the track when we are well positioned in the marathon, squandering our natural advantages.

In Toronto, failure during this period to make transformational investments in infrastructure became a drag on productivity and affected prosperity; this aggravated economic disparity and increased polarization: this exaggerated geographic divisions around car dependence across the urban-suburban divide; this became fertile ground for wedge politics and undermined the capacity for effective local and regional governance.

As a result, for all its admirable successes in other areas, Toronto fell behind in making the shift to a more sustainable future. With basic needs unmet and increasing disparities between rich and poor, we were developing a culture of perceived winners and losers, and harsh battles over reduced entitlements that severely inhibited stewardship, creativity, and innovation, critically needed for our success as a city.

Our successive administrations have inherited some serious challenges in the aftermath of the Ford years. We are clearly at a pivotal point in the life of our city. We need to get back into a virtuous cycle of proactive and inclusive city building. On parallel tracks in both the downtown and postwar suburbs, we need to extricate ourselves from the stifling postwar embrace of the automobile and move toward ways of living together in settings that are mixed, synergistic, compact, and walkable.

Transformation to a more sustainable urban future requires enlightened stewardship both inside and outside of city hall. Many of the challenges are partially internal to our city and partially external, like the impacts of globalization and the loss of industrial jobs, income polarization, infrastructure deficits, and climate change. Addressing them will depend on partnerships with all sectors, including sustained and meaningful engagement (and resources) from both federal and provincial governments.

In the end, I believe that the Ford years will be seen as a costly detour, a painful aberration, and Toronto's inherent strengths in social and human capital will prevail. If there is any silver lining to be found, it is that we may have been painfully inoculated by the trauma of the Ford years and awakened to the weaknesses his brand of divisive populist politics was able to exploit. I have often said that Rob Ford may have been the best community organizer Toronto ever had; his attacks on every progressive move the city was making jolted a generation into action to reaffirm the city's commitment to a positive future. This conflict also made Toronto more resilient. Citizens were motivated to come together to stop the worst of the

Ford agenda and to figure out ways to keep positive things happening. City Council also learned to work together across partisan lines. Another lesson, which has particular relevance for the present moment, is that there is no pre-ordained or inevitable path to progress. Cities do experience vulnerabilities and setbacks, and this period is a prime example. Toronto now has to do some serious rebuilding in the public sphere to restore that balance.

It is worth remembering the lessons of those years as Toronto enters a similar period of trial by fire under the oversight of the provincial government led by Mayor Ford's brother, Premier Doug Ford.

One thing to be learned is that there is no preordained or inevitable path to progress. Cities do experience vulnerabilities and setbacks and this period is a prime example. Ultimately, city building requires strength and depth in both the public and private spheres. Toronto will now have to do some serious rebuilding in the public sphere to restore that balance.

Amalgamation and its aftermath are a *fait accompli*, and we have no choice but to find a new way forward to heal the rift and perceived urban-suburban cultural divide that has now been subsumed within the larger challenge of equity and income polarization by geography. From an urban design standpoint, there are significant opportunities for positive change in the suburbs where their very weaknesses from a physical standpoint — too sparse and spread out — are almost the mirror image of those of the downtown core. That inner Toronto was expected to be a regional city on a modest, small-boned frame, never conceived to be so dense, so big, and so compact, and it is now experiencing a need to shoehorn in extraordinary growth and all manner of hard and soft infrastructure.

The very sparseness of the suburbs creates lots of potential. Suburban areas offer plentiful opportunities in the form of "breathing space," including wide rights-of-way that can be converted to complete streets with room for pedestrians and cyclists, vast areas of surface parking, and low-rise structures that can be re-colonized for mixed-use and mixed-income development that is intrinsically more affordable away from the overheated downtown real estate market. The key challenges are to equip these areas with adequate transit services, and to make vital local urban places with walkable streets, pedestrian-friendly neighbourhood shopping, daycare, community centres, and accessible services. The good news is that plans are emerging to tackle all of these challenges both in Toronto's inner suburbs and the surrounding 905* municipalities of the GTHA.

It turns out that we have distinctive strengths and resources to draw upon and special qualities to contribute to the broader urban project — not the least of which is our exceptional diversity, our unique sense of place, and a respect for each other that goes well beyond tolerance. The faces on the street and in schools from elementary to university and college levels throughout our city tell the story. Maybe a desire to live together peacefully in an increasingly conflicted, tribalized world is our most precious particularity. We have to be very careful not to destroy it.

This vast, multi-faceted birthing process is what I hope to capture, moving from the bigger picture of city-shaping forces — governance and leadership, change agents and invisible shaping hands, drivers both internal and external — to specific instances of change on the ground in a few selected places where transformation is taking place. Some of these I have had direct professional and personal involvement and experience with; in other cases, I have been an avid observer.

It is in this interactive territory connecting larger forces that the remarkable rebirth of our city is taking place, propelled by unprecedented diversity experienced in a way that makes us both an outlier and an extremely important progressive flag-bearer in a world that in many places seems to be reverting to something very dark and different.

With this book I have set out to cover this decisive period in the city's evolution, attempting to capture how Toronto becomes a new version of itself from the later part of the twentieth century into the twenty-first through critical modifications at the intersection of the physical city and the human and social life it sustains. I want to explore in some depth the manifestations of its accelerating growth spurt, the growing pains it is causing, how we are responding to them through a series of potent examples, and what that response portends for the city we may become. To paraphrase Winston Churchill's famous quote referring to the Parliament at Westminster, my dialectical circular thesis can be expressed as "we are reshaping our city and our city is reshaping us." In other words, as we change, we transform the

---

* The numbers 416 and 905, which are the telephone area codes for the City of Toronto and its band of surrounding suburban municipalities respectively, serve as shorthand labels for the respective areas.

places we use and inhabit; and they, in turn, transform us and the ways we relate to each other as city dwellers.

There are different valid ways of knowing or deciphering things, of capturing transformation. My approach is more nose-to-the-ground observation, rather than high level and analytical, although much is obviously to be learned through research and the systematic analysis of data. Through a number of accounts of tangible examples, I hope to capture some of the contours of this great, collective enterprise of city-shifting rebirth that is underway, including insights into how it actually happens. It is not a clean and simple process. The themes are complex and interwoven, exhibiting the characteristics of "organized complexity" — the critical observation that everything in the city is connected to everything else in ways that mirror habitats in ecology — introduced by Jane Jacobs in *The Death and Life of Great American Cities*. As a consequence, there wlll be some hard-to-avoid repetition, as themes appear and reappear in different contexts (which simply speaks to their inextricable connectedness).

One of the primary roles of cities is to innovate and improvise in solving problems, including, in our case, the challenging problems of success. Much of what comes next for the city will have to do with how we manage this growth spurt and respond to its multiple tests. I will use examples of progressive change as indicators, backgrounding their context while focusing on the real and particular. These are leading-edge exemplars, where new ideas and practices emerge, and they can demonstrate the potential for success in facing the next generation of challenges.

One of my inspirations for wanting to tell this story came from reading Joan DeJean's fascinating book *How Paris Became Paris: The Invention of the Modern City*. In her search for what gave that city its distinctive character, she turns to the seventeenth century, zeroing in on a few key events. These include the innovative Pont Neuf, the bridge to the Île de la Cité, which provided Parisians with a new kind of expanded public realm thanks to its broad expanse of walking surface for pedestrians protected from vehicle traffic — a place deliberately designed for mingling and social exchange. The Place Royale (today's Place des Vosges) and the master plan for the Île Saint-Louis are other pioneering examples of ordered neighbourhood plans, as is Louis XIV's removal of the city's defensive ramparts to give birth to Paris's unique form of tree-lined Grands Boulevards.

These were all dramatically new forms of public space, and spoke to the emergence of a "modernizing" city pursuing an urban ideal. In Toronto's case, however, the transformation can't be so easily attributed to single actors; instead, it's the result of a more democratic interplay between the invention of new kinds of social space and the emergence of an urban culture.

I hope to capture this process of change and invention through a number of noteworthy works-in-progress reflecting a made-in-Toronto learning curve. Together they form an overarching story of rebirth as our city redefines and rediscovers itself. Using these as indicators, my focus will be on how neighbourhoods coalesce and densify, how we change the ways we move in the city, how we expand our shared common ground, how we integrate nature into our altered conception of the city, how the vast new frontier on the waterfront becomes an integral part of the city, how our great institutions and actors embrace their roles as city builders, and how our suburbs become more urban.

Progress definitely does not occur as a simple linear progression. It is, at best, jagged and uneven. There are hard choices to be made on the way, and fierce debates as conflicting impulses compete and struggle with each other. Much is about the play of time. Capturing the longer-term vector of change in the city can be like watching water come to a boil. Ten years, a decade, is really the measurable unit that is truly meaningful. Change seems imperceptible, and then suddenly a change in degree becomes a fundamental change of state. It is often more evident through the eyes of outsiders who see the city only occasionally, and can compare Toronto with past versions of the city, and with their own urban centres.

Ultimately, the proofs of concept reside in the myriad examples that are appearing on all sides. They are best seen together as "film sequences" over time, not as still images. These places often start life as the exceptions, the icebreakers that are the leading edge of change where a different sensibility starts to be visible. As the instances both large and iconic and small and modest accumulate through a bumpy, uneven process the city redefines itself. Every city has its specificity — its air, its taste, its manners —

and Toronto, too, has its own special flavour; that is what this book is about. Toronto becomes Toronto; Toronto is reborn.

There is an aspect of consciousness-raising in naming and identifying this process. I bring a point of view to this task and it is not unbiased or impartial. I am urging Toronto to become its best self, to realize its great potential. It must recognize and capitalize on enterprising initiatives to drive the city toward betterment and improve the state of its well-being for all — and I will argue Toronto is, in fact, taking a big step up in the world of cities, as evidenced by the creative and inclusive city-building I see germinating in many quarters.

PART ONE ON THE GROUND

1

How Change Appears

Torontonians are now engaged in a massive exercise of reverse-engineering the city they inherited, recovering qualities that were being lost and moving forward in new directions, undoing constraints and strictures, demonstrating new possibilities, and making profound changes to build the city anew. This is a daunting task, but it is driven by the combination of powerful forces described in the introduction: demographic and social, economic and environmental, all constituting an irresistible *force majeure*.

The backdrop for this is a big shift in the nature of cities. Humanity is living through one of the most remarkable periods of transformation in urban history, as twenty-first-century cities worldwide are redefining themselves. In the post–Second World War decades, a complex convergence of centrifugal forces — anticity polemics, cheap energy, and the unreserved embrace of the automobile — led the majority of North Americans to live in auto-oriented suburbs. In a little over two-and-a-half generations, the form and nature of cities in North America was altered.

It is now round two, and we are in recovery mode. Cities are making a comeback. The re-embrace of urban living is not only motivated by a desire for the lifestyle that cities offer. It's also driven by the growing interdependence between nations and their major urban centres. In many cases, businesses no longer need to locate their operations in a particular region or even country to be close to its natural resources; they can, instead, locate these in whatever international location best suits their human resource needs. Such decisions, especially for the knowledge-based industries that are increasingly driving the North American economy, are to a significant degree based on the quality of life a particular location offers.

The old, post–Second World War model of the city no longer serves the needs of service- and knowledge-focused businesses and the workers they employ. But cities have a remarkable ability to adapt, and as a result, many of North America's cities are emerging in a new form. Cities are complex, heterogeneous, and perpetually unfinished, capable of being made and remade in each generation by many hands often acting autonomously. They are living things, demonstrating an incredible capacity to learn and to adapt by synthesizing feedback and making modifications based on what works and what is needed.

With its critical mass, its ability to bring different aspects of daily life together in close proximity, and a large, diverse population, Toronto is acting as a catalyst, fostering invention and innovation in myriad areas, while at the same time it is responding to those alterations, absorbing them as it reinvents itself. The actual increments of change range from the initiative of individuals starting new enterprises on a main street, or a small business start-up, or a new cultural initiative, to big transformative projects, both public and private: entire new neighbourhoods, or large civil works.

The trajectory for Toronto's rebirth has a particular direction. Stepping back from the fray, it is possible to discern a big arc of the city's revival, one that generally reflects the broader shift in many parts of the developed world, particularly in North America, that I described in *Walking Home*, but one that is in ways unique to us. This trajectory is not a straightforward one — there are many twists and turns — but the long-term trend line seems abundantly clear as we make the shift from growing out in low-density sprawl to growing inward and upward, filling in the voids.

Torontonians are dramatically altering the city region they inherited two-and-a-half generations ago, when planners and developers heavyhandedly chopped up the city into homogenous zones for living and working and tore out its heart with ever-larger traffic arteries — actions that separated the ingredients and lost the flavours of urban life. At the time, the city, like many others in North America, placed a massive cultural and economic bet on a set of dubious premises: cheap energy, the car, and the alleged benefits of suburban life. The city thinned out as it spread east, west, and north, filling in the boundaries of what was then Metropolitan Toronto; into Scarborough, North York, Etobicoke; and beyond into the 905 region. It widened the roads and built plazas, malls, and power centres that we had to drive to from isolated, car-dependent subdivisions.

Every adult needed a car for essential personal mobility, and as these cars multiplied, they overran the city, taking over the sidewalks in order to widen traffic lanes. Every aspect of life changed: the way we ate, the way we shopped (filling the trunk of the station wagon, or now SUV, once a week), the role of women, and the shape of households. Wheels replaced feet and drive-thrus replaced walk-ins. Life outside of office hours was sucked from the downtowns. And it seemed inevitable, like a force of nature; the widely shared concept of the "good life" based on the family car as the primary means of transportation was rarely challenged.

In the end, this set of ideas was tested to the point of failure in the rush to reshape the postwar city, and its "faults" — strains, unintended by-products, and collateral damage — were eventually plain to see. We are now moving inexorably from Paradigm A (the postwar embrace of the automobile and sprawl, separation of land uses) to Paradigm B (the adoption of the new compact, walkable, mixed, synergistic, sustainable model) on parallel tracks in the prewar City of Toronto and the postwar suburbs in the 416 and the 905.

How is this shift happening? Like a living organism, the city evolves in order to survive and prosper. The enduring frame of major infrastructure, the streets, the surveyed blocks, and basic form of the city (call it the hardware), along with the more ephemeral uses, individual buildings, and spaces (the software) change and evolve in relation to each other — albeit with different timelines.

We are now at a pivotal point in this transformation of the form and character of Toronto and its living patterns, one that is as profound as the one that took place in the second half of the twentieth century. Many people, young people in particular, are re-examining and recalibrating the value system they inherited from their parents' and grandparents' generations.

The new quest for proximity and convenience desired by this younger generation of employees and their employers in the knowledge economy — for mixed-use settings combining living and working, for convenience and access, and a more general awareness of the environmental and public health benefits of a more active, walkable lifestyle — is clearly helping to propel a turn toward desirable urbanity and a new, more broadly shared, understanding of what a city can offer.

These changes are cumulative and interactive, operating through a kind of organic call-and-response; each increment of change alters conditions and makes others possible. A neighbourhood grows denser, and as a result there are more feet on the street; a critical mass of shops open, drawing in more customers, which in turn draws employers and more residents. The unfolding process is circular and never-ending.

The "change agents" in Toronto, from top down to bottom up, represent a broad spectrum of diverse actors, including individuals, entrepreneurs and companies, developers, planners, designers, community groups, politicians, and civil servants. Some of these actors are small and agile; others are larger and slower. There are early adapters, pioneers, and others who pile on and follow. There are also resisters and holdouts — those who feel threatened by particular changes, don't see their benefits, or simply don't want to change — and then there are YIMBY (yes in my backyard) activists who want to leverage positive change. Increasingly, civil society actors, BIAs, NGOs, philanthropists, and activists like Cycle Toronto, Walk Toronto, Park People, 8 80 Cities, and Waterfront for All are making their voices heard.

In some areas with the most urgent needs, remedies are coming simultaneously from many quarters. There have been changes in government policy and programs, but also civil society groups have stepped up to advocate forcefully for more sustainable permanent change while taking direct action for such things as shelter for the homeless, safe injection sites, and food banks. Underpinning much of this change is support of the "city for all" perspective. An example: the Toronto organization 8 80 Cities, which focuses on mobility, advocates for a city that an eight-year-old and an eighty-year-old both can feel comfortable walking and cycling in. At a micro level, the StopGap Foundation intervenes to make entrances on main streets barrier free by supplying wooden ramps to overcome awkward grade separations: a simple but powerful expedient.

Change is also coming from the daily accumulation of personal choices and decisions: citizens, responding to opportunity and necessity, influenced by and influencing a marketplace of available options, choosing where to live, where to invest, where to raise a family, where to work, where to open a store; whether to work at home, to walk, drive, cycle, or take transit. All of these adaptations are interactive, reflecting "organized complexity," the idea that everything is connected to everything else.

According to the proverbial leaf-on-the-river theory, a twig that falls in the current at the headwaters can alter the river by the time it reaches the river mouth. The city is like that river, the joint creation of an infinite number of twigs. Over time, pools and eddies and clusters of shared experience and interests converge and find expression, and the shared gene pool of city life and culture grows with new additions.

Some of what is old is new again. Many activities, technologies, ways of doing things that were downplayed and rejected did not disappear entirely, remaining available as "holdouts" for future survival when course corrections were needed — such as local neighbourhood shopping, the streetcar, and the bicycle.

Seen from close up, this variability can seem confusing in our city region. But despite the fact that we still seem to be operating at cross purposes, at times actively pursuing both old paradigms and new ones, our long-term trajectory is shifting from reliance on highways and cars to overcoming our transit deficit and making the shift to cycling and walking.

Still there is a huge aircraft carrier to turn around. Toronto was significantly enmeshed in the postwar paradigm. As we seek to change our city we have to not only develop consensus around a renewed vison for the city, but also overcome a legacy of entrenched habits, rules and regulations, and practices in city hall, in senior levels of government, and throughout an interwoven network of financial institutions, developers, lawyers, builders, brokers, real estate agents, and contractors, largely organized to produce a city based on the postwar auto-oriented paradigm.

Now, albeit with a whole new set of challenges, a transformed city is already emerging from the old — and the shift is remarkable. Toronto's core population has exceeded historic highs after decades of loss and is growing at four times the rate of the surrounding suburbs. There is a perceptible generational shift as people vote with their feet, repopulating the prewar city of Toronto, and seeking their urban qualities in renewing portions of the larger city region. There's a new appreciation of the things dense, walkable, compact neighbourhoods have to offer (even while many aspects of the other paradigm are still rolling along on autopilot).

A new and visible liveliness in the city has much to tell us. Robert Kanigel's recent biography of Jane Jacobs, *Eyes on the Street*, makes the really interesting point that her famous title *The Death and Life of Great American Cities* is as much about death and life as it is about the city, and that what makes things "live" is the leitmotif that ties together her entire body of work.

What we are seeing in many areas of Toronto is an explosion of life and vitality, of lively dynamism jostling in the streets, animating the parks, the markets, the cafés. From a city with a core that was eerily empty a few short decades ago, we are rapidly becoming a more intensely urban place and in many ways inventing a more urbane way of being together with a style, a feeling that is particular to us. But it is not just about the volume and speed of growth, but how we harness and use it.

Almost surprising ourselves, we have become enthusiastic unabashed city dwellers, urbanites, especially our younger generation. We are flexing urban muscles that we didn't know we still had; rediscovering the joys of the *flâneur*, the city wanderer with no fixed destination; trying out new places; experiencing the amazing diversity; rubbing elbows with people of different ages and at different moments in their lives. But while this resurgence has interesting echoes of a simpler pre-automobile past, when our streets were animated and people lived closer to their workplaces, when Yonge Street was the dynamic locus of pedestrian life it is becoming once more, this is not just back to the future; there are major differences, new circumstances, and new opportunities opening up in a much bigger and more dynamic city.

The new city is much bigger, more vertical, with many more people. It's certainly extraordinarily more diverse. There are other big new shifts in play: rediscovering our waterfront; embracing our main streets and supporting local businesses; enjoying each other's cuisines and learning to love farmers' markets; exploring our vast network of ravines, our inverted mountain ranges (dramatically revealed by their vulnerability during Hurricane Hazel); becoming aware of the value of the Greenbelt and the Oak Ridges Moraine that envelop us and supply our drinking water; and taking to trails criss-crossing the city and beyond to discover nature in our midst.

Much of this change is pleasure, not pain or sacrifice. There is so much that is undeniably positive, yet we cannot afford to be complacent. With our successes have come significant new challenges, often dealing with problems noted above, like housing affordability and congestion, that are the unintended consequences of these successes. Life is getting richer and more interesting, but not yet for all. But first the good news, and there is a great deal to celebrate.

As it fills in, the city has become much more continuously walkable. It is recovering slowly from the postwar aftermath that brought wider roads for cars, a proliferation of surface parking lots, and an architecture of isolated objects set back too far from the sidewalks, pulling up their skirts and turning inward.

These trends are reversing as the voids are reclaimed with new, more extroverted buildings, designed with transparent and animated frontages, adding life and people to the streets. The distances seem to shrink as walking becomes more pleasurable, and intuitive connections between previously isolated places and neighbourhoods are revived, and new possibilities and synergies emerge. The thin soup of our urban presence thickens.

There is a surprising groundswell of interest in the older neighbourhoods, coming not from planning ideology or politics, but from practical choices about how individuals want to live — especially among young people. They are choosing, as much as they possibly can, to live in places where they can walk, cycle, or take transit to work. And they don't see that choice as a forfeit; they see it as being smarter about their life choices. Mainly what they are getting is more time. They hate the idea of sitting in the car for hours a day, stuck in traffic jams. If they can be in places where they can walk to shop, walk to work, or take public transit or a bicycle, this gives them more opportunities to spend time with friends and family. They better organize their lives, but they are not pretentious about it; it's a pragmatic response.

There is something new in Toronto that, if you haven't been here for a while, might really surprise you. The number of cyclists on downtown streets has started to resemble the scene in Amsterdam or Copenhagen, although it still largely lacks the supporting infrastructure. The city now has streets lined with sought-after bike rings all around the inner city — but, admittedly, never enough; it is becoming almost impossible to find a place to park a bike. A recent survey revealed that 55 percent of Torontonians use bikes at some point, and of those, 26 percent use them to go to work or school and to run errands. The others are using them for leisure. This is an astonishing increase over a virtual absence of cyclists a few decades ago.

Torontonians are embracing the intermingling of the places where they live and work — from the Central Area Plan, inviting people to live downtown, to the opening of the floodgates with the "Kings" initiative (which I'll discuss below), repopulating four hundred acres on the shoulders of downtown and permeating the entire downtown core and central waterfront and even the heart of the previously homogeneous financial district. Toronto now has 250,000 residents in the core, a number expected to double by 2041, not surprisingly because that is where there is walkability and proximity to services and infrastructure acquired through generations of sunk capital investment.

The city is transforming its previously isolated public housing projects — Regent Park, Alexandra Park, Lawrence Heights, and others — into denser, mixed-income neighbourhoods. This is no small accomplishment and not to be taken for granted. These social development plans are critical to their success for their inhabitants; it is about not just about physical transformation.

There is also an investment in the city's cultural institutions — the National Ballet of Canada, the Royal Conservatory of Music, Art Gallery of Ontario (AGO), Royal Ontario Museum (ROM), and many others. We are seeing a major new role for the arts and culture in the life of the city — participatory, interactive, democratized. Many of these cultural institutions are being pulled out of their institutional boxes into the public sphere. Libraries and other community facilities, such as schools and community centres, are being expanded into shared community hubs that host evening classes, put on special events, and provide access to equipment like 3-D printers.

The city's universities and colleges are also expanding: the campuses of the University of Toronto, Ryerson University, OCAD University, and George Brown College have all grown, enriching their neighbourhoods. The guiding mantra is a new openness to the city. New partnerships are being forged among these institutions, as well. For the city, these educational institutions provide a competitive advantage in a global economy, contributing special places and resources that enliven and enrich city life. For the institutions, the vibrancy of the city itself is a competitive advantage in meeting contemporary student expectations and providing services that enable scarce resources to be directed to academic programs. The proverbial win-win situation.

The streets are alive with all manner of festivals: Luminato, Nuit Blanche, First Night, Open Streets, and dozens of other festivals transform the city throughout the year. The city has become a perpetual stage, allowing its citizens to perform for and interact with each other. Torontonians have also become fanatical café patio denizens, spilling outdoors the moment the weather allows.

By moving its civic life into the streets, Toronto's established residents are taking cues from the newcomers from cultures that are accustomed to using streets as shared living spaces. Queens Quay has become our new waterfront promenade, a space for *dolce far niente*. Jan Gehl, an architect from Copenhagen, quipped that Danes were all becoming Italians as they took to pedestrian streets; so are we! The city is like a new dish, spiced with distinctive flavours from European, Asian, Latin American, and African sources.

Toronto is rapidly figuring out how to make good new neighbourhoods, learning from old ones — the city is on a learning curve as it tries to redevelop sites from the St. Lawrence Market area to the West Don Lands on the site of the Pan Am Athletes' Village, the Well,* Mirvish Village, the East Bayfront, and Regent Park. Because so many of Toronto's residents are living in smaller spaces, the city needs more shared public space, leading to an intense reimagining of the city. Seeing opportunities through fresh eyes, Torontonians are forging new connections in public space, moving to expand "common ground" with initiatives that are often the result of a groundswell of efforts from communities themselves.

---

* The Well, a seven-acre, mixed-use hybrid development on the southern flank of Wellington Street (on the former *Globe and Mail* site), is integrating a full range of uses on one site.

Residents are embracing and improving many of the city's 1,600 parks — with the participation of "friends of" groups led by Park People, a dynamic NGO that has gone national. There is an attempt to make the city greener as it gets denser, as new forms of public space appear, such as the Bentway in the previously ignored territory under the elevated Gardiner Expressway.

We are learning how to live with our weather, using the outdoors in all seasons, getting beyond the overreaction of the internalized PATH system that buried us underground throughout the downtown while giving the surface over to the car (solving a problem but creating a new one: the loss of street life).*

At the same time, we are being forced to face the need for greater resilience to climate change. Severe flooding events are requiring us to undertake major works that combine flood protection and open space expansion, such as the massive undertaking of rerouting the Lower Don River where it enters Toronto Harbour. These civil infrastructure projects open up opportunities to accomplish multiple goals: the protective landform shielding much of downtown, for example, has enabled the creation of Corktown Common.**

As all of these changes happen, however embryonic they may still be, the contours of a different kind of city are emerging. It is a greener, more interconnected city, one no longer so reliant on the car. It is more mixed, more vibrant, more dynamic; more densely populated, more sociable, and more productive. To champion this change, an intergenerational, loosely knit network of creative "city builders" has emerged — community leaders, university presidents, developers, politicians, and others — all with a set of loosely shared values and ideas.

As the shift is happening, Toronto is quickly becoming a magnet for creativity. And as the city builds a critical mass of innovators and innovative

---

* The PATH is a mostly underground pedestrian walkway network in downtown Toronto that spans more than thirty kilometres of restaurants, shopping, services, and entertainment. It provides pedestrian linkages to public transit, accommodating more than two hundred thousand business-day commuters as well as tourists and residents.

** A 7.3-hectare (eighteen-acre) park located at the foot of Lower River Street and Bayview Avenue on former industrial lands, Corktown Common has transformed an underutilized brownfield into a spectacular park and community meeting place featuring a marsh, sprawling lawns, urban prairies, playground areas, and a splash pad.

places for them to gather, this momentum is growing. Not inconsequentially, Alphabet's Sidewalk Labs chose Toronto from among cities around the world for its urban test bed.* While this new project has generated much excitement, it has also led to an important reflection about the role of technology in the city.

Another telltale event occurred when Amazon issued a call in 2017 for cities to compete for its second headquarters, with fifty thousand employees. Toronto's response to this call sent a significant signal of the city's growing self-confidence. Unlike many of its American counterparts, which were somewhat desperately offering free land, tax subsidies and writeoffs, and a great variety of other financial inducements, Toronto put together a regional bid with its neighbouring cities simply stating: Come if you wish, we have the talent, the quality of life, and the physical and social infrastructure, including, not inconsequentially, public health care. No inducements, your choice. Toronto has begun to understand that it has something of inestimable value. And while the bid was not successful, it was a serious contender.

Toronto is less and less a branch plant and more and more an original producer. Many notable ideas have been pioneered, incubated, and exported in Toronto — Artscape (a not-for-profit organization dedicated to producing space for artists), CSI (the Centre for Social Innovation), BIAs, and Luminato. Our city is becoming the subject, not just the stand-in, in films like Sarah Polley's *Take This Waltz*, and there are similar proudly local manifestations in music, photography, literature, and theatre.

Toronto is far from perfect (or perfectible). Constantly under construction, it feels eclectic, ad hoc, and "accidental," not orderly or formally grand, although it has its special places. It is certainly not conventionally beautiful in an ordered, composed way. It has a kind of homely frontier roughness — exterior hydro poles and streets strung with wires, buildings of all sizes and shapes cohabiting streets — but it is incredibly robust and energetic. It embraces modernity and struggles to retain its heritage, but the most interesting places occur where styles mix and overlap in eclectic combination.

---

* Sidewalk Toronto is a joint effort by Waterfront Toronto and Alphabet's Sidewalk Labs to create a new kind of mixed-use, complete community on Toronto's Eastern Waterfront, beginning with a new neighbourhood called Quayside.

It is fascinating to examine how Torontonians have described themselves over time, from a narrow and penny-pinching "Hogtown," to puritanical "Toronto the Good," somewhat more positively "The City that Works," and now Drake's "the 6ix"; and what next? This changing self-perception can be traced through the influences of our formative moments in recent years: the actions of the Reform Council of the 1970s, the traumas of amalgamation, the Ford years, the big fights — the Spadina Expressway rejection, the defeat of casino resorts on the waterfront. The city's ever-shifting architectural iconography also provides a view of the city's evolution. Examples include the city's escalating skyline — the construction of the iconic TD Centre and the other bank towers, the building of the monumental CN Tower, and, more recently, the astonishing proliferation of ever-taller condos and office buildings; the refurbishing of our emblematic public buildings and spaces — New City Hall, the AGO, the city's universities and colleges, and the new waterfront parks; the revitalization of Regent Park; and the increasing vibrancy of the city's streets.

The truth is, for cities, branding is as branding does. While words, images, logos, and concepts do matter a great deal, they ring hollow without corresponding deeds. It is the vital narrative of place that makes a city unique and special. You can't just graft on a false story or an empty one. Torontonians now know much more about themselves; their self-image and self-understanding are more mature and confident. They have to some extent internalized a better understanding of how a city works and its "organized complexity." What Torontonians do for a living is shifting dramatically as they begin to use their brains and not just their muscle, and make the transition to an economy based on renewables, resting more lightly on the earth, developing their human resources first and foremost in the city.

Torontonians are constantly struggling, of course, with what the city can and cannot achieve alone, how they relate to their regional hinterland, the increasing power of city-regions, but also their dependence on federal and provincial levels for resources and policy direction, as well as global externalities beyond the city's borders. Yet in many respects, the city itself is a great innovator. It can take credit both internally and externally for very real accomplishments at a city level without arrogance or narcissism. Toronto, after all, reshaped Canada's national housing strategy and the lending policies of CMHC (Canada Mortgage and Housing Corporation) in the 1970s with City Home and the St. Lawrence neighbourhood, when it pioneered new forms of financing and management for non-equity co-ops serving a full spectrum of incomes.

Perhaps the best news is that there has never been greater interest in "city building" in Toronto. The details of plans for the city are no longer just "insider baseball," shared amongst professionals, developers and others with a vested interest in the money that can be made from the transformation of Toronto. There is now a shared societal interest in them and a focus on their impacts engaging a very broad constituency as we keep up with changes almost the way we follow our sports teams. *Metro Morning* on CBC radio, Toronto's most popular morning radio show, has been the constant soundtrack for this evolution, with a succession of hosts from Joe Coté to Andy Barrie and Matt Galloway who have kept the city informed on a daily basis about the current wave of paradigm-shifting initiatives.

The city is a world in intense, non-stop motion. More and more players are drawn into the fray as plans call forth other plans. It is an evolving ecosystem — physical and human, interactive — with hundreds, in fact thousands of creators operating by trial and error. Some initiatives succeed, some don't; some morph into something else as they reshape the urban culture, adding new references and touchstones. Some have well-known authors and origin stories, as when occasionally a unique, flamboyant entrepreneur like Honest Ed Mirvish arrived on the scene, making an indelible impression. Other ideas arrive anonymously. Some are transplants that take root. Others are entirely homegrown and native. Mostly, they are serial creations.

The backdrop is rarely a *tabula rasa*, a clean slate. Torontonians are continuously building and rebuilding the city on the city that already exists. This legacy of context provides both constraints and opportunities. The previous layers, the surveyed pattern of streets and blocks, structures and open spaces, institutions and collective memory, provide a rich inheritance of palimpsests.

The city is immeasurably more appealing when these traces of former lives — built legacy, natural features, and human stories — are preserved and revealed in their present and future selves. They tell us a great deal about who we are; in some cases, they inspire and enable things that would otherwise not be possible; they shape an identity that makes us more interesting to ourselves and others. They provide a competitive advantage in a world of sameness.

Torontonians have fervently declared our aspiration to be a city that is equitable, diverse, inclusive, productive, sustainable, and welcoming. These visionary goals are certainly not unique to Toronto. They are to be found in some form in the planning documents of almost all contemporary cities. A set of common forces affects many cities in the developed world as we collectively make the big paradigm shift from a mid-twentieth-century, auto-led exodus from city cores, and heavy-handed urban renewal in those city cores, to the new vision now in the early decades of the twenty-first century. Many cities are participating in a rediscovery of the discarded virtues of the prewar city — compact, walkable, and mixed in use — in combination with the new. The fact that Toronto is dealing with circumstances similar to those of many cities around the world does not necessarily make those circumstances easier to face. Torontonians can't take this current positive direction for granted. While there may be a promising historic trend line, there are constant struggles in the trenches as we reshape the city.

Toronto has a very big to-do list. One of the biggest challenges in moving forward is the problem of recombining how we live and work while also dealing with diversity, ensuring that Toronto truly is a city for all. Toronto needs to modify its existing, rather restricted, street network to better accommodate pedestrians, cyclists, transit vehicles, and drivers. Developers must be made to ensure that their projects contribute positively to the urban fabric. The city has to find innovative ways of expanding public space; as it grows denser, it needs to overcome barriers and create new forms of open space networks. Toronto must adapt to climate change, not by attempting to overpower nature but by working with natural processes. The city must be made healthier for all citizens. The citizens of Toronto have to figure out how to overcome the great divide caused by amalgamation. And finally, Torontonians need to summon the will to invest in the hard and soft infrastructure urgently needed to make the city work.

Our personal mental maps of the city must constantly be redrawn as visible and tangible changes continue to appear. The result is often patchy and uneven; alterations are dispersed throughout the city through the work of individual projects by developers, the city itself, social entrepreneurs, non-profits, public-private partnerships, and individuals. Over time, these microcosms of change accumulate and connect, and the physiognomy of the entire city alters. It is revealing to see how this process happens piece by piece in real time and space, and how it modifies our perception of the city as a whole and our sense of what is expected and possible. Through this churn we get glimpses of change.

In the following chapters I want to focus on some potent examples: icebreakers, early indicators that demonstrate particular themes relating to how we live and move in this new city. They are a combination of ordinary and special places that point the way. Each is a leitmotif for a particular theme. Admittedly, these examples are personal choices; some I have had direct involvement in, others I have been following carefully. But I believe they have general relevance. Perhaps they are exceptional right now, but hopefully they have the capacity to expand our sense of the possible.

2

Neighbourhoods Coalesce

A leisurely twenty-minute walk west of the heart of Toronto's financial district at King and Bay, a broad stretch of Wellington Street leads to a small green oasis called Victoria Memorial Square. It is a space with a rich history, one all but lost to memory a couple of decades ago. From 1794 to 1863, this square was the cemetery for the garrison of Fort York. To this day, it still contains approximately five hundred unmarked graves. Since the 1880s, however, it has been operated by the city as a public park.

Looking to the east, looming office towers are in plain view. They might as well be a world away, though. On a sunny weekend afternoon, this once desolate and empty park is newly full of bench sitters, sunbathers, dog walkers, frisbee throwers, runners, and yoga classes. All the benches are full, and even though their number has been recently doubled, there are still not enough. A small playground on the edge of the park overflows with the young families who have repopulated the area.

On weekday mornings and afternoons, there is a steady rush hour flow of pedestrians criss-crossing the park on their way to and from work in the adjacent downtown core and the neighbourhood itself, on its relatively new interlacing wishbone pathways. Plaques that line these walks inform visitors of the noteworthy origin of the square as the burial ground for Fort York, the outline of which has now been delineated with granite strips as part of a redesign. The few remaining headstones that were lying flat and deteriorating from acid rain have been rescued and mounted vertically with identifying inscriptions. Increasingly, walking tours of the curious visit the park to learn about its special place in the city's history.

Two decades ago, the edges of the park were ill-defined, blending with the forlorn parking lots that surrounded it. Today it is almost entirely surrounded by new, mid-rise residential buildings forming a complete enclosure, most evident at night when the lights from the buildings provide a warm and welcoming intimacy, complementing the lit walkways in the park itself.

In 1997, my friends and colleagues Howard Cohen and Lloyd Alter were launching their first development venture on Victoria Memorial Square, and Howard invited me to visit his sales office on my way to the airport. With some optimism about what the future might hold for the neighbourhood, my wife, Eti, and I took the leap and bought a unit overlooking the park along with some other friends. We moved into 20 Niagara Street in 1998, where we have lived ever since, giving us a unique vantage point of the extraordinary transformation that has occurred.

This reborn neighbourhood is called Wellington Place. It reclaims the original name given to the ambitious development plan laid out by the city in 1837, which included a grand, tree-lined boulevard (now Wellington Street West) that connected a dumbbell of squares to Clarence Square at Spadina (designed as a site for the lieutenant governor's residence) and ran westward to Victoria Memorial Square at Portland.

Some grand homes were initially erected on large lots, but this process was soon arrested when the Northern Railway arrived with its Toronto passenger depot and shops on landfill south of Front Street in the mid-1850s, radically altering the character of the area. The railway's presence produced some railway workers' housing in the 1880s, still in evidence on Draper Street (where Lieutenant Governor of Ontario Lincoln Alexander was born in 1922 to West Indian parents). That housing construction was also interrupted, this time by the 1857 commercial depression, whose effects were felt for a decade during which very few new buildings were constructed.

Next in the series of dramatic shifts came a period after 1900 when manufacturing, drawn by the railway, began to move in, and the area's character changed from residential to predominantly industrial. Some of these industries had been forced out of the downtown by the Great Fire of 1904, while others sought to erect their factories near a good supply of labour. Of all the streets in the area, Wellington Place (today's Wellington Street West) was the best suited for redevelopment since it was lined by big, old houses on good-sized lots.

With the advent of industry, the appearance of the area changed, coming to resemble its present form, with substantial, mid-rise, loft-like buildings constructed largely between 1905 and 1920. About the same time, on the south side of King Street, west of Spadina Avenue, some other large, handsome factories were erected for "name" clients. The entire area had rapidly become an industrial powerhouse for Canada from which a wide range of manufactured goods of all types were exported by rail.

Following the Second World War, however, this bustling industrial area gradually lost its steam. Industry abandoned downtown Toronto and many of the factories and warehouses were torn down, replaced with parking lots. Only a few isolated businesses hung on and there were almost no residents or pedestrians. The stage was thus set for the Kings Initiative, as the remaining legacy of industrial buildings proved remarkably well suited to post-industrial mixed-use.

In a massive turnaround, Wellington Place and its immediate neighbours in the Garment District neighbourhood and the Niagara neigbourhood have been steadily filling in for the past twenty years, as the remaining stock of solidly built, early twentieth-century mercantile buildings are repurposed for new workspaces and dwelling units and the population grows by leaps and bounds. In tandem, retail offerings have gone from almost non-existent to meeting virtually every daily need, from food shopping to hairdressers and hardware, all within easy walking distance. It is now common to see residents walking (not driving) home with bags of groceries.

During the day, the old brick and beam buildings, and now some new purpose-built office buildings, are busy with the comings and goings of the people who work there. At night, things really spring to life. Clubs and restaurants fill with patrons; sometimes a rowdy scene spills out into the streets at closing time. All of this has sprung up in what were once empty warehouse spaces. This mix is not static, though; buildings are changing occupants; some uses are gradually displaced by others as the area fills in.

The population of residents and workers keeps growing, and walking and cycling are increasing exponentially. Each layer of new development is becoming more ambitious in combining living and working spaces and adding amenities.

A powerful momentum of change has been unleashed. New business ventures of all sizes and shapes, along with an eclectic mix of professional offices and services, continue to sprout up in great profusion throughout the area; likewise, many new restaurants and cafés are serving local residents, employees, and visitors.

The public realm of streets and open spaces is also evolving to meet new needs and pressures. Aside from the two squares of Wellington Place, there was very little green space. Now, in addition to a few strategic new park acquisitions secured through redevelopment, a potent new opportunity has been identified to add to the public realm. A number of these new Wellington Place projects are providing a finer grain of connectivity by breaking up the very large blocks in the area through a combination of repurposing existing lanes and introducing a new network of pedestrian mews and passageways. Interiors of the large blocks that were closed and inaccessible are becoming open and porous; very long walks around the block are shortened. This is creating many new opportunities for small-scale enterprises and animation, allowing for a valuable fine-grained counterpoint to the surrounding larger grain of the industrial era.

With this increased mix of living and working, an area once filled with single-use workspaces, occupied for very specific and limited times, has become a vibrant 24/7 neighbourhood. As renovation and new building advance and the population increases, streets that had been monopolized by heavy truck traffic and parking access are being incrementally modified to accommodate vastly increased use by pedestrians and cyclists. The grand boulevard of Wellington Street, with its original tree-lined promenades and generous forty-five-metre right-of-way, had been subverted by surface parking lots within the boulevard. Today, it is being reclaimed as green space in keeping with that earlier vision.

Both ends of this stretch of Wellington Street have been modified in telling ways. At the eastern border, where once there was no safe way of crossing Spadina Avenue to get to Clarence Square, there is now a heavily used pedestrian-activated light. No longer is it necessary for the hundreds of pedestrians to tempt fate by running across six lanes of fast moving traffic and LRT lines.

To the west, the awkwardly staggered intersection of Portland and Wellington had a wide, sweeping radius combining two intersections to allow for free-flowing traffic and was similarly dangerous for the volumes of crossing pedestrians. With the help of then city councillor Adam Vaughan, the city was prevailed upon to straighten out this pair of intersections, add sidewalk space, and make vehicles stop. This last change helped to ensure that there is eye contact between drivers, pedestrians, and cyclists. Subtle changes like this are completely changing the "reading" of the crossing, giving priority back to pedestrians.

All of this has happened in a relatively short time. Wellington Place has gone from being an undervalued no man's land to a dynamic, multi-layered neighbourhood, and Victoria Memorial Square has been transformed from a neglected, scraggly patch of underutilized space into the area's much prized, active green heart. A whole new generation of buildings has come, with over thirty new projects in the last twenty years filling in the voids. Wellington Place has become denser, populated by mid-rise buildings, while for the most part retaining its important legacy of heritage structures, and this process is not nearly finished.

How did this rapid transformation come about?

The foundation for the transformation of Wellington Place was laid some twenty years earlier by the Kings Initiative, championed by then mayor Barbara Hall, which had liberated Wellington Place from traditional planning restrictions. This initiative had been conceived shortly after her election in 1994 by a group she convened including Jane Jacobs, me, Chief Planner Paul Bedford, economist Gary Stamm, and developer Bob Eisenberg. In a rare and compelling example of what could be called "subtractive urbanism," the Kings Initiative removed an unhelpful zoning prohibition against the mixing of residential and commercial land use to allow people to live and work in two large, previously moribund, industrial areas straddling Toronto's core.

The "Kings" (King-Spadina and King-Parliament) cover four hundred acres bisected by King Street on the shoulders of Toronto's financial core. These areas had served as successful manufacturing districts until the mid-twentieth century. They entered a period of accelerating decline from the 1970s to the early 1990s, as manufacturing migrated from multi-storey buildings in the city core to low-density, single-storey structures in highway-oriented suburbs.

Meanwhile, Toronto's zoning regulations were still aimed at protecting receding traditional industry, and prohibited most modern development activity, including residential development. Despite futile attempts to restimulate these traditional employment uses, industrial vacancy rates increased, and property owners began to demolish heritage buildings to reduce their property taxes. The writing was on the wall.

Faced with the inevitable attrition of valuable building stock as well as the sterilization of a very large, strategically located land resource, the strategies of the Kings Initiative were relatively simple: remove traditional strictures by deregulating land use in the affected areas, and abandon the industrial policy strategy in favour of a new, flexible regulatory system controlling only built form so as to encourage reinvestment for a broad range of contemporary mixed land use. In other words, the new zoning provisions were aimed at building shape and size, instead of buiding use. Planners were less concerned with what was happening in buildings, and more interested in the ways buildings fit in their lots and shaped their surroundings."

In 1995, the Kings were re-designated as "regeneration areas," and by April of 1996, City Council had approved the necessary planning and zoning amendments to implement the new vision: encouraging new reinvestment, creating housing opportunities, and allowing for creative spaces for new business development in mixed-use settings. This radical plan (which came at little public cost) has had enormous impact. As of 2018, over fifty thousand new residential units have been built in the Kings area, and there are many more on the way. There were already 58 percent more jobs in the Kings than existed before the initiative, as well as a growing variety of new businesses, shops, and services, often in existing buildings. More than half of the Kings' residents walk to work.

Though obviously the right choice in hindsight, the new planning policies and zoning alterations of the Kings Initiative represented a dramatic departure from the way planning had been done in Toronto. The old approach had relied on highly specific land-use restrictions, segregating work from living. But these restrictions had not been keeping pace with either the emerging desire of both residents and businesses to combine work and living spaces, or the changing real estate market in those areas of transition, where industry had fled.

In addition to shifting zoning priorities away from controlling the uses in the buildings and toward their built form, the new policy attempted to emphasize neighbourhood context and bring greater attention to public spaces and pedestrian amenities, recognizing that improvements to the public realm would be required to make these industrial districts more attractive to new businesses and residents. Along with a relaxation of land use policies, Community Improvement Plans (CIPs) were adopted by City Council in 1997 for both the King-Spadina and King-Parliament areas. These plans focused on enhancing heritage character, improving the quality of public spaces, and increasing public safety.

The rediscovered and now lively Wellington Place neighbourhood, in the heart of the Kings, has been a direct beneficiary of the bold plan to transform the Kings some twenty years earlier. In 2017, former mayor Barbara Hall and I led a well-attended Jane's Walk through the area to tell the story to a rapt group, many of whom were young people who now live and work in Wellington Place, but had no idea how their neighbourhood had come to be. (Named after urban activist and writer Jane Jacobs, these free walking tours are held annually in hundreds of cities around the world during the first weekend in May to coincide with her birthday.)

While the Kings Initiative has been generally successful, some growing pains — problems of success associated with redevelopment that exceeded expectations — are also starting to appear, including strains on the city's ability to control the scale of buildings and to fund the public improvements necessary to keep up with the pace of change.

One of the most important groups in ensuring that development of the Wellington Place area remains on track is the Wellington Place Neighbourhood Association (WPNA), formed to represent the interests of the new people who were coming to live and work in the area. (In the interest of full disclosure, I am the current chair of the association.) Right from the outset, this group's work has complemented the city's top-down policy shift and has served as a critical ingredient in the success of Wellington Place.

For over eighteen years this association has worked with a succession of local councillors and city staff to shape and guide change during this critical period of neighbourhood revival. It has engaged with every developer who has invested in the area to improve the quality of design, secure public benefits, and ensure respect for the rich heritage of the area, providing a tailored community checklist of issues and opportunities for each site under consideration.

Early on, the WPNA joined its neighbouring associations to successfully fight off a potentially devastating expressway incursion through the heart of the neighbourhood. While accepting that change is both inevitable and desirable, the WPNA's vision and modus operandi has been to work in partnership with the private sector and the city to revitalize the entire Wellington Place district in a way that builds on the area's legacy and respects its unique underlying historic structure.

The community's initial focus was on the public realm, bringing to light its key hidden asset, Victoria Memorial Square. One of the WPNA's very first initiatives was to take a lead role in the restoration and improvement of the square as a public space. The community funded a landscape plan, built on the square's historical significance and natural beauty, which called for regrading, lighting, pathways, trees and plantings, furniture, and playground equipment — and a visible public commemoration of the rich history it embodies. Then, with the support of the area's councillors, the group developed a program of rehabilitation and interpretation using development impact fees that has resulted in a treasured amenity for those who live and work in the area and a cultural attraction for all citizens and visitors to the city.

In 2002, Jane Jacobs wrote the following in a letter to the association, which now appears on a plaque on a pair of chairs in the square dedicated to her memory: "In gratitude to the Wellington Place Neighbourhood Association: Victoria Memorial Square will be an urban jewel, rescued from a wasteland of neglect and forgetfulness. It beautifully ties the city's earliest roots into a living, caring, revitalized community. The whole city is made richer by this enlightened act of stewardship."

With an eye to the future, the WPNA remains alert to Toronto's mounting city-building challenges while still aiming to maintain the unique scale and quality of the neighbourhood. This requires both advocacy and, when necessary, pushing back hard in the face of sometimes inappropriate development proposals. Recognizing that its neighbourhood is not an island in a rapidly evolving part of the city, the WPNA is also committed to working closely with neighbouring associations to play a constructive role on larger issues critical for the future health and vitality of the entire community, including expanding housing opportunities and providing increased amenities, such as parks, playgrounds, daycare, libraries, and schools, for a diverse and growing population.

Those who wish to move forward must first understand how they arrived where they are. The association was extremely fortunate to have as a founding member Scott James, Toronto's former city archivist and head of the Toronto Historical Board. With the assistance of Steve Otto, one of Toronto's most knowledgeable city historians and a key member of the Friends of Fort York, James was able to help new community members appreciate the rich, multi-layered history of Wellington Place and Victoria Memorial Square, beginning with their origins as part of a military reserve, which prohibited the erection of private buildings in an area defined by the cannon range from Fort York.

Wellington Place provides a great example of a living history, where every era has left its mark, providing a rich, ongoing narrative of city building from the eighteenth-century burial ground to the unfolding present, which residents and visitors can literally still "read" in their surroundings. The city's initial ambitious plan to create a generous public realm at the neighbourhood scale in 1837 — the pair of nineteenth-century squares and their connecting greenway — still provides the neighbourhood's framework, the essential glue that ties the area together and a context from which the most recent developments can draw their identity.

The revival of the "Kings," and of Wellington Place in particular, is a fitting tribute to Jane Jacobs. When my wife and I first moved to 20 Niagara on Victoria Memorial Square, the first legal new residential building in the King and Spadina area (a direct product of the Kings Initiative), we picked Jane up and brought her to see our new place. As always, she was very curious about everything that was happening. We went out on our sixth-floor balcony overlooking the park to survey the neighbourhood, and she stood rapt with her hands on the railing and talked about the struggles to get the plan approved at city hall. She then said, with a broad smile, "I just can't wait to see how things turn out." Almost twenty years later, I still feel the same way.

For the past two decades, Wellington Place has provided a useful test bed for learning how to build the "new city," the "new neighbourhood," on top of the one that already exists. It's an exercise in taking advantage of the sunk capital in hard and soft infrastructure we inherit from previous generations, capitalizing on the area's inherent qualities without overwhelming them through overdevelopment. This is an ongoing struggle; success is a magnet for more development.

In many respects, the rebirth of Wellington Place fulfills the vision of the even earlier pre-Kings Central Area Plan of the mid-1980s, which advocated bringing a live-in population back to Toronto's then somewhat sterile and homogeneous nine-to-five downtown core. The change is happening incredibly fast, with cranes on the sky everywhere and every vacant lot seemingly under construction. While Wellington Place is a unique example, *sui generis*, it has much to teach us that is broadly applicable as the city's development takes on a new intensity.

In previous decades, following the prescriptions of the modern movement, Toronto had blown its neighbourhoods apart into work and living zones separated by long commutes. Now Toronto is rediscovering the virtues of mixed-use communities. This change in thinking was led by the success of the adaptive reuse of former warehouse and factory districts like Wellington Place. To achieve a greater mix and density in the older areas of the city, Toronto's planners have had to alter the lens of consideration for planning and design, changing from a focus on individual buildings, or even clusters of individual buildings, to the totality of the environment they form, the dense and compact heterogeneous neighbourhood.

In stark contrast to the bounded suburban layout of residential cul-de-sacs located around a local elementary school and surrounded by arterial roads with a shopping plaza and some multi-family buildings at the edge, most often created by a single developer, the heterogeneous neighbourhood is something much more organic, intensively mixed and made by many hands. Diverse urban neighbourhoods have "weak borders," permeable, interpenetrating, and changeable over time, open to interactions with their neighbours and changes in use.

Wellington Street in 1983. Industrial obsolescence had left an eerie emptiness in the streets of Wellington Place, which had been largely abandoned by the major industrial users that had populated the area with factories in the early decades of the twentieth century.

With the advent of the Kings Initiative — a major change in city policy that permitted mixed-use zoning — a new life and vitality started to appear in the area as residents and workers went about their daily routines in reoccupied older buildings and new ones that filled in the gaps as surface parking lots disappeared.

Victoria Memorial Square in 1913. Isolated and almost lost to memory in the mid-twentieth century, this historic square began life in 1794 as the burial ground for nearby Fort York and was reconfigured to form one of the bookend squares of Wellington Place in 1834. For many decades it sat largely empty and neglected in the wake of departing industries.

Now the vital heart of a dynamic new neighbourhood, Victoria Memorial Square has become the shared green space and community living room for the neighbourhood, offering respite and relaxation and a glimpse into the area's rich history for a growing number of new residents, employees, and visitors.

Wellington Place, mixed by its very nature as an eclectic recycled warehouse district, is a great demonstration of what this looks like at a neighbourhood scale. Uses and daily patterns begin to overlap and intertwine to mutual advantage, allowing new relationships and synergies to emerge. The adaptive reuse of older buildings is releasing a pent-up potential, allowing things that want to happen to occur. My favourite local café, serving residents and workers, can operate from 7:00 a.m. to 2:00 a.m. with a changing menu and clientele following the rhythm of the day. As we completely collapse the boundaries between living and working, a useful analogy from ecology that captures the idea of the neighbourhood as a mixing chamber is the *ecotone* — a transitional zone between two adjacent biological communities, containing a rich variety of species characteristic of both.

Instructive examples of this fine-grained mix pepper our older, lower density neighbourhoods, where, before segregated zoning took hold, corner stores, workshops, small-scale restaurants, and local pubs thrived within the neighbourhood fabric. One example is the symbiotic combination of the Monarch Tavern and San Francisco Foods on Clinton Street in Little Italy, where you can buy a great sandwich and take it next door for a beer in the midst of a much-loved residential neighbourhood.

Thanks to its mix of old and new buildings of all sizes and shapes, Wellington Place provides many opportunities for these kinds of small neighbourhood outlets and enterprises, tucked in among the larger ones, that would be very difficult to establish in an entirely new setting. Week by week, month by month, these show up in unexpected places on the street frontages and, increasingly, in laneways and mid-block passages. Popular co-working spaces and co-living spaces, combined with live-work arrangements within dwellings and the growth of the sharing economy, are pushing the boundaries of current planning regulations and restrictions. Technology itself is a powerful change agent for radical mix, providing new opportunities for flexibly managing and operating mixed-use buildings.

Many of the more practical reasons we may have had for wanting to separate living and working spaces in earlier periods — the negative environmental and health impacts of industry, for example — are no longer relevant in the new economy. To some extent what is old is new again, but in an entirely different way. The next step, inspired by these adaptive reuse models, is to make new places with new buildings, developing structures that are as adaptable as these early twentieth-century warehouses still are, with malleable, loft-like spaces.

Key questions arise, such as how fine-grained is the desired mix? Is it coarse-grained at the scale of the neighbourhood, like Liberty Village, with side-by-side residential and employment areas that are still very separate; or does the mix of living, working, and shopping become more intimate, within blocks of contiguous buildings; or finer still, within buildings themselves, stacked vertically or horizontally; or even further, on floors of integrated use, interchangeably blended?

It is ultimately far more efficient to build "full life-cycle" neighbourhoods designed to self-renew with a mix of demographics and living options from the start, so that people have the option of growing up in a neighbourhood, starting their careers there, raising a family and growing older without being forced to move away when their life circumstances change. For example, in this type of neighbourhood, seniors can move from houses to apartments, or from larger to smaller apartments, without moving away from the community to an isolated seniors' residence. This "aging in place" also allows younger people to keep entering the community, replacing older generations; the schools don't suffer from severe overcrowding or emptying out as one age cohort passes through.

The benefits are multiple and obvious: better use of scarce resources and human capital, tapping the skills and knowledge of elders, who are able to play useful and productive roles in the community, and the creation of more opportunities for younger people to get a foothold in the community. Age-integrated neighbourhoods smooth out demographic peaks and valleys of need for facilities like schools, daycare, and community centres, making them more financially sustainable and responsive.

The shift to radical mixed-use has major implications for developers who were highly specialized in one market niche in the previous paradigm, with expertise in financing and building stand-alone office buildings, condos, rental buildings, or retail complexes, and whose financial plans were based on such specialization. This shift is forcing forward-looking developers to form joint ventures or diversify internally to meet escalating market demand for mixed-use integration within their projects.

Projects like the Well, a seven-acre, mixed-use hybrid development on the southern flank of Wellington Street (on the former *Globe and Mail* site), are integrating a full range of uses on one site. The Well, which may be the most ambitious mixed-use endeavour in Canada, is a multi-party developer collaboration, led by Steve Diamond of DiamondCorp, which specializes in residential buildings; Tridel, an additional residential developer; Woodbourne Canada Management; Allied Properties, a REIT (real estate investment trust) whose developments offer office space; and RioCan, a retail developer. The scheme takes the form of seven small-footprint, mixed-use "blocks," framing a fine-grained, mid-block pedestrian network animated by retail. It will include a public daycare and an on-site linear park, an additional north-south park connection on a site across Wellington Street linking to an adjoining development with connections to King Street, and a westerly neighbourhood park link to Draper Street.

When completed, there will be as many as twenty thousand people living, working, and shopping on this 7.8-acre site. The site will also provide parking for over two thousand bicycles. With so many new residents and employees in close proximity there is a push for public amenities, such as schools, community centres, daycares, parks, playgrounds, and the whole array of community service facilities. Here and elsewhere, the benefits, both in terms of savings through shared use and convenience through co-location, are driving a push to create consolidated community hubs instead of scattered individual facilities on separate parcels of land. The new combined Public and Catholic School and Community Centre complex in CityPlace, adjacent to Canoe Landing Park, is a leading example. One step further is the incorporation of a variety of these facilities within the lower floors of mixed-use buildings, like the new "embedded" YMCA, located within a recycled City Works structure on Richmond Street, which is combined with residential floors above.

As planners struggle to keep up with and choreograph Toronto's massive growth and its changing land use, dealing with the impacts and trying to ensure that the new creation is sustainable, there are clear implications for municipal governance. Acknowledging the phenomenal growth of the downtown core, at a rate some four times greater than the city as a whole, then Chief Planner Jennifer Keesmaat launched an exercise in 2017 called

TOcore to address the problems of success and the urgent need to augment both hard and soft infrastructure: services and utilities, transit, social infrastructure, schools, daycare, community centres, and parks and recreation. These are complex challenges requiring unprecedented levels of teamwork, connecting traditional silos, new uses of financial tools, and partnership arrangements.

One of the most challenging problems of Toronto's success in attracting development has to do with maintaining balance and distributing growth in the face of enormous development pressures. The infusions of new life that higher-density buildings bring into older areas raise critical issues, such as the compatibility of new structures with existing ones, and the impact of these changes on the comfort and well-being of the area's existing residents. The residents, businesses, and additional street life that accompany these new buildings are a good thing, but too many bulky new buildings can bring so many changes that the very qualities that make the area successful in the first place are undermined. Transitions in scale, facing distances between buildings that affect light and privacy, and contextual relationships between old and new are critical.

The current wave of development in Toronto is unevenly distributed, causing enormous spikes in height in a few concentrated areas, like parts of the King-Spadina area, the Yonge Street corridor, and the waterfront. Two or three of the downtown wards are absorbing the lion's share of new growth, leaving many areas untouched where infusions of development would actually be beneficial. An industry fixation on achieving great building height in places where it is not always appropriate — something inspired to a significant degree by the greed of land speculators — has become a particular Toronto problem. We have equated growth with extreme height in some areas (towers of ninety and one hundred storeys are in development), while preventing it almost entirely in other areas sometimes dubbed the "yellow belt" (the colour on planning maps for "stable residential areas"). There we succumb to pressure from some homeowners who resist any redevelopment and intensification, even if it involves buildings of modest size. This very uneven pattern of development — very tall towers in a few, concentrated areas of the city and no real increasing of density in most of the city — was exacerbated in the past by the now defunct Ontario

Municipal Board's unpredictable rulings, and an adversarial culture that pitted developers against citizens (and often city government).

The antidote to such uneven hyperdevelopment is "spread." Tall buildings definitely have their place, but in the "space race" for height we have too often overlooked the benefits of the mid-rise scale, the "missing middle." Getting to a more sustainable and equitable distribution will require directing growth to more places in our city, and this will require overcoming the sometimes unreasonable resistance to necessary change, getting to "yes in my backyard" (YIMBY) in more places. Then Toronto can more comprehensively realize the opportunities for positive neighbourhood building throughout its urban fabric.

Wellington Place has become a rare Toronto example of a dense fabric of robust, mid-scale old and new buildings. It has largely bucked the high-rise tower–podium format that has become Toronto's prevalent form of redevelopment. As of this writing, there are some developers who keep challenging the limits in Wellington Place, but hopefully the line will be held. A city like Toronto needs variety in its built form and neighbourhood character; one size need not fit all. Wellington Place demonstrates that is possible to achieve sustainable density in different ways, and that spreading this density more evenly can have real benefits, creating a viable, human-scaled setting for neighbourhood life while drawing inspiration from a rich local history.

City building is a multi-generational, serial exercise. One of the things that has made Wellington Place special is its layered history, a history that has left behind many physical artefacts and traces, beginning with the unique block pattern formed by the original 1837 plan with its two squares, some 450 metres apart. This distinctive configuration of public space has endured and stirred imaginations over time, giving rise to multiple projects, lining it on all sides, that seek to enhance its quality and draw a shared identity from it. It has been revived, not just in order to preserve the feature as a kind of cultural memory but also to give it new life. In its new form, it has been refreshed in ways that its original "framers" could never have imagined as a vital neighbourhood spine.

If we look hard enough, almost every redeveloping neighbourhood has a legacy of embedded histories with unique traces to build on. These may take the form of heritage buildings, civil structures, or idiosyncratic spatial relationships and street configurations. All can provide meaning that anchors the new in both time and space. Respect for heritage is not just a matter of preserving individual structures or parts thereof, but of interpreting those traces and artefacts and weaving them into meaningful new patterns, and, in the case of buildings, contrasting the old with the new so there is no confusion created by a too literal mimicry.

We have learned the value of paying attention to those idiosyncrasies and found places — a secret garden in the middle of a deep block, or a covered carriageway — as the Wellington Place neighbourhood keeps evolving organically. The mix of old and new buildings, and the fact that ownership is so fragmented, is ensuring a genuine and desirable diversity of use and architectural expression, avoiding the monotony that can come with large land assemblies. Against this backdrop, a new generation of contemporary buildings is emerging. Some are standouts, some are simply background, but as they complete the street frontages, the sense of spatial continuity is increasing, and walking on neighbourhood streets feels more satisfying.

City building is, above all, about expanding and enhancing the public realm we share. The city sidewalk and the first ten metres above it in clear view of pedestrians are where a sense of place is formed. We are increasingly focused on how new growth animates the streets and adds to the richness of public spaces, how well it works with its neighbours, and how it enlivens and plays off what was there before. It is about the in-between spaces the buildings frame, the ground floor uses they provide, the provision of public spaces, services, amenities, and services at street level.

Not only what appears on the exterior, but also the diversification inside buildings is rapidly evolving. From an initial period of residential construction, which focused almost entirely on producing identical, very small condo units aimed at a particular market niche consisting of transient young people with no or few children and a high level of absent investor purchasers, the bell curve of options is broadening. New living arrangements accommodating a broader cross-section of the population are being provided, with large, two- or three-bedroom units making dwelling units and buildings family-friendly.

Along with design innovation, there is also a greater diversity of tenure options, with more purpose-built rental entering the market, meeting a need that was fulfilled by rental condos but in a more sustainable way, better built and better managed. The major challenge, however, reimains the issue of affordability in accommodating the full spectrum of the population, particularly for young families. Inclusionary zoning, or other strategies with real teeth, need to be implemented in a meaningful way (but more on that later).

The challenge of fully realizing a fully mixed and sustainable new form of neighbourhood sensitive to context requires creative problem solving. Rising expectations for design excellence, and an increased sophistication on the part of the community, are shifting the conversation from very limited and reductive considerations of height and density to a much broader range of issues, including sustainable building practices and the enhancement of the public realm.

I have been working on a generation of new projects in the Kings area with progressive developers who are committed to city building, employing talented architectural firms like KPMB from Toronto and BIG from Copenhagen and 3XN from New York. Thanks to the work of professionals of this calibre, the gene pool of building typologies is expanding, moving beyond the limited gamut of well-worn templates like the tower-podium to include new building types in the mid-rise range, such as contemporary interpretations of the internal, shared courtyard.

Building programs have always been complex, but today they are more so, as greater attention is now paid to what happens at street level. The first generation of condo buildings paid scant attention to retail. It was not part of their business model. The few spaces that were provided were too shallow, with low ceilings, and rarely accommodated more than dry cleaners and the odd convenience store. Now, condo development co-ventures with experienced retail developers, and increased population and demand means these lower level spaces are being taken seriously, generously dimensioned with high ceilings and a much greater range of tenants.

Compression, tightening up spaces, filling in voids, and the needs of a growing population force designers to come up with ways to use space more effectively. Planning policy objectives can't be realized by just checking boxes in isolation, one issue at a time. Achieving perfection in one area may undermine another. Optimizing an ambitious set of neighbourhood building goals involves making trade-offs among competing objectives for heritage, parks, urban design, planning, and transportation, and maintaining a focus on the integrity of the whole neighbourhood, not just the individual project in its own terms.

When it works, creative architecture and landscape design can contribute to true city building, not just offering new looks or styles, but fundamentally new approaches to making great urban places by expanding the vocabulary of public space. Well-designed buildings raise the bar and transform entire neighbourhoods.

One of the most important lessons from the experience of Wellington Place is that sustained community engagement is an essential ingredient of successful transformation. Outcomes are vastly improved when we manage change democratically, tapping local knowledge, and inviting community voices to be heard in a decision-making process that is not just top down and developer driven. The Wellington Place Neighbourhood Association has played this role effectively in a rapidly unfolding, dynamic process.

This engagement is even more critical in light of the extreme development pressures being felt in some parts of Toronto. The problematic role of the Ontario Municipal Board (more on that later) has forced communities to pay for lawyers and expensive hearings, an issue the province has tried to address with the new Local Planning Appeal Board Tribunal (LPAT). It remains to be seen how effective the change will be.

The key for WPNA was to be proactive. There is a four-legged stool involved in managing change — the local councillor (in our ward system), city staff, the developer and designers, and the community. By getting ahead of the curve, anticipating change and advancing a community vision in this four-way dialogue as opposed to reacting after the fact to plans that have been baked, there has been a much greater opportunity to shape results.

WPNA made it known that it was willing to engage in informal "pre-application" discussions with developers before the required formal statutory process of consultation begins, including developing a tailored community checklist for each site to be shared with the other parties. Most critical was the fact that the neighbourhood association was not just focused on one building at a time but maintained a holistic view of the whole neighbourhood and its larger context.

Looking more broadly, we need to accommodate much more diverse housing for a growing population in viable neighbourhoods. There are not enough older rejuvenating neighbourhoods to accommodate all of this growth, and we risk undermining them with overdevelopment, but the good news is that there is still a great deal of room and many untapped places for Toronto to grow without depending on either low-density green-fields sprawl on the urban fringe or excessive hyperdevelopment concentrated in a few small areas.

Despite the dramatic concentrations of high-rise development and the many cranes on the skyline, Toronto is not as dense as we think it is overall, not even in the top thirty when it comes to city-wide density of people per square kilometre. By a recent count there were 4,457 inhabitants per square kilometre in Toronto, compared to just over 11,000 in London and New York. Tokyo had 14,796 people per square kilometre. In Canada alone, Vancouver and Montreal were both considered denser than Toronto, with 5,493 and 4,916 inhabitants respectively per square kilometre.

Our problem is that the density is so unevenly distributed. As urban design expert Jonathan Barnett has quipped, "it is not just how dense you make it, but how you make it dense," and, I would add, where you make it dense. One of the things that Wellington Place has demonstrated is the potential for the missing middle ground to meet that need. Wellington Place's success could be replicated in a number of areas in the city, developing in a compact, mid-rise form without recourse to tall towers.

A great opportunity to apply these development principles exists in the future transformation and reuse of the vast reservoir of Toronto's waterfront lands, former industrial sites, and other obsolescent landholdings that dot the city, such as malls and plazas and their large parking surfaces. While Toronto does reasonably well in established areas, one of the greatest challenges is to get our arms around the need for all-embracing holistic neighbourhood building in these "new places."

It is obviously easier to achieve the mix and intricacy of a vital prewar neighbourhood where there is already a "there there," made up of past layers providing inherent complexity and variety, as was the case in Wellington

Place. It is much harder to apply these lessons to the establishment of new and emerging places that are conceived and developed from scratch within relatively short time horizons.

It's easy to intellectually grasp the importance of shifting our focus from the development of individual buildings to the creation of new neighbourhoods as dynamic, evolving entities, but how do we actually do it? A major challenge has to do with overcoming the way we have fragmented the roles involved in city building into the proverbial silos. Different entities are responsible for narrowly defined slices of the urban environment — the streets, the buildings, the parks, the services — with different reporting relationships, budgets, timetables, rules and regulations, and desired outcomes.

The disappointing result of such "silofication" in many newly redeveloped areas has been a certain sterility. Yes, there may be density, but the result is often still lacking in true urbanity, active public space, and vibrant street life. Instead, there are empty plazas and dreary sidewalks with a few chain outlets for the bare necessities of life — fast food, dry cleaning, and "convenience" shopping — with scant encouragement for pedestrian life.

Will these relatively new places eventually become more alive; will they age and fill in, taking on a patina and richness not yet evident? Will children ever play here? Will there be shops, cafés, schools? Can people grow old here? Or will norms and standards, bylaws, leases, and deeds prove too rigid and inflexible to allow for evolution and change? In short, will these areas ever be pieces of "real city"?

Can we introduce all of these missing ingredients — the grain, the intricacy, the importance of the public realm and community services — into the next generation of new places? We are on a steep learning curve to remedy this failing and reassemble the pieces of the urban fabric into meaningful wholes. Inevitably these large projects are phased over years, if not decades. As we shift the focus from infill of older neighbourhoods to deliberate neighbourhood building, each phase of development should contain the full DNA of livability, with places of work, places of living, places to play, public spaces, access to transit, and access to shopping, where people can enjoy a high quality of life.

The good news is that, while still more the exception than the rule, some good precedents are accumulating. A trajectory of consciously orchestrated, diverse, sustainable neighbourhood building has been emerging in Toronto, from the St. Lawrence neighbourhood in the 1980s to recent efforts like Regent Park and the "precincts" being developed by Waterfront Toronto in the West Don Lands and East Bayfront, along with much more focused efforts to insert *ex post facto* the missing ingredients and facilities in areas like CityPlace (where my initial skepticism is being gradually overcome) by the introduction of more housing mix, parks, new schools and a community centre, and live–work retail at street level.

Perhaps the most significant challenge is whether we can realize our fundamental aspiration to be a "city for all" in a world where economic disparity seems to be growing. And what can the city do in the face of this? Gentrification, bringing with it the displacement of lower income residents (and of low-overhead small businesses by heated real estate markets), has become an ugly term. But it is almost impossible to stem the growing desire of those who can afford it to be in compact, walkable neighbourhoods as the great game of musical chairs unfolds and the hand-me-downs become the auto-dependent first-ring suburbs. Confronting this dynamic will require bold and proactive solutions.

Who can afford to live in the most successful parts of the city, those with the most amenities and services? Can people afford to live in or near the community where they work, or are they forced into long commutes? Can we create and maintain an inherently diverse city fabric? This gets to the heart of social cohesion, and may be the Achilles heel of our newfound success. It has the potential to undermine all the rest if we don't address it. We need to build a true and stable mix into our neighbourhoods, devising ways to ensure the affordability that the market does not produce when left to its own devices. We need to combine a range of tenure options, spanning the gamut from market housing to social housing, with tenure options including purchase and rental at different levels.

The work of Toronto Community Housing in transforming a number of troubled public housing projects into mixed-income neighbourhoods may be leading the way. Surprisingly, these revitalization projects are producing some of the most "complete neighbourhoods" we have in the city, not only in terms of income mix but also in terms of the full range of attributes of a complete neighbourhood. Regent Park is a prime example. Its revitalization can be viewed as a bellwether of the kind of city Toronto aspires to be — equitable, diverse, inclusive, productive, sustainable, and welcoming.

Regent Park, on the east side of downtown Toronto, is one of Canada's oldest and largest public housing projects. Despite the name, there was never a "park" to speak of in Regent Park; instead, in its original form, the development consisted of a combination of bleak, three-storey walk-up housing blocks and some high-rise slabs, each with a small piece of lawn, and a few rather bedraggled parking lots scattered between them. In 2002 I was part of a collaborative team commissioned to prepare a comprehensive redevelopment plan for its renewal and reintegration into the surrounding city as a mixed-income neighbourhood. There had been a number of failed attempts to renew Regent Park leading up to that point, so there was a lot of skepticism about the new scheme. But the stars had realigned with the creation of the consolidated Toronto Community Housing Corporation that owned and managed the project.

With a committed staff led by CEO Derek Ballantyne, TCHC, now the largest social housing provider in Canada and the second largest in North America, was demonstrating real leadership and innovation in its approach to rejuvenating the deteriorating social housing stock that makes up its large portfolio. The largest of its efforts was Regent Park.

Right in the heart of Regent Park there is a new aquatic centre, now arguably Toronto's best and most popular public swimming pool. It feels like it has always been there, yet this aquatic centre didn't exist just a few years ago. The site it occupies was in the centre of the previous version of Regent Park, isolated and insulated from the surrounding city, with not much to attract outsiders, certainly not those looking for an afternoon of leisurely family recreation.

On a blustery afternoon two days after Christmas 2016, I met my daughter Anna and my then five-year-old twin grandsons, Martin and Isaac, for a swim at the aquatic centre. When I got there, the kids were already in the water, totally engrossed. The centre is large, welcoming, and bright, with big windows to the west overlooking the park. The shallow, generously sized kids' pool was comfortably warm, with sprays and bubblers and variable depths for kids of different heights to find their footing. Next to the kids' pool there is a hot tub, a larger adult pool with lanes for serious swimmers, a waterslide, and a continuous ledge for those who want to sit and watch.

Looking into the interior of Regent Park, one of Canada's oldest and largest postwar public housing projects, from Dundas Street in 1972. Occupying two large superblocks with no internal streets, this project was completely isolated from the city neighbourhoods around it.

Seen here in 2012, the revitalization of Regent Park reintroduced local streets and a mixed-income population and brought new buildings and life, including a major grocery store at the corner of Parliament and Dundas, animating this once-sterile corner, serving local residents, and contributing to the amenities in the larger neighbourhood.

Despite its name, there was no real park in the original Regent Park — only a series of surface parking lots and residual green spaces. A new six-acre park now forms the neighbourhood's heart along with the new aquatic centre, visible on the left, one of the best and most popular swimming pools in the city.

Sitting out on Regent Park Boulevard on a summer evening enjoying the "Regent Park Film Festival — Movies Under the Stars," adjacent to the Daniels Spectrum, a vital cultural hub for the revitalized neighbourhood.

We parents and grandparents were squatting, kneeling, and floating in a few feet of water, putting us at eye level with the kids, who were ducking under water, trying their strokes, laughing, playing, splashing each other and their adult companions, propelling float boards, and generally having a grand time. We were a polyglot bunch; all around me, other swimmers spoke a huge variety of languages, including English (more often by the kids).

The change rooms were universal cubicles, not segregated by sex, convenient for families and also light and airy, with common showers and lockers of different sizes. Some of the little kids took showers in their bathing suits, others unselfconsciously stripped down. A little boy, just older than my grandsons, naked and with no towel, somehow wandered from the showers and was in momentary distress not seeing his parents; he was scooped up by my daughter Anna, who guided him back to his relieved father.

The lifeguards and other staff were personable, friendly, and welcoming. The use of the pool was free. It all seemed so normal, natural, and deeply satisfying. I had a sense that some, like my family, had come from other parts of the city to enjoy this very special pool, while others were from the immediate neighbourhood. While this was a mixed group, other swim times are reserved for women and children, when blinds can be drawn for privacy.

Outside the window on that December day, we could see a six-acre park with hard and soft surfaces, play equipment for kids of all ages, a terrace for seating, rows of saplings that will grow and provide shade, community gardens, and even a pizza/tandoori oven. Across Dundas Street was the Daniels Spectrum, housing, among other things, the Show Love Café, the Centre for Social Innovation, the Regent Park Film Festival, Native Earth Performing Arts, ArtHeart Community Art Centre, Pathways to Education, the Regent Park School of Music, and the Collective of Black Artists.

Where there had been almost no retail in Regent Park, now at the other end of the block was Paintbox, a restaurant café doubling as a music venue and providing catering services; and continuing down the block, a Royal Bank branch, a FreshCo grocery store, a Tim Hortons around the corner, a locally owned shawarma shop, a birthing centre, a health clinic, a Shoppers Drug Mart about to open, and many more businesses to come, all mandated to employ local people. Across the street on the west side of the park there is now an adult learning centre staffed by faculty from several universities and colleges offering free university level courses.

A little farther afield, we find a new sports area, including a cricket pitch and hockey rink. The local Nelson Mandela Park Public School has had a facelift and shares its site with a new community centre. Nearby, an older repurposed building houses a media centre, where young people learn radio, TV, and film production. A former Christian Resource Centre, next to but separate from the former Regent Park, has done its own ambitious renovation and shares space with a Muslim centre serving the homeless and those in need.

On all sides, attractive new buildings contain a combination of fully subsidized, rent-geared-to-income rental units equal to the number that existed in the old Regent Park, as well as new condo and market rental units that more than double the previous population. It is hard for the untrained eye to tell which building is subsidized and which is market rate. The new mixed-income neighbourhood contains a mix of higher buildings and townhouses served by new Toronto-style laneways that in many cases double as play spaces for neighbourhood kids. The transformation is at midpoint in a series of phased buildouts and is ahead of schedule due to demand.

This emerging neighbourhood is a work in progress, a stage along a shared learning curve that involves a growing cast of creators, committed individuals, and groups working in government, the private sector, and philanthropic organizations. It is all about partnerships. How did this transformation come about?

The master plan we developed was conceived in 2002–2003 as a framework for revitalizing Regent Park. But it wasn't just a physical plan. It also dealt with financial viability, social development, tenant relocation, and environmental sustainability. The circumstances seemed right: a long-standing desire to improve Regent Park after multiple false starts, the fact that the city around it seemed ripe for positive change in this central downtown location, a willing if somewhat skeptical tenants' group, and positive reception from surrounding neighbourhoods.

The deliberately simple framework laid out public spaces, streets, and blocks, the central park, building sites with general provisions for heights and densities and mix of housing types and tenures, and a methodology for engaging private sector developers to implement the plan. At its core was a conviction about the potential for creating a successful mixed-income neighbourhood based in part on an earlier positive experience with the St. Lawrence neighbourhood (albeit one that had been created from whole cloth not the transformation of an existing public housing project).

Regent Park had been created in the post–Second World War era as a classic example of "garden-city" urban renewal. *Farewell Oak Street* (1953), an NFB (National Film Board) production moderated by Lorne Greene about the creation of the new Regent Park Public Housing Project, perfectly captured the prevailing mood and beliefs. It shows the poor conditions in an inner-city "slum" that is being demolished to be replaced by a squat and stripped-down version of towers in the park on superblocks formed by removing neighbourhood streets. It introduces the families moving into their new apartments, and makes extraordinary claims for the salutary effects this project will have on their lives, poignantly capturing the naive faith in its guiding principles that was common at the time. Unfortunately, in the end the cure was far worse than the disease it proposed to deal with.

From the outset of the revitalization effort begun in 2002 it was clear that the key to success would be engaging the people of Regent Park and the surrounding neighbourhoods in ways that would make them truly committed to and part of the process. This was a 100-percent low-income community of rent-geared-to-income rental housing. It was also home to a high proportion of newcomers to Canada; over 65 percent of its residents had been living in Canada for fewer than ten years. The plan was about more than just replacing the buildings; it also aimed to use the revitalization to empower the community through an innovative approach to community involvement in all stages of the transformation.

Three rounds of workshops were carried out in seven languages, with local community animators assisting residents through whispered interpreting and help accessing information. The result was enthusiastic participation from more than two thousand residents, who provided detailed feedback that was both pragmatic and insightful. A set of community planning principles was hammered out that encapsulated the key ideas and continues to underpin daily decisions as redevelopment proceeds.

The most important principle reflected in our design approach was the aspiration to become a "normal" city neighbourhood. Equally important was the reassurance that rent-geared-to-income units would be protected in the mix, and that tenant relocation during the reconstruction period would guarantee people could come back if they wished. There was, and is, a strong sense of community in Regent Park. We were able to tap into the tremendous pride of the residents and their attachment to the Park and to each other. Equally impressive was the pull of the environmental theme, and the across-the-board desire to be "green" in new ways.

This exercise demonstrated that it was possible to generate broad and enthusiastic support for reintegrating this neighbourhood by reintroducing local public streets, creating generous new park spaces, aligning buildings along those streets, and providing increased opportunities for employment, education, and cultural and community facilities. The plan that emerged was based on a pattern of small urban blocks framing a major new six-acre central park and greenways linking a series of smaller public spaces with the neighbourhood schools.

Through a rigorous developer selection process, the Daniels Corporation, led by President Mitchell Cohen, with broad experience in social housing, was brought in through a competitive process as a uniquely qualified master developer. Critical to their success has been the full and sensitive embrace of the social development plan along with the normal range of development activities including marketing and construction.

One of the attributes of Regent Park was its strong sense of community solidarity, even in dire circumstances. The massive change to make way for new construction was seen as both traumatic and hopeful at the same time. The way this was experienced by the residents is chronicled in a powerful music video entitled "Spectrum of Hope," a collaboration of Mustafa Ahmed, a.k.a. Mustafa the Poet, a rising spoken-word poet from the Regent Park neighbourhood, and internationally known jazz pianist Thompson Egbo-Egbo, also from the "Park."

The story of the Regent Park transformation was also told in a moving stage production written by Mitchell Cohen (also a musician and composer) in collaboration with members of the Regent Park community. With a powerful combination of words, music, and dance, "The Journey" documents Regent Park's nearly seventy-year history through the eyes of local residents. Not only was the show inspired by the real-life stories of Regent Park residents, it was performed by artists and young people from the local community with a guest performance by renowned singer and actress Jackie Richardson.

The fully integrated, $1-billion-plus, fifteen-year Neighbourhood Renewal Plan is still in progress to turn the entire Regent Park neighbourhood into a safer and healthier mixed-income community of approximately 12,500 residents. The project has six planned phases, and entails replacing almost all existing buildings with a denser fabric and reconstructing the streets and underground infrastructure to reconnect the neighbourhood to the existing grid pattern that surrounds Regent Park.

Phases one and two are complete, and phase three is well underway. Along with the mix of market condominiums and rental (affordable rental and rent-geared-to-income) buildings that will make up the redeveloped area, as well as the retail and services mentioned above, there is a municipally licensed daycare. Additional phases, which will include more market condominiums and rental units, are on deck. There will be more new commercial uses than the plan originally anticipated based on market demand, as well as more community amenities.

Regent Park is breaking new ground architecturally; the developers of the project adopted a deliberate strategy of using different design teams for almost every building to reinforce the sense of a diverse city neighbourhood. With a strong commitment to design excellence, the first phase was initiated with invited competitions involving creative design firms who were eager to participate in giving form to this highly ambitious and innovative project.

The review of these submissions and all subsequent phases of the evolving plan have been overseen by a Design Review Panel (DRP), which includes members of the Toronto Society of Architects, the Ontario Association of Landscape Architects, Ontario Professional Planners Institute, an urban designer (myself for the first thirteen years), TCHC representatives, community representatives from Regent Park and the community at large, and an environmental sustainability engineer. City of Toronto staff provide administrative support and serve as observers.

This multistep process involves return visits by the developers and their design teams with the opportunity for refinement of proposals leading to consensus around a final project.

A compelling example of the value of this oversight was the invention of what is now known as the "living lane," which came about through the Design Review Panel's intervention. The panel noted that a utilitarian blind service alley between two rent-geared-to-income buildings and two market condo buildings had the potential to be a critical component of shared public realm. It became a design assignment in its own right. A "fit out" of pedestrian-friendly improvements, including paving, street furniture, and landscaping, was created; added to these were cycling facilities and live–work spaces. In the creation of all of these, attention was paid to the architectural treatments to give scale and identity to this "found" space.

A special feature of the taller rental buildings, carefully reviewed by the DRP, is the design of the lower level roofs for use by residents of the buildings. These rooftop areas serve as both children's play areas — laundry rooms are conveniently situated adjacent to allow parents to keep an eye on the kids — and community gardens for food production. These kinds of family-friendly features rarely appear in market condominium buildings.

The revitalization initiative is predicated on the premise that great neighbourhoods require sustainable design practices and structures with high standards of energy efficiency. In terms of building systems and technology, the new buildings at Regent Park will be some of the most efficient in Canada. All of the high- and mid-rise buildings, both the Toronto Community Housing rental and the for-sale market condominiums, are designed to achieve Leadership in Energy & Environmental Design (LEED) Gold certification.

The Regent Park Revitalization Plan received the 2003 City of Toronto Urban Design Awards, Honourable Mention, and the 2003 Canadian Institute of Planners Excellence Award. The Regent Park Revitalization Plan Urban Design Guidelines received the Ontario Professional Planners Institute (OPPI) 2005 Award for Excellence in Planning.

The transformation of Regent Park has been guided by some basic shared values and aspirations, but so many of its elements were not part of the original plan. Beyond the housing itself, almost none of the facilities and amenities described above, including the aquatic centre, were conceived or even anticipated at the time the initial plan was made. With each step, as confidence has grown, the range of facilities has gotten richer and more varied.

In the summer of 2016, my wife and I took the Chilean minister of sports and her assistant on a bicycle tour ending at Regent Park. When I explained what Regent Park had been before its revitalization, she marvelled at what had been accomplished, at the quality of the buildings and spaces, and the range of facilities. But what struck her most was the mix of incomes, and the variety of languages heard and faces seen on the streets.

The transformation of the area has been so successful that the renewed Regent Park public housing project may prove to be one of the most livable and kid-friendly neighbourhoods in Toronto. Its range of shared neighbourhood-enhancing features far exceeds what can be found in most fully market-developed new neighbourhoods, where each individual building may contain an internal resident-only exercise facility and meeting room, but neighbourhood amenities are lacking.

While the Regent Park revitalization plan came about in response to a particular situation, there is much it can teach us about how to provide more affordable housing options for a diverse population and how to equip an evolving neighbourhood with the array of services and facilities needed for a mixed population. Although in every project the proportion of affordable housing to market-value housing may vary, and although the specific funding mechanisms to provide subsidies may change, there is clear evidence that mixed-income development works and must be a critical component of neighbourhood building.

We are once more challenging ourselves, as we did in earlier periods when Canada and Toronto were great innovators in pioneering such mixed-income neighbourhoods. Now, the need for creative housing solutions is more urgent than ever, and government, their agencies, and even private developers are working together to find those. Toronto Community Housing is leading the way in many respects, with revitalization projects including Regent Park, Alexandra Park, and Lawrence Heights, but some private developers are also responding to a greater range of needs in their projects. The province and the city now need to find viable ways to introduce broad-based inclusionary zoning to enable similar efforts throughout the city.

As Toronto attempts to make the shift from segregation by income to integration, it should be aiming to create a seamless city fabric that accommodates people of all ages and conditions within neighbourhoods, not in isolated patches — including the growing population of seniors and young families. The city needs to deliberately create mixed-tenure-form neighbourhoods — neighbourhoods that integrate affordable and market-priced rental units at close quarters with owner-occupier options — and create them throughout the city, rather than simply let market forces separate and fragment society by income, age, and origin. It is a matter of enlightened self-interest, fairness, and solidarity. One of the next ambitions for Regent Park is to have that mix occur not only building by building, but also within buildings.

If the city is able to address the challenge of inclusivity, these examples — the regeneration of the Wellington Place neighbourhood in the Kings, some of the exemplary new waterfront neighbourhoods, and the revitalization of Regent Park — may be seen as key milestones and indicators on the road to a flourishing of mixed, vital, and successful Toronto neighbourhoods.

3

Changing How We Move

Queens Quay Boulevard, Toronto's premier waterfront thoroughfare, has taken on a vibrant new life. When weather permits, it hosts a steady parade of walkers, some purposeful, others meandering. Individuals, multi-generational families with strollers and picnic gear, and gaggles of friends move along the strip, enjoying the sights and activities to be found there. Undulating timber WaveDecks grace the numerous slip spaces overlooking the harbour. Their stepped profiles serve as informal grandstands for watching the passing crowds or gazing over the water at the first-time canoeists and kayakers practising their strokes in the Rees Street Slip before venturing out into open water.

Queens Quay has taken on an entirely different look and feel. There are still some kinks and adjustments to be made, and the new arrangement has taken a little getting used to, but there is no denying the new strip is a success, allowing better access to the lake for pedestrians and cyclists alike. Whether they are getting to work or just strolling for pleasure, many people are now able to enjoy the visceral, liberating feeling of riding a bike or walking along Queens Quay on a generous, protected path.

The space reallocated to non-motorized movement has been vastly increased, and it is being used, enthusiastically and to great advantage. On any good day, especially weekends, it feels as if the entire city has come down to stroll, ride, and generally hang out on Queens Quay. Crowds populate the adjoining quays and open spaces, such as the outdoor stage at Harbourfront Centre, the beach at HTO Park, and the very special Music Garden inspired by Yo-Yo Ma.

Queens Quay is one of the few places in the city where cyclists and pedestrians can be at relative ease and transit is accessible and convenient. Benches, bike rings, and trees line the promenade, providing shade and seating for creature comfort. New markings, like the embedded maple leaf motifs in the paving stones in the broad promenade, add a touch of artistry; traffic signals for cyclists, subtle level changes in the pathways to signal caution, and colourful patches delineating crossings all remind different categories of users to acknowledge each other, and speak to an expanded vocabulary of signs and signals for the intense mingling of users on a shared street.

The street has been radically reconfigured into four parallel strips. To the south there is a generous pedestrian promenade; beside it is separated lanes that allow for a steady stream of cyclists and in-line skaters moving at different speeds. Riders in full spandex on specialized bikes race along while others, moving at a more leisurely pace, roll by on bikes of all sizes and shapes. Next to the cyclists, the waterfront LRTs glide by in their own two-track right-of-way (which is not in the usual positon in the middle of the street) en route to Union Station, Exhibition Place, or Spadina subway station at Bloor Street. Finally, to the north of the tracks, the original four lanes of traffic have been compressed to two.

The remade Queens Quay has picked up pre-existing relationships, weaving them into a new pedestrian-oriented pattern, and added some new ones. Old driveway access points to the roadway had to be accommodated and previous patterns persist still, but new habits and perceptions have formed and have quickly become normalized. In the street's original configuration, the buildings lining Queens Quay had minimal retail, situated as they were next to a heavily travelled traffic artery with narrow, awkward sidewalks and dangerous conditions for cyclists. Now the edges of the street are changing as new businesses and new life appear in ground floor spaces, taking advantage of the increased foot traffic. Temporary uses, such as the Artisan Market stalls in HTO Park, enliven parts of the promenade. The streets that run perpendicular to Queens Quay, including Dan Leckie Way,

Queens Quay in 1976. The street was transitioning from a utilitarian artery serving port-related industry, with heavy rail down its middle, to a post-industrial people place for a new era. The row of concrete pipe sections with trees marked "Harbourfront Passage" were a first gesture at the introduction of public access to the city's central waterfront.

Queens Quay in 2015, fully transformed into a popular and well-used waterfront thoroughfare, welcoming pedestrians and cyclists. This was the result of an international competition for its redesign; the winning entry introduced a generous greenway promenade, an LRT in its own right-of-way, and separated bike lanes. It has become Toronto's "Corso" on the water's edge.

Top and bottom: With a more generous sense of space and ease, a growing population of downtown residents and visitors has begun to use the street as their "front porch on the water," exercising sociable urban muscles they didn't know they had, and adjusting to a new sharing of the right-of-way by all users.

Rees Street, and Simcoe Street, now deliver more pedestrian traffic to this newly desirable destination. Plans for new parks adjacent to Rees Street, reclaiming a parking lot on the north side of Queens Quay and at York Street, replacing a highway ramp, are in the works.

The impact of this transformation has been remarkable. Flash back a few decades and Queens Quay would be barely recognizable. While still a student in the School of Architecture at the University of Toronto, I had a job with my professors Jeff Stinson and Carmen Corneil in their small firm's office in the original Terminal Warehouse building on Queens Quay, before its massive conversion into the current mixed-use Queen's Quay Terminal with its condos, offices, shops, and restaurants and the Fleck Dance Theatre. At the time, this fading industrial port area was already starting to lose its industrial base. Shipping had largely stopped using the port; container ships had become too large for the St. Lawrence Seaway and the piers. But occasional freight trains still rumbled down the middle of Queens Quay, serving the various remaining industries with spur lines.

In fact, these trains came right into the lower level of the Terminal Warehouse adjacent to its only restaurant, the loading dock café for workers in the building. This enormous concrete structure with its cold storage wing (later removed) along the southern flank was just beginning to be colonized by small, makeshift offices and studios like the one I worked in, accessed by improvised labyrinthine passageways. Across the way, in what was to become Harbourfront Centre, the Direct Winters trucking company was still in operation. The area was noisy, dusty, and largely off limits to the public. The idea of a publicly accessible waterfront was already in the air, but its realization was still far off.

How did this radical transformation happen? It began in 1972, with the expropriation of eighty acres of obsolescing waterfront along Queens Quay, from York Street west to Bathurst Street, by the federal government under Prime Minister Pierre Elliott Trudeau. The intention was to convert the area into a cultural and residential district for Toronto, with art galleries, performance spaces, boating areas, and parks.

Subsequently, and in lockstep with this cultural infusion, virtually all the surrounding formerly industrial lands along this stretch of the harbour were converted by the Harbourfront Development Corporation, which brought in private developers to produce a series of condominium towers overlooking Lake Ontario. A waterfront community was forming in fits and starts but major controversies arose on the way as the public reacted strongly to some of the projects — seen as "a wall of condos" — and expressed deep concern about the loss of public access to the waterfront. Eventually these objections led to major changes in the city's approach to waterfront development, as I will describe later.

At the centre of this conversion, through a process of trial and error, Queens Quay emerged in stages as a new kind of street for Toronto. First, heavy rail was removed from the street and replaced with a streetcar line. A portion of Queens Quay itself was realigned and then realigned again, pushed back to provide more park space on the water's edge, which included the Music Garden.

Meanwhile, pressure was mounting for more and improved public space on the waterfront. In 2006, a decision was eventually made to hold the Toronto Central Waterfront Innovative Design Competition, managed by Waterfront Toronto, which included the potential for a redesign of Queens Quay. I was on the jury. While some of the submissions focused primarily on the slip spaces, we were captivated by the winning proposal from the Rotterdam landscape firm West 8, which teamed with Toronto firm DTAH to bring Dutch know-how and a level of boldness to a complete redesign of the public realm. Their vision included moving the light rail tracks on one side of Queens Quay next to a generous, multi-use greenway incorporating the Martin Goodman Trail, the fifty-six-kilometre, multi-use path that runs along Toronto's entire lakeshore from one end of the city to the other.

This highly audacious plan for Queens Quay needed some proof of concept, and so a pilot version called "Quay to the City" was installed for two weeks, with temporary landscaping and public art. It was an enormous success: the public got to experience the exhilarating feeling of moving freely on the wide greenway that was carved out of the right-of-way, and traffic still managed to flow. After an environmental assessment, the plan was approved.

Finally, in July 2012, Waterfront Toronto began the major reconstruction of Queens Quay West. This complex project was like open heart surgery on an urban scale. Access had to be maintained; the streetcar was replaced with buses for the duration of the construction period. Eventually, the two traffic lanes south of the streetcar tracks were eliminated between Spadina Avenue and York Street to extend the multi-use Martin Goodman Trail with a double row of trees, benches, and the generous pedestrian promenade.

On June 19, 2015, after what seemed like an interminable wait, the fully redesigned Queens Quay opened to the public and Torontonians were able to experience a new kind of place, a major artery reconceived as a great public space where pedestrians, cyclists, transit vehicles, and cars share space in ways that reflect a completely different set of priorities. Reversing the traditional pyramid, in which vehicular traffic was given highest priority, a new model was created that put pedestrians first, followed by cycling and transit. And, yes, there are cars in two lanes, but the wide lanes and large radii of the curbs at intersections to ease traffic flow were tightened, and crosswalks were enlarged to improve the safety of pedestrians. In a few decades, Queens Quay had gone from being an industrial artery for heavy rail and trucking, to a heavily used automobile commuter artery, to a new kind of grand and sociable waterfront boulevard.

This first phase of the Queens Quay makeover established a template that is now being carried across the entire waterfront, extending east to the eight-hundred-acre Port Lands, the last great waterfront frontier undergoing transformation. There, even more generous space for walking and cycling will be needed in order to accommodate the anticipated greater numbers of pedestrians and cyclists who will use the area. That 2006 competition brought emerging best practices of street design to the waterfront. Together with the WaveDecks, a first manifestation of the competition, the reconceived street formed a connecting lifeline, giving the city the unfettered experience of a bold and generous waterfront "greenway."

By completing one of the last missing pieces of the Martin Goodman Trail, Queens Quay also linked together other emerging green networks — streets, trails, squares, indoor and outdoor gathering spaces, and parks leading to and across the entire waterfront. The speed at which the new Queens Quay was adopted and populated made it clear how powerfully it had addressed an unmet need. The revamped Queens Quay gave Torontonians a new way to experience this unique location and the amazing diversity of the city, affording them the opportunity to rub elbows with people of different ages, backgrounds, and interests. This newfound breathing space offered respite from the pressures of traffic and access to an unbounded horizon at the water's edge. For many, especially those without cottages to escape to, the waterfront has become an in situ "resort," and Queens Quay Toronto has created its own version of a relaxed and sociable urban *paseo* or *corso*.

The redesign of Queens Quay has much to say beyond itself about the evolution of our city. Street rights-of-way represent over a quarter of the land area of the city. How the city uses that space goes a long way toward determining how its residents experience the city and each other. While Queens Quay is a special case, in some ways it also can be seen as a prototype. In the mid-twentieth century when Toronto became a driving city, it focused on highways and major arterials as the primary way of getting around. This went hand in glove with the separation and specialization of land uses — living and working spaces were sited farther and farther away from each other, hence there was more driving. Residents were driving from place to place for specific purposes, but rarely overlapping on foot in public spaces, and the streets reflected that.

In searching for auto-oriented efficiency, cities invented the stand-alone profession of traffic engineering, which focused almost exclusively on moving cars efficiently. For a time this became the most powerful discipline in city building. Downtown city streets were largely devoid of pedestrians for most hours of the day, and cars had their own way. To keep things moving, the city widened lanes, narrowed sidewalks, and widened intersections, favouring vehicle flow and lengthening pedestrian crossings, scouring streets of any extraneous elements in order to avoid friction. In the process, we correspondingly diminished the streets' role as shared social spaces.

With vastly increased population in the city core, this whole paradigm tested to failure. It was clear that the overreliance on the car had become self-defeating. The city became saturated; there was simply no room for more cars. For over sixty years, transportation planners have tried to slay the congestion dragon by facilitating traffic movement; but with history as our guide, we know that when we build more and wider roads, we only invite more congestion. Right from the start, the lanes fill up as traffic increases with each successive round of road widening. The only thing that really works in big cities is getting more people out of their cars, shifting the focus to moving people rather than vehicles. We can move more people per hour on streets designed to also serve pedestrians, cyclists, and transit users than we can when they are dedicated to the private car.

The congestion that Toronto is experiencing is a measure of its success as a city, but that congestion comes with a heavy price. As Toronto's Board of Trade continually points out, the city (and the region) is overrun with cars and is paying a huge economic opportunity cost for congestion, quite apart from the heavy personal toll it takes on daily commuters. Toronto has exacerbated the problem through a long hiatus of insufficient investment in transit even as its population grew. So it is no surprise that severe problems are now endemic, experienced as extreme overcrowding on the Yonge subway line, along with widespread vehicular gridlock. Something has to give. From this perspective, the transformation of Queens Quay is part of the much larger second paradigm shift under way; it is a pioneer and a bellwether of what is yet to come throughout the city.

Overcrowded streets can be dangerous. Congestion leads to evident frustration and bad behaviour, but more than that, the conflicts are life threatening. With the vast increase in the number of residents, a growing number of walkers and cyclists are competing with drivers for limited space and daily conflicts are producing record levels of fatal collisions and injuries. In Toronto in 2017, a pedestrian was hit by a car every three and a half hours, while a cyclist was hit every seven hours and ten minutes; and these were just the cases reported to the police. It should be noted here that these conditions produce bad behaviour on all sides: reckless risk-taking drivers, multi-tasking pedestrians who text obliviously while crossing the street, and kamikaze cyclists who weave recklessly through traffic and on sidewalks in their own bubbles.

It is all very well to say people should just follow the rules, but what rules? The fact is that mid-twentieth-century streets, inadequately designed for the volume and variety of new users, send ambiguous signals. How should a cyclist make a left turn at an intersection on a busy street? Go with the traffic and get in the left lane, or join the crosswalk, conflicting with ped-estrians? It isn't obvious. Should cyclists stay off the sidewalks even where the lanes are too narrow and fast-moving traffic is treacherous? Improvising is dangerous and anxiety-producing when there is no shared understanding about how to navigate the streets and sidewalks. This is clearly a case where we both need to change our behaviour — for instance, make eye contact and pay closer attention to each other — and also redesign the limited space available in the rights-of-way for the greater good, rather than seeing it as a zero-sum game among competing users.

Redesigning roads and the rules of traffic use, and improving walking, cycling, and transit will not only go a long way to helping to lower the number of pedestrians and cyclists hit by cars. These changes will also im-prove the general health of residents by reducing other, less well understood forms of collateral damage, the unintended by-products that come with automobile dependency. Even low-emission vehicles contribute heavily to the pollution that afflicts city dwellers. And the unhealthy consequences of a sedentary, car-dependent lifestyle are clear. Driving everywhere, even if you also drive to the gym or health club, is no substitute for walking as part of a daily routine, nor is it a solution for serious health challenges like obesity, hypertension, increased levels of diabetes, and heart disease. Of course, changing behaviour to embrace a healthier lifestyle isn't easily done for some. We're also facing a time when baby boomers who have grown up with the car as a way of life are approaching an age at which many can no longer safely drive. Giving up the car keys is traumatic for seniors, as they are forced to give up their car-enabled independence with few other mobil-ity options. Providing those options is clearly the solution to this problem — for seniors and others.

The city is now at a tipping point. Some beneficial change has occurred, but much more needs to be done. A change in priorities and practices and the development of a new way of thinking about how we move in the city are essential. A number of recent studies have confirmed the public's de-sire for change and the benefits of confronting these new realities. Toronto Public Health's newly published report *The Walkable City* surveyed 1,525 residents of the city and its boroughs and found that 74 percent strongly preferred a pedestrian-friendly neighbourhood over one that's car oriented.

A report by the Brookings Institution in Washington, D.C., revealed a clear correlation between walkability and real estate values. The more walkable a street is, the more valuable its properties become.

The goal is clear, but finding the route to it is difficult — this is a wicked problem to solve. We need radical urban surgery, and not just in a few isolated cases. But change on the ground does not come easily. It means overcoming entrenched habits and dealing with the complex design and logistical problems of reworking infrastructure and street spaces while keeping things moving in the meantime. Queens Quay is both proof of concept and part of a critical city-wide learning curve. The impetus came from the unavoidable fact that the increasingly popular but isolated waterfront could no longer be a place that most people would drive to. Its very popularity forced change. There had to be a solution that resulted in more users and less cars. That was the key.

By shifting from thinking of the street as a utilitarian artery to treating it like a shared social space, we vastly increase its capacity to serve multiple purposes, enhancing our lives as city dwellers. Today the connecting spine of Queens Quay is becoming more lively and animated, with new, active retail uses framing the sidewalks. Limited vehicular traffic is still there but it is mixed, with pedestrians, cyclists, transit vehicles, cars, and trucks all sharing the right-of-way. There are frequent crossings and the narrower lane widths, and the pattern of frequent intersections and crosswalks encourages eye contact and sharing of the street space. It is becoming a lively and engaging place in the city, contributing in numerous ways to our health and well-being.

Queens Quay is a leading Toronto example of getting to what are called "complete streets," but it remains one of the few exceptions that prove the rule. The city still has a tremendous job of catch-up ahead. Changing how Toronto moves is one of the major items on our collective to-do list; we urgently need to replace auto dependency with forms of mobility befitting a city of our size and density.

It goes hand in glove with all of the moves in neighbourhood building described in the previous chapter — building a better mix and density of living, working, and shopping — which in turn reduce the number and length of trips by car and the time between destinations. With proximity and density, it becomes more and more practical and economical to live without a car or have very limited use of one. Attrition in car use, as we know, is inevitable, and it is already happening in places where people do have viable options.

This shift involves a massive reorientation of investment in our public rights-of-way. The result is a whole new generation of innovative street design. Primary consideration goes to pedestrians, then transit, then cyclists, and finally cars, which are still present but no longer occupying their former place of priority. This shift produces a city that looks and feels different.

When we examine cities around the world that have been designed for walking, cycling, and riding transit, we see people living more sustainable lifestyles. In the mid-twentieth century it was the Dutch in particular who kept faith in the bike as a major form of movement, and they and the Danes have led the way in developing bike culture and design. Copenhagen, a northern city like Toronto, has distinguished itself through its sustainability innovations and very high quality of life. It has returned much of its street network to pedestrians and cyclists, and is achieving a 50-percent share of commuting trips to work by cycling.

Bikes are increasingly used in combination with other modes of transportation for longer journeys. They're either brought along for the rest of the journey, or picked up at the end of the trip through bicycle-sharing programs. New York now has 220,000 daily cycling trips, and this number is increasing dramatically. Similar changes are underway in Portland, Bogotá, San Francisco, Berlin, and Barcelona, among others. Over one hundred cities now have ubiquitous bike-sharing stations.

By promoting these alternatives and making safe and comfortable spaces for cyclists (and pedestrians) in shared rights-of-way, we make room for more efficient, less congested driving when an auto trip is genuinely necessary. The old model — giving cars priority — makes efficient driving impossible. The great examples, cities like Amsterdam and Copenhagen, have developed some of the most sophisticated designs for shared use, with fully separated lanes for cyclists, pedestrian priority crossings, and signals adapted to all users. Seeing these solutions in action, it's obvious that when there's more clarity, all users tend to be calmer and more considerate. Peer pressure and follow-the-leader behaviour kicks in — at intersections, waiting at lights, et cetera. There's less of the stress and danger that comes from uncertainty. Toronto is still in the very early stages of making that transition, but Queens Quay represents an important step toward Torontonians developing that collective learning from shared experience.

Toronto can also learn from cities in the developing world. In India, for instance, the seemingly impossible non-stop rhythm of streets works because of constant eye contact among pedestrians and the drivers of an unbelievable variety of conveyances — cars, trucks, buses, rickshaws (motorized and pedaled), bicycles, motorcycles, and mopeds. This phenomenon relies on low-tech human interaction as a complement to the minimum of essential signage and signals, and has been taken up in the latest, sophisticated, European-engineered streets, which are sometimes called "naked streets." On some smaller-scale streets, reducing the number of traffic signs can actually encourage eye contact and increase pedestrian safety.

We also need to overcome our hurried self-absorption and see each other when we share space in transit vehicles — increasingly crowded subways, streetcars, and buses. We need to become much more considerate of the growing numbers of the less able: seniors, for example, who are downtown dwellers, or parents with children, or pregnant women. Small gestures go a long way: giving up a seat, offering a helping hand, or giving directions.

Toronto is facing a classic chicken-and-egg problem: form (in this case, street design) follows function (streets that are safe), and function follows form. To break the impasse, the city urgently needs viable alternatives. To shrink our roads and get out of our cars, and redistribute the space in the street right-of-way we have to make major shifts in the modal split by giving people more attractive options. A vastly expanded public transit network is essential, along with intercity rail. Transit must take many forms and scales, not just subways and light rail but a range of solutions, including small-scale, highly responsive bus service and shared vans on flexible routes. Other alternatives are needed too. Rental car share services for essential trips and carpooling already play significant roles in the urban transportation mix, and as mentioned above there has been a dramatic increase in walking and cycling.

We need to provide infrastructure and support for modes of transportation other than cars. Disincentives for car use are also necessary. Restricting the size of roads as well as access to them — the King Street Pilot Project is a good example of the latter — go some way to reducing vehicular traffic.* Market pricing for parking is another powerful inducement for people to adapt.

While our current culture and infrastructure present serious challenges, I am convinced that we will ultimately see excessive auto dependency as a mid-twentieth-century aberration; there is not really a viable alternative to making the shift to other transit modes. We know the adjustments we need to make to achieve a more sustainable balance of options: on the land use side, more compact, denser, walkable places with greater mix; on the mobility side, more modal choices, better transit, more frequent headways. The question is how. Toronto can't give up its auto dependency by going cold turkey.

The way out of exaggerated dependency on the car will undoubtedly be incremental, messy, and uneven, based on big and small moves; there is no easy technological fix, no silver bullet(s). Change will require a complex basket of tools and solutions. We will need to ease out of the web of current planning and design solutions that have been built around the car while we take steps to introduce more options by remaking the urban fabric as we expand the range of mobility options in cities.

The process is already well underway in Toronto. As density and the mix of land uses increase, amenities become more accessible, and it becomes more practical and economical to make very limited use of a car, or even to live without one. After several generations in which our cars defined us, some 23 percent of households in the city now apparently don't own cars, and an even higher 46 percent are car-free in the core. For many, preferred neighbourhoods are measured not by how big or grand the houses in them are, but by their proximity to the grocery store, the transit stop, the playground, and, in some cases, how big the trees are. Paradoxically, with greater density, the city's residents can also rely less on public transit. It becomes feasible to walk and cycle to pick something up for dinner or take the kids to daycare if the facilities are close to where they work or live.

---

* A pilot project in which the flow of cars and other private vehicles is restricted (but not banned entirely) to enhance the flow of streetcars. Transit reliability has improved significantly, while local access to parking garages is maintained at all times. Condominiums, businesses, et cetera, are being maintained, as are designated passenger loading zones and taxi stands.

Top and bottom: Prior to the Kings Initiative, King Street West, with its typical twenty-metre right-of-way, had streetcars in four lanes of mixed traffic and few nearby residents. As residential development moved in, King Street became the spine of one of the most intensely inhabited areas of the city's core. Congestion was agonizing, and something had to give.

Top and bottom: A unique, made-in-Toronto solution emerged in the form of the King Street Transit Pilot, eliminating through traffic and freeing up space to improve transit service while providing more space for pedestrian life in the liberated curb lanes.

But not everything can happen in self-sufficient "urban villages." To shrink our roads, get people out of individually owned private cars, and redistribute the space they presently monopolize, we have to give people better ways to get around. We need a set of linked strategies in a multi-modal world, ranging from walking and cycling to transit and, yes, cars. Many of us will at some time or other use most if not all of them. To accomplish this, cities can offer both carrots and sticks, expanding alternatives in some areas while shrinking auto dependency in others. Queens Quay demonstrates how this can work. It points the way to a sophisticated approach to the problems of phasing and adaptation, of taking incremental steps, monitoring progress, and allowing for behaviours to change, easing out of the current paradigm and into another.

The case for moving to a new era of sustained investment in complete streets and multi-modal mobility seems straightforward, doesn't it? Yet Toronto is caught in a tug-of-war. Innovations are happening piecemeal as we inch forward, but they are not happening fast enough. One of the biggest stumbling blocks is that government must lead in making the shift, and the city is too frequently caught in political gridlock, one of the uncomfortable outfalls of its forced and uncomfortable amalgamation in 1998. The rebalancing that must occur is not a "war on cars" (as some suburban politicians would still have it), but a natural and inevitable step in our evolution.

All the knowledge, technology, and precedents are there but we are frequently held back by politics, and progress is at best sporadic and controversial. We are too frequently waylaid by the politicization of major transit investments. That has become a major stumbling block, and as a result the city is often unable to make long-term plans based on factual information. Through the unfortunate lens of wedge politics, every move to make improvements is too often seen as a zero-sum game, so we go back and forth, reversing direction. Opinions about transit investments and bike lanes become symbolic "them and us" markers attached to downtown "elites" or suburban "drivers."

Two of the most obvious and costly recent casualties are an irrational commitment to the one-stop Scarborough subway, which costs more and provides less than light rail but has become a symbolic trophy, and the relocation of a portion of the elevated Gardiner Expressway to shave a few minutes off a suburban commute for a very small number of drivers when removing it was clearly the superior and more economical solution recommended by all of the professionals involved in the project.

This is a complex love-hate issue that touches a deep cultural nerve. Many who have grown up with the car see it as a key part of their identity. For some, driving speaks to a sense of personal liberty. But is liberty the freedom to be behind our own wheel at all costs, or at some point would we rather be liberated from the tyranny of rising gas prices, traffic jams, and long commutes? There will undoubtedly be different answers to these questions for some time, but even the most diehard drivers have a vested interest in getting some of their fellow drivers off the road to free up space.

The tangible benefits of making the change are enormous. The fundamental paradox is that those who have to drive — those who have no choice — and those who for whatever reason insist on driving should be the greatest proponents of this paradigm shift. There are many compelling reasons to change, from public health to environmental impacts and convenience, but even if we focus narrowly on the status quo, the best solution for drivers who want to get where they're going faster is to provide a better range of alternatives, including transit, walking, and, yes, cycling. When we think about moving the highest number of people in our limited rights-of-way, creating more space for walking, cycling, and transit makes perfect sense.

Every additional trip we take on foot, on a bicycle, or by public transit frees up significant space for drivers, since the "footprints" of these other modes are so much smaller. The cyclist beside you is not the car in front of you; the bicycle locked to a ring at curbside means one less parking space is taken. Driver, cyclist, and pedestrian are complementary rather than mutually exclusive categories. Most of us are all of the above at different times. It is crucial to analyze the proportion of the time we use each mode and identify the trip types where the car is genuinely needed. For other trips, we can make more efficient choices.

Despite the potential for political gridlock, we have to look at the evidence and keep being inspired by successes. The City of Toronto, for example, reported that the new downtown bike lanes along Simcoe, Richmond, and Adelaide Streets have dramatically increased — in some cases tripled —

the number of cyclists using those routes. This has occurred without impeding car travel along the same stretches; in fact, the city's report shows car travel times have generally improved at the same time the number of cyclists using the streets has grown. Queens Quay represents another important verifiable milestone in the transition to a more sustainable, livable future. It currently serves five hundred cyclists per hour, the highest number in the city thus far. By rearranging priorities and reallocating space — putting people at the centre — it demonstrates how we can think differently about the street spaces we share. Toronto is slowly making its way down this path, albeit still hampered by divisive identity politics.

What we really need is a determined carrot-and-stick policy of phased auto reduction, incrementally making prioritized transit investments in areas of greatest need. The cities that are making this shift most gracefully and rapidly are emerging as the big winners, with improved quality of life and economic competitiveness. When I was working in Amsterdam in the mid-1990s, that city was at a crossroads. While Amsterdam had always embraced walking and cycling, cars were choking the city centre. Historic canal edges were cluttered with parked vehicles, and pedestrian-vehicle conflicts were occurring everywhere. So, the city adopted a phased policy of year-by-year "auto reduction," incrementally removing parking spaces while adding bicycle lanes and decreasing wait times between trams. People were soon amazed to discover that they could actually hear their footfalls in the city again.

In Toronto, Queens Quay must not remain a one-off exception; it must become the new rule. Periodically, all of the streets of our city are rebuilt, their surfaces — sidewalks and roadbeds — repaved, their underground services and utilities renewed. Every opportunity should be taken to systematically incorporate the characteristics of shared or complete streets into the ongoing annual processes already in place for infrastructure renewal.

Each aspect of a road's surface and sub-grade components (the parts below the surface) has a limited shelf life. This cycle creates an opportunity for incremental change, as pedestrians and cyclists stake their claims for a greater place in these public rights-of-way. "Roads," which were remodelled in the postwar decades as the almost-exclusive domain of traffic engineering, have the potential to be reconstructed through this process of periodic renewal as complete streets serving all modes of travel.

The most dramatic example of how aging infrastructure can be transformed comes from the concrete-and-steel elevated expressways, ramps, and approaches that have been exposed to intensive use (and in northern cities, to road salting) for about fifty years. Faced with the cost of maintaining or rebuilding these structures, it is natural to question whether it makes sense to keep them. Unlike regular streets, these structures cannot easily be adapted to mixed use. While they do perform important functions for the transport of goods, they're designed primarily for private automobiles, and, as such, they discourage urban density. The elevated Gardiner Expressway is a complex example. Parts of it, like the stretch adjacent to Fort York now forming the Bentway, cannot come down for a variety of reasons and so have been restored, whereas other parts farther east could be removed.

Deciding what to do with such structures is never easy. Removing them would involve major costs, dislocations of traffic and population, and logistical challenges, not to mention the rallying of the necessary political will. But they are decisions worth making. The cost of replacing these aging structures, when added to the opportunity to gain access to all the lands they occupy or sterilize by their presence, will often outweigh the costs of making the change.

Numerous cities have reached this conclusion, and they've engaged in elevated highway takedowns. Most famous, perhaps, is the extraordinary Big Dig in Boston. But there are other examples: the Embarcadero Freeway in San Francisco and West Side Highway in New York both literally collapsed, one due to an earthquake and the latter due to its deteriorating structure. Neither was replaced. To these we can add the Central Freeway, San Francisco; Fort Washington Way in Cincinnati; a portion of the Gardiner Expressway in Toronto; the Alaskan Way Viaduct in Seattle; Harbor Drive in Portland, Oregon; and the Cheonggyecheon Highway in Seoul, South Korea.

Another such example is the removal of the Cogswell Interchange in Halifax, a complex piece of multi-level highway infrastructure that was cutting the city off from its waterfront. I became involved in this project in 2016, advising the local chapter of the Urban Development Institute (UDI), a business-led group, on its advocacy for this important initiative. The removal of the interchange was a logical step in the effort to reconnect

Halifax's downtown to its surrounding neighbourhoods. Doing so would repair past damage by overcoming physical barriers and creating major opportunities for positive redevelopment.

While there have been exceptions, with now over a hundred examples of such highway removal or downsizing to evaluate, transportation researchers have generally found that areas affected by these changes improved and prospered, and also that the redistribution of traffic onto other facilities and transit has worked when the alternatives have been well planned in advance and well managed.

So, aging expressways offer the city one opportunity to institute change. There are many others. A number of pilot projects have been created or are in the works; it is hoped that these will lead to long-term change.

Building on the success of Queens Quay, one such pilot project was the highly successful Celebrate Yonge, which ran in 2012. For four weeks, a lane on Yonge Street was closed to traffic and the space was given over to pedestrian use and sidewalk cafés. Other examples include the temporary seasonal sidewalk widening John Street, and the recent, also successful, King Street pilot to improve transit performance by removing through traffic and adding pedestrian space.

New York City offers another example: in 2009 the city initiated a pilot project that involved removing all motorized vehicles from a section of Broadway, the great diagonal thoroughfare slicing through Manhattan. Cars and trucks were removed from the stretch of the street around Times Square and the impact was carefully analyzed. It was determined that this section of road was not needed for the flow of traffic in the area; the surrounding grid of avenues and streets was capable of accommodating the increased traffic. Broadway, from 23rd to 59th Street, was then transformed into a remarkable high-amenity pedestrian space; as well, bicycle lanes were added on 8th and 9th Avenues in an impressive move led by then transportation commissioner Janette Sadik-Khan with the full support of Mayor Michael Bloomberg. These bold pilot projects are often the best way to introduce the public to the potential benefits of very significant change.

Created around the same time, New York City's Street Design Manual has been guiding this transition away from auto dependence toward alternative means of getting around by cycling, walking, and using transit, with great success throughout the city's five boroughs. Essential in this process is the adoption of a standardized "pattern language," preferably one based on international signs and symbols, so that information encoded in pavement markings, signage, and traffic signals for vehicles, cyclists, and pedestrians can be easily recognized by all users. Part of the initial confusion and growing pains on Queens Quay stemmed from users' lack of familiarity with the new coding. But as the kinks are worked out and this signage becomes more common and consistent throughout the city (as it is already in others), navigation on shared streets will become second nature.

Citizens often lead the way in these innovations. Despite the lack of safe and comfortable spaces to ride, there has been a remarkable uptake in cycling in Toronto in recent years. While the number of regular riders is increasing, it is nonetheless still small, reflecting a lack of comfort with the current state of the city's cycling network.

Land-use changes affect transportation choices, since there are now thousands more people living downtown, and closer to where they work, than even a decade ago. This new proximity helps to make auto independence practical. But the city is struggling to keep pace with its citizens' demands for a more equitable apportionment of space in public rights-of-way. Forty-six percent of downtown residents walk and cycle to work these days. They need more space on the streets. The "bottom-up decisions" of the city's denizens are creating pressure for change, necessary for driving the fundamental rebalancing of the city's transportation network as we undo the intrusive "cars first" postwar interventions. In this process of learning we are revisiting solutions from our own past, from other cultures' traditions, and from new discoveries elsewhere in the world.

A vastly expanded public transit network is the *sine qua non*. Many European and Asian cities have already made great advances in integrating high-speed intercity rail, commuter rail, expanded subway networks, light rail, and the innovative use of bus technology to give urban dwellers and commuters a range of effective transit options. But because of our massive investment in highway building and our lower energy costs, North American cities, Toronto among them, have dragged their heels on this front, and we are now struggling to catch up.

But retooling for transit has to start with the recognition that this is not just an engineering problem. Making this change requires integrated city building, not just more hardware. A greater number of people living and working in an area obviously increases the financial viability of high-performance public transit. Historically, suburbs were built around streetcar lines and intercity rail, since the vested self-interest of transit service providers required riders in "transit-oriented development," and this symbiosis is still the foundation of best practices in many parts of the world. Somewhere along the line, however, these activities got uncoupled in North America, with sprawling land use driven by the car proceeding in tandem with expensive, "disconnected," stand-alone transit investment unsupported by density.

It is also not about prioritizing one mode of transportation at the expense of others. Mayor Rob Ford's call for "subways, subways, subways" was an enormous red herring, dismissive of the many appropriate and cost-effective ways of providing transit, from heavy rail to light rail (LRT) and bus rapid transit (BRT), that can be calibrated to the population density and the form of the community being served.

Toronto is embarking on a major reinvestment in our regional transportation network, developing the Regional Express Rail (RER) with the goal of transforming GO from a rush hour commuter service to a two-way, all-day regional transportation service. Over two hundred projects worth over $16 billion are now under development. But we are still falling short in the key area of linking transit, land use, and urban form so that we can fully leverage that next round of transit investment. There must be a full integration of the "Big Move" provincial program, which lays out the proposed regional transportation network, with "Places to Grow," a provincial policy that indicates where major growth should be distributed around the region, and recommends but does not require transit-oriented development. (It remains to be seen what level of commitment the Doug Ford government at Queen's Park will bring to implementing this network of transit initiatives.)

There is a pressing need to re-establish this vital linkage if we want our public funds to augment ridership, support effective regional planning, stimulate economic development and job creation, create real estate value for the public, and guide more sustainable forms of growth and promote social equity. (It is often the underserved populations at risk who end up in the least-served places.) In Toronto's case this will require organizational change, expanding the role of Metrolinx to play a proactive developmental role on public lands along lines and at stations and stops.

All of this additional public transit is not going to entirely replace the car; some part of the population will continue to need cars. So we must also develop transitional systems and solutions that can cope with the highly dispersed, polycentric pattern of living that we have inherited in the Toronto city region. But the way in which we access cars is also changing. Self-driving automated vehicles (AVs) are already here; the question is how we will use them. In a worst-case scenario, as a replacement for the privately owned automobile, they could become the great enablers of more unbridled sprawl. Hopefully, instead, they will become adjuncts to the transit system, providing critical missing links for the proverbial "last mile" that is difficult to serve in low-density areas with conventional transit vehicles.

We are increasingly able to use our handheld devices to access all forms of transportation in real time, enabling us to use a bicycle, a car, a ferry, a train, a subway, a bus — eventually with total fare integration.

Not fully appreciated is what will happen to all the parking in light of these changes. As the postwar world took on an auto-dependent form, North Americans developed an almost insatiable need for parking, and so there was a proliferation of surface parking lots, above-grade structures, and ever-deeper, hugely expensive below-grade parking caverns. Toronto is saturated. Over time, the proportion of space consumed by parking began to equal and then overtake the actual floor space used in buildings themselves. The average parking space today occupies approximately thirty square metres, and suburban ratios for office and retail use often requires four to five spaces for each one hundred square metres of occupied space. "Solving parking" is often the key to unlocking value in new, more sustainable forms of mixed-use development.

Once more, this is a problem of getting from A to B. Transitional steps involve sharing parking among uses with different daily demands, such as office and retail, and reducing parking requirements for development as more people move to alternative ways of getting around. Parking is costly, and market pricing for parking is a powerful inducement for people to abandon their cars. In the private sector, the market for parking can adjust according to law of supply and demand. Slower to adapt are public sector requirements, like zoning, and legal provisions in covenants and land eases, which reinforce the status quo by imposing high parking ratios. Malls are often locked into commitments to their tenants to provide long-term surface parking. Interestingly, one of the most difficult nuts to crack in this regard consists of public-sector agencies that have built unrealistic expectations for free or highly subsidized parking into union contracts.

Road pricing is another powerful tool for using market dynamics to foster change. As the range of non-auto options expands, a number of cities, including Singapore, London, Stockholm, and Milan, have introduced congestion pricing, charging tolls on routes leading into the city. This has been most successful when combined with readily available information about different modes of transportation, including carpooling programs.

A comprehensive package of these and other inducements, including promoting the advantage of not spending hours stuck in traffic or paying for expensive parking, can encourage people to choose more sustainable ways of getting around and to opt for housing closer to work. Likewise, businesses can be encouraged to move their offices closer to residential centres. While most observers acknowledge that the spread of congestion pricing to other cities is inevitable, the great challenge for politicians is to communicate its benefits to reluctant electorates. We have tried but so far failed to introduce road pricing in Toronto through tolls on major highways. Even when Mayor John Tory proposed it and City Council voted for it, the provincial government turned down the city's request for approval for the initiative, a decision that pandered to suburban drivers. But tolls will eventually have to come.

How well and quickly Toronto makes the key moves to reduce its unhealthy and unsustainable dependency on the automobile will play a dominant role in determining its future prospects for economic prosperity, environmental sustainability, and social harmony. Leadership in tackling these complex and intertwined issues must come from many quarters. Government has a crucial role to play, as do the planning, design, and engineering professions; the providers of transportation services; communities; and private-sector partners. All must work together to seize the opportunities to make the inescapable shift to a more sustainable balance in the way we move.

On March 2, 2010, thirty urban leaders representing a broad range of interests gathered at Grano Restaurant to discuss the growing perception of conflict within the field of transportation planning. We noted that the media had frequently fostered a divisive sense of two camps fighting against each other for space in streets. After many hours of discussion, we agreed upon a statement that aimed to diffuse the perceived conflict and build a consensus on this highly charged issue:

> We do not believe that there is a "war on the car." The Complete Streets model strives to provide room for everyone including drivers, cyclists, transit riders and pedestrians. It's simply about offering choice, and ensuring that everyone can travel safely. If there is a war, it's just a war on old thinking. A war on inefficiency. A war on traffic. A war on pollution. Cities around the world are making this shift with great success, improving the quality of life for all of their citizens and their competitiveness as places to live, work and invest.
>
> To describe transportation issues in Toronto as a conflict between drivers, cyclists, and pedestrians is a divisive approach that does our city a disservice and misses the whole point. There are not two Toronto's, comprised of cyclists or drivers. In fact, statistics show us that those who own bicycles are more likely to own cars than those who do not. We are one Toronto. We drive, we ride and we walk. The goal of Complete Streets is to ensure that our streets are designed to safely accommodate all users.

Signed,
Jehad Aliweiwi • Executive Director, Thorncliffe
Neighbourhood Office

Yvonne Bambrick • Executive Director, Toronto Cyclists Union

Rahul Bhardwaj • President and CEO, Toronto Community Foundation

Matthew Blackett • Publisher and Creative Director, Spacing Magazine

David Crombie • Chair, Toronto Lands Corp.

David Crowley • Vice President, Halcrow Consulting Inc.

Julia Deans • CEO, Toronto City Summit Alliance

Susan Eng • Vice-President, Advocacy, CARP

Jane Farrow • Executive Director, Jane's Walk

Luigi Ferrara • Director, School of Design at George Brown College

Adam Goddard • Composer

Eti Greenberg • Wellington Place Neighhbourhood Association

Ken Greenberg • Architect and Urban Designer

Paul Hess • Professor, Geography and Planning, U of T

Ed Levy • Senior Transportation Consultant and Transportation Engineer

Roberto Martella • Owner/Operator, Grano Restaurant

Dave Meslin • Founder, Toronto Cyclists Union

Shawn Micallef • Senior Editor, Spacing Magazine

Eric Miller • Director, Cities Centre, U of T

Steve Munro • Transit Advocate

Gil Peñalosa • Founder and Chair, 8 80 cities

Dylan Reid • Co-chair, Toronto Pedestrian Committee

Nancy Smith Lea • Director, Toronto Coalition for Active Transportation, Clean Air Partnership

Adam Vaughan • City Councillor, Ward 20

This still rings true. The good news is that societal attitudes are changing across perceived divides. As an interesting sidebar, on August 9, 2018, a surprising EKOS survey was released, pointing to a new consensus forming in Toronto when it comes to traffic safety and protected bike lanes. This poll put many clichés to rest. The alleged split between suburbs and down-town, driver versus cyclist is diminishing . Almost nine in ten respondents are concerned about road safety. Seventy-seven percent of people living in the former City of Toronto want lower speed limits, but so do 68 percent of North York residents. Speed reduction has majority support everywhere in the city. And while this was most popular among people who cycle, it's also supported by a majority (59 percent) of those who list "car" as their main mode of transport. There is wide support for separated bike lanes across the board and this was not just a young person's issue; bike lanes enjoy the backing of 79 percent of those aged fifty-five years and older. Change to a more bike-friendly city will take time, but the momentum is there.

4

Expanding Common Ground

It felt odd lacing up my skates for the first time while sitting on a bench under the Gardiner Expressway. I was a little wobbly (after years of not skating) but once I joined the procession of skaters of all ages and skill levels on the ribbon of ice, weaving through the structural "bents" (holding up the elevated Gardiner Expressway), it all came back. The experience of being there on skates was exhilarating and surprising as I looked up at the impressive height of the highway deck some five stories above, or at the familiar earthen ramparts of Fort York on one side and the neighbouring towers across Fort York Boulevard on the other. High above me, unseen traffic sped by, drivers oblivious to what was happening below.

There were newly planted trees in the islands formed by the 220-metre-long figure eight of the skate trail; containers had been arranged, in the middle of what was still a construction site, with sheltered skate rental, lockers, a pop-up vending stand with hot chocolate and cider, benches, and firepits. After the first few turns around the trail I bumped into Waterfront Toronto CEO Will Fleissig, his wife, Wendy, and their daughter Mia, and we chatted casually as we skated as if we were strolling down a familiar street.

It felt both entirely natural, as if it had always been there, and totally unexpected at the same time, almost like a pilfered pleasure in a former cavernous no man's land. Something so familiar had turned into something completely different. The highway above had all but disappeared, and in its place another reality had materialized in the void on the ground.

The opening of the Bentway took place on the weekend of January 6–8, 2018. It was one of the coldest weekends of the winter with temperatures hovering around -30° Celsius. I had been involved in this project for years, and I couldn't wait to see how it would actually work. In the event, some twenty thousand Torontonians came out to brave the cold that weekend. It was remarkable to see them bundled up, enjoying a choir, watching an amazing demonstration of breakdancing on ice by a young Scarborough group, and discovering the artwork enlivening the space. Mayor John Tory and councillors Joe Cressy and Mike Layton officiated at the ribbon cutting, along with Judy and Wil Matthews, whose extraordinary donation had made all this happen. Intense curiosity quickly turned to a sense of wonder and pleasure as the skaters took to the ice for the first time. The reaction by Torontonians as reflected in media attention and all forms of social media was overwhelmingly positive and enthusiastic.

The Bentway project — its name, selected through a public naming project, derives from the "bents," the structural framing of combined concrete columns and beams that holds up the highway deck — was launched in 2015. The project was designed to exploit a great untapped resource that sat, previously ignored, in a highly strategic location. No longer a symbol of division, the almost two-kilometre stretch of the elevated Gardiner Expressway from west of Strachan Avenue to Spadina has been reclaimed to frame and shelter a great new civic living room — one with a five-storey-high "roof canopy" — shared by the seven neighbourhoods it touches. It has transformed this lost space from a psychological and physical barrier into a connection, from a back to a front, from hostile and off-putting to welcoming.

It is a new kind of hybrid public space that doesn't exactly fit into existing categories: not exactly a park, a square, or a trail, although it has elements of all of those. Not only in its form but in its operation it is breaking new ground, imagining the possibility of a new kind of cultural landscape beneath Toronto's Gardiner Expressway, celebrating its monumental presence by inviting a new generation of use and activity. An elevated highway and a surprising "people place" were revealing, in their startling juxtaposition, a new quality of heightened experience. This kind of contrasting reality speaks to how we are beginning to reclaim perceived wastelands in the city, expanding the realm of the possible as life in public surfaces in new and unexpected places.

In describing the Bentway, David Crombie pointed me to the provocative concept of a "unity of opposites" used by Karl Marx to define a situation in which the existence or identity of a thing (or situation) depends on the coexistence of conditions that are opposite to each other yet dependent on each other in a field of tension. The Gardiner Expressway may not depend on the existence of the Bentway to serve its function, but the city, needing both the benefits of a major transportation corridor and enhanced communal recreation area, depends on the relationship between both to achieve two important objectives, one of which was not even acknowledged when the expressway was originally created.

In 2011 I was watching the remarkable transformation taking place in this vast area of the city west of downtown with great interest. A vast churn was underway as the major industrial plants on sites occupied by household names like Molson, Massey Ferguson, Inglis, Canadian Pacific, and Canadian National were closing, making way for a wave of redevelopment. I put forward an idea in an article in the *Fife and Drum*, the Friends of Fort York newsletter, about a new and enhanced role the fort and the space under the highway could play in this radically altered context.

Fort York had miraculously survived onslaught after onslaught. Cut off from its historic relationship to the lake by over a half kilometre of landfill, marooned in a sea of heavy industry by the nineteenth- and early twentieth-century rail corridors, and again by the mid-twentieth-century construction of the elevated Gardiner, it had experienced a number of near misses, including proposals to run a streetcar line right through it, and even to relocate it entirely to accommodate a straight alignment for the highway. Thanks to its fervent defenders, it had miraculously endured in the eye of the storm. At the time, much of the fort's surrounding grounds were occupied by a tree nursery serving the city's Parks, Forestry and Recreation Department, plus a visitor parking lot.

This was an "aha" moment for me. Fort York was sitting there, relatively intact, at the epicentre of one of the fastest-growing areas of Toronto.

With its forty-three acres of space, including a military cemetery, it was a green oasis, albeit disconnected, little known, and undervalued. It was tightly flanked by the elevated Gardiner Expressway and its colossal undercroft, sheltering an extensive no man's land hugging the ramparts where the original shoreline had been.

It was a treasure hidden in plain sight. With my article I included a rough sketch showing where all the new development was occurring — the then emerging new Fort York neighbourhood, the west end of CityPlace, the southeastern portion of Liberty Village, Garrison Point on the Ordnance Triangle, and the north side of the rail corridor from Spadina Avenue to the southern flank of the Niagara neighbourhood — and argued that the combined open space of historic Fort York and the space "under Gardiner" could be a kind of new central park for this band of rapidly emerging neighbourhoods.

Redevelopment in this highly strategic central location was mostly taking the form of dense high-rise buildings with little open space. These immediate neighbourhoods were eventually to house some seventy-seven thousand residents (and now more on the way), including young families with several children, a high percentage of whom were new arrivals to the country. With radical growth and the need for public space, necessity became the mother of invention.

The challenge was that the available open spaces were severely truncated and cut off by an accumulation of transportation barriers — the bifurcating Georgetown and Lakeshore rail corridors, the elevated Gardiner Expressway, and the awkward disconnect at the Bathurst Street Bridge — all of which made it extremely difficult to move around the area. Distances on foot were short in every direction, but the perception was "you can't get there from here." Some moves were already in play to overcome these barriers. The proposed Fort York Pedestrian and Cycle Bridge was designed to provide a critical link across the rail corridors from the north; but this only dealt with one direction.

In the east-west direction, the linear space under the Gardiner held the key to overcoming the barriers that had isolated and fragmented these lands for many decades. It could provide the missing link for a much larger open-space network, connecting all of the emerging new neighbourhoods to each other and to the Lake Ontario waterfront.

It would connect Fort York, with its generous landscape preserving vestiges of historic Garrison Creek and recall of the original Lake Ontario shoreline, to plans underway to extend new "green fingers" — to the east under the historic Bathurst railway bridge and, to the south through the new June Callwood Park — to a multi-modal trail that will run under the Bathurst Street Bridge along the rail corridor, connecting to the new Puente de Luz Pedestrian Bridge (a.k.a. Yellow Bridge) at Portland Street and Dan Leckie Way. By treating the "under Gardiner" as a linking public space, all of these existing and new ingredients would add up to a great deal more than the sum of their individual parts.

Reclaiming the space under the Gardiner would accord a new prominence to Fort York and its grounds at the heart of this complex geography, repositioning this valuable asset as the anchor of a set of new neighbourhoods that derived their identity from the relationship. I saw it much like the neighbourhoods surrounding the Citadel in Halifax; the historic El Morro fortifications of Viejo San Juan, Puerto Rico; the ramparts in Quebec City; or Fort Henry in Kingston. Appropriating this unused asset to provide increased amenity and daily pleasure for tens of thousands of Torontonians and visitors would be a wise investment in the future. At least that was my hope. And it wasn't until some four years later that it would begin to come to fruition.

It took an extraordinary act of civic generosity and willingness to take a risk. Judy Matthews and I were friends and colleagues from our days in the Planning and Development Department at the City of Toronto. She and her husband, Wil, an investment banker, are dedicated urbanites and long-time Torontonians. Their profound love for Toronto had led them to a unique form of philanthropy with a focus on public space. They had previously lent their support to the Music Garden on the waterfront and the Evergreen Brick Works, among other projects. Most significantly, they had made an anonymous (at the time) donation to enable the transformation of St. George Street on the University of Toronto campus in partnership with the city and the university. The success of this project had encouraged them to look for other opportunities that would make a difference.

In April of 2015, I got a call from Judy. She and Wil were searching for a legacy public-realm initiative and were very particular in their requirements.

They were seeking to do something that would be more than a discrete public space, a park or square that might in itself be quite delightful, but rather an opportunity that would be catalytic and have a significant impact stimulating change beyond itself. I immediately thought of the "under Gardiner" potential and described it to Judy, who was intrigued. Shortly after, my wife, Eti, and I went for a fateful walk with Judy and Wil who, as they put it, "were not in the habit of hanging around under expressways"; but standing under the monumental space formed by the bents, they were captivated by its power and the vision for its adaptive reuse.

This was the beginning of a remarkable journey to reimagine and reclaim this forgotten stretch of land beneath the Gardiner Expressway as great civic space. The bulk of the land under the Gardiner adjacent to Fort York was in public ownership as part of the city-owned National Historic Site, so this would have to be a public-private partnership. The next step was to prepare some very preliminary concepts to present to the city. I suggested teaming up with the highly innovative and talented team of young landscape architects Marc Ryan and Adam Nicklin, who had come together to form the firm Public Work. Judy and Wil agreed, and Marc and Adam embraced the concept with great enthusiasm. We immediately set to work in a highly collaborative effort.

We landed on a simple way of illustrating what was a very complex project: producing a three-dimensional concept plan that lifted the "cover" off the Gardiner, revealing the space below, highlighting its shifting and unique relationships to context along its two-kilometre length and how these could be exploited to provide a highly diverse set of experiences in a public space. Although there were no perfect parallels, we gathered a number of the most relevant precedent images we could find to convey its potential. We also prepared a high-level estimate of the capital cost of the project, which was $25 million.

With this material in hand, we prepared for meetings with Mayor John Tory and the two city councillors, Mike Layton and Joe Cressy, whose adjoining wards 19 and 20 straddled the project area. We benefitted from a wonderful piece of serendipity — the city had already embarked on a $150 million investment in the restoration of this part of the Gardiner structure, ensuring structural integrity for many decades to come, a fact that we could leverage in our proposal; with the city's investment this was actually a $175 million adaptive reuse project.

In July of 2015 we were able to meet with the mayor and the councillors and the project was once again wholeheartedly embraced. The Matthews agreed to put up $25 million for the capital cost based on a "cut our cloth to suit" estimate. The city was asked in return to do three things: to make best efforts to complete the work in calendar year 2017 (there was some slippage, but we came close); to appoint a high-level "point person" to coordinate city efforts and city staff (the mayor designated Deputy City Manager John Livey, who was exemplary in the role); and to provide a substantial financial commitment to ongoing Program, Operations, and Maintenance.

This agreement in principle initiated a period of feverish activity from July to November, when we were able to stand on the site with the Matthews, Mayor Tory, and the councillors to publicly announce the project. Many city staff had worked tirelessly with our team to flesh out the details of the project, addressing technical issues to be resolved and identifying the necessary approvals to be secured. Remarkably, confidentiality was maintained until the announcement.

We were breaking new ground not only by creating a new kind of public space, but also by pioneering a new funding and delivery model for the capital project and an operating and stewardship model for the space once it was created. With legal assistance on both sides, the city and initially the Matthews Foundation proceeded from a simple term sheet outlining areas of responsibility to a more elaborate Memorandum of Understanding and ultimately a full Land Use Agreement for occupation of the site. City Council approved each of our progress reports, and each time it was given unanimously.

The detailed design for the Bentway has been brilliantly executed by Public Work, with Marc and Adam, and their associate Lauren Abrahams as project landscape architect, supported by a host of talented technical consultants. I have continued to play the role of urban designer and strategic advisor, supporting the Matthews on all aspects of the project as it evolved from inception to full operation.

Innovating on all these fronts and in record time would never have been possible without extraordinary co-operation from the city. It is challenging to name all of those who played a critical role, but in addition to Mayor Tory they included ward councillors Layton and Cressy and the rest of City Council; guidance from Deputy City Manager John Livey; close collaboration with Fort York and its very able Manager David O'Hara; and the work of city staff in many departments, coordinated by David Stonehouse and Pinelopi Gramatikopoulos of the Waterfront Secretariat. Given the cross-cutting complexity of the project, staff from Planning, Urban Design, Parks, Forrestry, and Recreation, and Transportation Services (responsible for the integrity of the Gardiner structure) all played vital roles.

Waterfront Toronto was an essential third partner. The Matthews Foundation did not have the capacity to implement the project, get approvals, procure contractors, and manage construction; but Waterfront Toronto, whose geographic area of interest fortunately included the Bentway, had this expertise. John Campbell, then CEO, readily agreed to become a third partner and with his retirement, his successor Will Fleissig enthusiastically took on this role. Key staff members at Waterfront Toronto, including David Kusturin, Chris Glaisek, Pina Mallozzi, Shannon Baker, and Lynne Postuma, devoted a great deal of time and energy to overseeing project execution including an extensive public engagement process and construction supervision.

A critical part of the invention of the Bentway was the exploration of stewardship models. How would it be managed? What would its relationship be to city hall and to the many constituencies it would serve?

Once again, the Bentway was to be a pioneer in Toronto, providing a new model of stewardship and funding of public space by setting up the non-profit conservancy that is working in partnership with the City of Toronto. In the early days of planning for the Bentway, Judy and Wil Matthews joined my wife and me on a visit to New York. There, in addition to visiting the High Line and various other innovative projects, we met with Betsy Barlow Rogers, the founder of the Central Park Conservancy, and her husband, Ted, to get advice based on the Central Park experience.

We learned about the way the conservancy has been structured to combine the resources of the City of New York and philanthropy, including its education and service programs, which provide groups and individual youth with hands-on opportunities to learn about Central Park and help preserve and maintain its landscapes. Through activities that are both

The undercroft of the Gardiner Expressway formed a vast, underutilized space hidden in plain sight on the edge of historic Fort York, surrounded by emerging new neighbourhoods on all sides; here seen in 2017.

educational and fun (such as gardening alongside parks department employees), participants develop a sense of stewardship for Central Park and, by extension, other natural environments. We were suitably impressed and encouraged to come up with a made-in-Toronto model.

Considerable thought was given to a range of stewardship options. Ultimately, we decided that an arm's-length not-for-profit "Bentway Conservancy," the first urban version of its kind in Canada, offered the right combination of nimbleness, flexibility, and community responsiveness based on successful precedents. It is a new model of governance and stewardship for public space in our city. The conservancy, as an independent organization, will operate, maintain, and program the space. This was a significant departure for Toronto, and many of the implications had to be worked out and built into the agreements with the city. While the model was embraced, another immediate challenge was that before the conservancy had a board or staff, a number of important tasks had to be performed including initial community outreach, planning for operations, and staff recruitment.

Reimagined as the Bentway, the Strachan Gate at its west end can host a great variety of events, in this case an informal gathering during the opening launch, Bentway Block Party, on August 25, 2018.

Sunday Social at the Bentway with the Canadian National Brass Project on July 8, 2018.

Artscape, a Toronto-born organization with great experience in the management of cultural spaces, generously agreed to step into the breech to "incubate" the fledgling conservancy over an eighteen-month period. Ably led by Tim Jones and Pru Robey, that incubation was completed with the appointment of the very skilled and experienced CEO Julian Sleath, who has assembled a highly competent staff and taken on all aspects of programming, operation, maintenance, and development, reporting to the Conservancy Board. Anchored by the Matthews family and the two ward councillors, the board is still adding new members, including me.

The annual operating budget of the conservancy is made up of a combination of the promised city support, which was advanced for an initial eight-year period, and a blending of additional philanthropy and sponsorship.

The success of the Bentway was buttressed throughout this collaborative birthing process by the unique public-private partnership between the Matthews family, the City of Toronto, Waterfront Toronto, and for a period Artscape in its incubating role. Enabled by the generosity of Wil and Judy Matthews and inspired by their vision, it is being realized through the unstinting efforts of many parties. It has demonstrated that when there is a will and a purpose, impressive breakthroughs in teamwork can be achieved to accomplish something new and different. Rather than dwell on all the non-conforming aspects of this challenging project, which might have easily become stumbling blocks, these players mobilized talents and solved problems with a "yes we can" attitude that was supported and encouraged from the top.

The phenomenon of taking something built for one purpose in the life of a city, and, by challenging preconceptions, turning it into something else is not without precedent. It is a matter of seeing the familiar with fresh eyes, often spurred by pressures demanding radical innovation and reappropriation. I have likened this kind of mind-shift to conceptual artist Marcel Duchamp's "ready-mades," the bicycle wheel or the urinal presented as found objects in a gallery; by changing their context, he caused us to see them in an entirely new light. In analogous fashion, the hard-to-meet deficit of public space is leading us to reimagine previously neglected or underutilized infrastructure such as the Bentway, seeing an elevated highway as the covering (and shading) canopy of a generously dimensioned civic space.

A familiar historic example of this kind of repurposing is the removal of fortifying walls surrounding medieval cities. Paris is a prime example. These city walls were originally designed for defence, but as armaments evolved and the city expanded, the redundant fortifications were demolished, and their vacated footprints converted into Grands Boulevards, which became defining features of the modernizing city. Or a more contemporary Parisian example: the banks of the Seine transformed seasonally with truckloads of sand into "Paris Plages," making the city its own summer resort.

Similarly, the Bentway will reconnect visitors with the many traces of this unique and evolving landscape. It is exceptionally positioned to bring the city's multi-layered history to life, from Indigenous occupation, to a strategic military location protecting the harbour with Fort York, to the arrival of the railway era in the mid-nineteenth century, to the mid-twentieth-century highway, up to its current role as an active transportation artery linking former industrial lands and new post-industrial neighbourhoods along the city's waterfront.

As a late chapter in that evolution, the elevated expressway was an object we loved to hate, and for many good reasons, as a brutal heavy-handed intrusion in the urban fabric, trampling on its surroundings. Yet seen from below with fresh eyes, its sturdy supporting structure is a thing of strange beauty, forming a magnificent space. It was this quality that my colleagues at Public Work and I wanted to exploit.

The plan we developed reinterprets this portion of the Gardiner Expressway's neglected but grand underbelly defined by the heavy-duty rib cage of concrete post-and-beam structural elements (bents) supporting the highway deck. The ever-so-slightly curved free-standing colonnade they form bends sinuously around Fort York, opening up perspectives that are only fully revealed as you move through the space. The approach was not to radically change this, but to embrace it and reveal its intrinsic qualities and rugged character.

The Bentway demonstrates the possibility of a new kind of multivalent cultural landscape beneath the highway deck by celebrating its monumental structural presence. At 24 metres wide and 14.5 metres high (five storeys), the dramatic proportions of this 1.75-kilometre-long space present endless opportunities for diverse programs. As a great "civic living room" for the underserved neighbourhoods surrounding it, the Bentway will facilitate a sharing and overlapping of activities in a dynamic public space that links physical and cultural communities, neighbourhoods, and people.

The Bentway's design interventions play off its found condition, with subtle accents of colour, texture, and the play of light to enhance its muscular quality. The space has been outfitted like an immense stage set. Power and lighting make the monumental frame of the Bentway "adhesive," with rigging that allows programmers to hang things off the bents using specially designed friction clamps that don't penetrate the concrete surface. Ground-level treatments vary from hardscape to softscape, creating different, flexible, non-prescriptive spatial configurations, which offer maximum opportunity for improvisation and discovery.

Each section of the Bentway has been exploited for its particular properties. At the west end, Strachan Avenue passes under the Gardiner at a higher level, which at one time accommodated a tunnel for the Grand Trunk Railway; that tunnel will eventually serve as a connection to Liberty Village, the GO station, and Exhibition Place. This higher elevation provides a natural mezzanine that has been exploited to form a descending, stepped timber stage, enclosing a green room and public washrooms below. To the south and overlooking the stage, an earthen amphitheatre has been shaped from mounded capped fill that had to be removed from the site.

Moving east, the parking lot for the Fort York Visitor Centre doubles as a hardscape plaza that can be programmed, leading to a generous Events Dock boardwalk in a "liquid" landscape of tall grasses. That area connects to the visitor centre through notional "piers" recalling the original water's edge, also available for programming in association with the fort. Next, the figure-eight skate trail doubles as an all-season venue with a water feature and a plan for mist curtains framing the trail within the bents. To the east again, there is an active plaza next to the abutment of a new pedestrian cycle bridge over Fort York Boulevard.

Director of Programming Ilana Altman and her staff have brilliantly exploited the possibilities of this monumental stage set to demonstrate the extraordinary range of programs the Bentway can accommodate. They've used the space to do things that could happen nowhere else, at scales ranging from the most intimate, such as individual dancers exploring the "bentscape," to small-scale performances and conversations, to expansive and monumental events like the remarkable Waterlicht, a dream landscape created by Dutch artist Daan Roosegaarde, which used a combination of LEDs and lenses to simulate the power and poetry of a flood resulting from climate change. The work attracted thirty thousand visitors who wanted to experience the powerful, though illusory, sensation of being under water.

The Bentway does not stand in isolation. The expansive green lawns of the fort and the space of the Bentway offer rich program opportunities for combined use. This seamless overlap with the National Historic Site creates a fluid, connected landscape that also allows vegetation to thrive within the Bentway, which functions like an immense, linear shade canopy. It provides welcome shade when the sun is high in midsummer, but its height means the sun's rays can reach well beneath in the shoulder and winter months. The sound of highway traffic is attenuated within the Bentway itself, shielded by the deck above, although the syncopated rhythm of vehicles going over the expansion joints is a reminder of its presence.

Across the pedestrian cycle bridge, the multi-use trail of the Bentway will weave through and connect a series of already publicly accessible spaces under the Gardiner tightly sandwiched between adjoining residential buildings. It provides continuity across several north-south streets to Canoe Landing Park in CityPlace, where it rises up a slope to connect with the new Bishop Macdonell Catholic School and Jean Lumb Public School and community centre in CityPlace. Then it gently descends to Spadina Avenue, where there are plans for another pedestrian-cycle bridge.

The Bentway will be a unique gathering place and a forum for social engagement, artistic experimentation, and creative expression. Events will range in scale and scope from the simple and everyday to the extraordinary and one of a kind, but all will encourage a sense of discovery, openness, and shared community experience. Over time, a connective cultural precinct will emerge, a place that invites and inspires creativity in a uniquely Toronto way.

It can be outfitted to house a kaleidoscope of all-season activities, including the unique all-season skate trail and multi-use trail, gardens, gathering and play spaces, public art installations, cafés, public markets, art fairs and exhibitions, creative workshops, festivals, theatre, musical performances, and other recreational amenities. A summary of the Bentway Conservancy's programming principles captures this spirit and ambition: events should be *Accessible* — deliver free and inclusive year-round programming; *Connected and Discoverable* — unite diverse communities through shared immersive, artistic, and educational experiences; *Generative* — encourage creative and community partners to embrace the site's unique conditions, histories, and possibilities; and *Participatory* — encourage visitors as active agents rather than passive audiences.

The Bentway is responding to a powerful, emerging trend for innovative programming in public spaces as artists and creators seek direct dialogue with the city to reach broader, more diverse, and unexpected audiences. The working mandate of the Bentway also expresses this symbiotic relationship to the evolving city as a cultural project:

> The Bentway is a new public space and programming platform deeply rooted in Toronto's urban fabric. It is a project both *of the city* and *about the city*, working to deliver accessible, participatory and responsive programming at the intersection of arts and urbanism. Through the lens of culture and recreation the Bentway explores Toronto's changing urban landscape as well as the opportunities and issues that unite cities across the globe.

The Bentway launched in a series of staged openings in 2018. As it opened, it transformed the way the public perceived this formerly neglected vacuum. This entire area of the city had been like an island, cut off by the Gardiner and railway to the north and Lakeshore Boulevard to the south. By reconnecting the severed neighbourhood fragments around it, the Bentway has initiated a process of call-and-response, opening a new dialogue among its neighbours on all sides.

Thanks to the Bentway, previously disconnected places are starting to form a new whole as the central void becomes a site of new opportunities for social interaction. With this critical missing link in place, the rapidly densifying new communities of Liberty Village, Niagara, Wellington Place, CityPlace, Waterfront, Fort York, and Exhibition Place surrounding this kilometre-plus stretch of the Gardiner are now more tightly linked; you can now "get there from here" to shop, to access transit, to get to school, or to meet with friends and neighbours.

The Bentway Conservancy is actively pursuing funding for future phases to expand its reach along the Gardiner to the east and west. Its first priority is to build the already-designed pedestrian cycle bridge over Fort York Boulevard, which will be suspended on cables from the Gardiner structure to form a belvedere, a special vantage point overlooking the historic grounds of the fort. Second, an extension of the skate trail is in the works from its current 220-metre length to a full kilometre under Bathurst Street to the Mouth of the Creek Park. Third, a westerly extension into Exhibition Place is planned, utilizing the currently enclosed "cubicles" under the Gardiner as a cultural hub and gateway into the grounds and a link to the GO station at Liberty Village.

The projects that will follow these steps will be even more transformative. In part stimulated by the Bentway, an even larger web of connected trails and green spaces is emerging around the entire perimeter of the combined rail corridors extending from Bathurst to Strachan. Linked, these will form a unique green and connected cultural precinct in this formerly truncated and inaccessible industrial landscape.

This network will include the Garrison Creek Park west of Bathurst; eventually the Rail Deck Park; Stackt, a container village for markets and artisans on the former lead smelter site on the west side of Bathurst at Front; the redevelopment of the former abattoir with a public edge on the rail corridor; the repurposing of the former Symes Road incinerator (nicknamed the "Destructor") as a cultural venue; the extended Stanley Park on the former Works Yard against the corridor; the new park at the tip of the Ordnance Triangle; and Trillium Park on the east edge of Ontario Place. Eventually, it will also include the Fort York Armoury (currently leased to the Department of National Defence), with its remarkable vaulted interior, which has the potential to be transformed to a cultural or community use.

The Bentway grew out of a particular response to need and opportunity in Toronto. But this is also a case of simultaneous discovery. An extraordinary gathering at the High Line's offices in New York in June 2016 brought together the creators of a new generation of public space projects from across North America in cities as diverse as New York, Philadelphia, Washington, Atlanta, Miami, Austin, Houston, Dallas, Los Angeles, Chicago, Seattle, and Toronto to share experiences. Despite their particularities and differences, they had a common interest in repurposing found post-industrial spaces — bridges, elevated highways and transit lines, rail lines, viaducts, neglected riverbanks and bayous, urban expressways from above and below, transit stations and floodways — in new and remarkable ways by forging new kinds of public-private partnerships to bring new resources to the table, and in the process inventing new models to manage and program them.

When such broad, simultaneous discovery occurs, there are usually compelling reasons. A nexus of interrelated "drivers" is now reaching a tipping point. On the one hand, the return to cities with an increasing desire for urban living is producing pressures of density and changes in the spaces we occupy. Living in smaller spaces is leading to a greater need for more shared public space. Meeting this need is thwarted, however, by high land costs; it's increasingly difficult to acquire substantial amounts of land for traditional parks. Instead, we're turning our attention to large and strategically positioned post-industrial spaces, often obsolete or underutilized.

This need for more space is accompanied by a change in how we perceive and use that public space. The kinds of experiences we seek in public space are also changing, more fluid, interconnected, less static and bounded, leading to new forms like linear "greenways" and supporting the shift from the auto paradigm to active movement — cycling and walking. Reflecting public health concerns, as well, getting us back on our feet as we seek more active lifestyles.

There is also a desire to overcome the barriers that divided the city. We're seeking connectivity, moving from social isolation to more "common ground." This is supported by a wave of civil-society initiatives and a groundswell from communities themselves, who are also expressing a desire for "greening," getting us closer to nature throughout the city and not just in isolated pockets. This in turn relates to our need for increased climate change readiness and the need to retrofit or replace aging twentieth-century infrastructure.

The combination of all of these factors is leading to an intensive re-imagining of the city — seeing it though fresh eyes. In the process, we are changing our mental maps of the city, moving from the perception of public space as a collection of discrete and isolated green spaces to a view that sees interconnected webs or matrices of space, with elements that arise organically from existing forms and rediscovered, underutilized spaces. The Bentway embodies all of the above.

Reinforcing this enlarged sense of the public realm are the major new roles for arts and culture in public spaces. A democratization of major cultural institutions has occurred; there has been a moving out into the public sphere, and participatory interaction with these institutions is now encouraged. The Bentway is a prime example of how Toronto and Canada have progressed in this regard, and how we are now more open to creative governance models for public spaces. Just five years earlier, creating an arm's-length conservancy to manage public space would have been almost impossible in Toronto.

While there were clearly significant differences among the projects presented in the initial meeting of the High Line Network — distinctions between organizations, projects, and communities — they had much in common in the ways in which they responded to these drivers. There was real interest in continuing the conversation. Out of that initial encounter came the idea of using the network as an ongoing vehicle to share experiences and best practices, engage in advocacy, and communicate the power of these ideas and approaches to a broad range of audiences.

We also spent considerable time discussing the broader implications of our initiatives and the responsibilities that come with the stewardship models we are developing. Public-private partnerships and philanthropy bring many powerful advantages: increased resources; the ability to address the urgent need for public space nimbly and flexibly in innovative, unique, and exceptional ways; the opportunity to "prototype" new forms and hybrids that do not neatly fall within traditional public-space categories; and the potential for new and exciting ways of engaging communities in new models of stewardship.

While it is clear that these initiatives have the potential to bring enormous positive impacts for their host cities and local communities, they also raise important questions about roles and responsibilities. What are the over-arching goals and priorities, and who gets to decide? Whom are we serving? How do we meet the changing needs of cities, residents, and communities, and where do these projects fit in the discussion of larger social issues?

A second, smaller meeting aimed at solidifying the network and flesh-ing out its goals and purposes took place in Toronto at the Bentway in September 2016, and one of the things we tackled was an attempt to artic-ulate a common definition of the phenomenon:

> The creation of new kinds of public space reappropriating and repurposing previously neglected or underutilized lands and infrastructure in the hearts of cities, bringing new re-sources to bear, providing much needed democratic accessi-ble public space and an expanded range of ways of using it, often linear overcoming barriers and reconnecting commu-nities; supporting healthier lifestyles and greater integration across real and perceived divides; providing new support and stimulus for existing and new neighbourhoods, enlarged op-portunities for expressions of arts and culture; developing new stewardship models rooted in local communities while pioneering new forms of public-private partnerships.

We concluded that this phenomenon is more complex than might be realized at first blush. There is an important ethical dimension that must shape our work in negotiating these complex questions and relationships. We identified three pillars — economic, social, and environmental — on which the whole enterprise rests, with an overarching concept of equity and shared benefits that apply to all three.

We wrestled with the meaning of democratic, accessible, and inclusive public space, acknowledging that in many situations our initiatives have significant impacts on existing communities of poverty, and also the poten-tial for displacement through gentrification. We talked about the obligation to respect the places and people that are already living in and around the sites we want to transform, and the need to work with those affected com-munities to secure a stake in outcomes by building civic capacity, working with a broad range of other actors. We stressed that this commitment to addressing the full spectrum of society should be reflected in diverse boards and staff, as well as in the nature of programming.

We acknowledged the ultimate role of cities themselves as defenders of the public interest and the need to work in close partnership with public agencies, parks departments, and transportation departments, working out our place in the ecosystem of public spaces. These new entities are clearly not a panacea intended to supplant or diminish the commitment of governments to the public realm. Rather, they present an opportunity to strengthen that commitment by adding to the resource base, taking on projects that otherwise might not happen, and pioneering new models of shared community stewardship and engagement.

We concluded with a list of best practice issues and topics to be explored in depth at our next gatherings: governance, programming, community development, value capture, funding, and design. Representatives of projects from cities around North America would consider these issues together, through shared lenses and perspectives, but with close attention to their particular circumstances. Those meetings are now ongoing and the Bentway is playing an active role.

Toronto shares all of the conditions that have led to this innovative generation of High Line Network projects: the convergence of change drivers, and the intense need for, and constraints in, expanding the public realm. Great parks and open spaces are the hallmark of a great city. Given the lack of availability and the cost of land in Toronto, conventional methods for acquiring additional parkland in a high-price real estate market won't always work. This invites the question of what our next public spaces will be as we evolve into a great and densely populated city. We do have a wide range of existing parks, from expansive legacy parks, like the Toronto Islands and High Park, more intimate neighbourhood parks like Trinity Bellwoods, gardens and historic squares like Victoria Memorial Square, natural waterfront parks like the Eastern Beaches and Western Beaches, as well as a vast array of neighbourhood parks, some sixteen hundred, in fact.

A brilliant new round of renewal of existing parks, and creation of new ones, is underway in some areas. There is now a refurbished Grange Park behind the Art Gallery of Ontario with unique children's play structures, and Berczy Park with its crowd-pleasing dog-inspired fountains; recent additions along the waterfront include Sugar Beach, with a sand beach and sturdy pink beach umbrellas; Sherbourne Common with its water filtration artworks; Corktown Common with a working wetlands; and Trillium Park with its cavelike rock formations. And at the other end of the size spectrum, there is the new Rouge Park, the country's largest urban national park, and the new sixteen-kilometre Meadoway, which utilizes a Hydro corridor to link Rouge Park to the Don Valley.

These spaces, however, even combined with existing spaces, don't come close to fully meeting the city's growing need, as important demographic cohorts — immigrants and migrants, young people and empty nesters (and increasingly now young families) — are creating a Toronto that is literally bursting at the seams. A key demand of city residents, expressed over and over in community meetings about intensifying development, is for more and improved open space as part of an expanded public realm.

This desire for more and better public space in Toronto is practically palpable. It may have seemed at one point as if TV, shopping at the mall, and, more recently, the virtual world of screens, home entertainment centres, text messaging, e-commerce, Facebook, and chat rooms, all increasingly claiming our time, would kill public space, or make it redundant. But while it may have been tempting to see the demand for public space as on a downward spiral, that dire prognosis seems incorrect. There is pressure to increase the amount and quality of public space, notwithstanding those trends.

We have outgrown the limited amount of dedicated public space that is our inheritance from a much smaller City of Toronto (and its amalgamated suburbs). Space for new conventional parks is scarce, and current land values extremely expensive. Even with "carve outs" and land takings from development, and cash put into a park reserve fund, traditional means of buying discrete parcels of land to create new parks are strained.

This is our dilemma. How can Toronto get ahead of the intense development curve to shape a dynamic and growing city around a forward-looking program for expanding the public realm? The Bentway, and the other projects in the High Line Network, may offer some clues. To use the momentum of change, we will need creative solutions that anticipate and exploit new opportunities to complement conventional means like land acquisition and development "takings." It is not only about the quantity of public open space — in conventional planning terms, we have been focused on the square metres of parkland per inhabitant within a given radius — and while this is important, it is actually more important to focus on the quality and usefulness of that space and how it enhances our lives.

The "commons" (the shared public spaces in our cities) is essential to our well-being as social creatures. It could, in fact, be argued that it has become the bedrock foundation for a new generation of city-building efforts in Toronto. Public space has been at the core of every project I have ever worked on, from putting the parks in Regent Park, which, despite its name, never had them; to reconnecting St. Paul, Minnesota, to its origins on the Mississippi River; to reappropriating abandoned piers on the Brooklyn waterfront to create the Brooklyn Bridge Park; to giving the public access to the edges of the harbour islands in Amsterdam. It is the starting point and the critical leitmotif of effective city building.

Public realm in this sense refers not only to publicly owned spaces in the city fabric. It also includes streets, small parks, squares, plazas, and trails, and the larger spaces provided by urban parks (some of which may be privately owned but publicly accessible), which in combination typically make up half of the city's land area. The correlation between the character of these spaces, the unique sense of place they provide, and the health and vitality of the city has long been recognized. Shared common ground, where we come together face to face, is what makes cities livable and productive and makes democracy work in heterogeneous societies like ours — especially as we learn to live in smaller spaces set in denser, more walkable settings, and find our way toward a more sustainable future.

Public spaces are as varied and specific to place as the urban cultures that have given birth to them. They come in all sizes and shapes. The best ones have a living, ongoing symbiotic relationship with their host cities, from the traditional *piazze* and *campi* of Italian cities, the *pleins* of the Netherlands, or the *places* of France, the *plazas* and *paseos* in the Spanish-speaking world; to the traditional great urban parks in the hearts of cities, like Central Park in NYC (and all the great Frederick Law Olmsted parks for that matter), Chapultepec Park in Mexico City, and the Bois de Boulogne in Paris; to the new carved-out spaces like Millennium Park in Chicago and the repurposed pedestrian laneways of Melbourne.

City parks and squares have emerged as a potent new focus for community allegiance, civic pride, and neighbourhood identification. The desire for quality in the public realm goes hand in hand with a renewed appreciation of the city's physicality, moving from the abstractions of statistics to the qualities of space and place. There's a new public confidence and interest in design. Even where government faces challenges in providing and maintaining such spaces, civil society in the form of communities, individuals, the private sector, and institutions is stepping up in a kind of groundswell with support for the "commons," from high-profile efforts like New York's Central Park Conservancy and now the Bentway Conservancy in Toronto to hundreds of more modest "Friends of" organizations. Partnerships have become the way to accomplish what government could no longer manage alone.

This is not about a frill or non-essential "nice to have." There are powerful drivers behind this push, including the environmental imperative, the need to accommodate more active lifestyles, the need for personal and social space, and the need for competitiveness in a knowledge-based or creative economy based on quality of place. In the face of this array of new forces, we are seeing the reversal of many of the major tendencies and projects of mid-twentieth-century urban and suburban planning, which devalued public space. This reversal is provoking a wide-ranging reconsideration of priorities and practices.

This is particularly relevant for Toronto. As we grow denser and more diverse, we have come to understand that expanding common ground is critical for our continued success as a productive, socially harmonious city drawing investments, businesses, residents, and visitors. We are, after all, a city where over half the population was born elsewhere. If cultural homogeneity is no longer an option, how do we live together? An indispensable precondition for peace and harmony is to have places and spaces where we tread the same sidewalks, see each other, simply walk to a park or public square to meet friends, take our kids to play, walk our dogs, and through unscripted interactions learn to cope with our inevitable differences and understand our commonalities. Virtual space does not replace that. As with many other earlier communications advancements — telephone, movies, television — new technological capabilities are absorbed and become complementary to this still-basic need for face-to-face encounters.

Encountering the "other" in public has something fundamental to do with self-actualization. As philosopher Hannah Arendt observed, humans appear before others in public in order to be recognized. Personal identity is exposed and revealed. This "revelation" of identity cannot happen in isolation; it cannot result from self-reflection alone. Our public self is revealed in a public place. In our city, we cannot help being aware that we have been born into a world that is inhabited by many others who are different from ourselves. We can also see that, in large part, we benefit from that reality and thus we consider it a positive condition of our shared lives as city dwellers.

A pervasive desire for some form of sociability in true public space seems to meet a fundamental human need. On a personal level, many of us have a longing for the unscripted possibilities — a life of absolutely "no surprises" is deadly dull. Too, the experience of seeing and being seen among our peers in public confirms our own place in the universe as humans and the connectedness of things. In true public space we can reveal and communicate our uniqueness as individuals and at the same time recognize the differing identities of others. These interactions, even when they provide something as simple as awareness and familiarity, speak to our collective viability as an urban society. In the absence of public spaces where such mingling can occur, problems of exclusion can easily arise. When citizens do not meet their fellow citizens — in all their variety — there emerges the very real danger that the unknown "other" will be seen as in some way threatening. In our heterogeneous city, we have an obligation to ensure the existence of a space for communication and interaction among all citizens; and it must be inclusive enough to allow access and use by everyone.

There is an important political dimension, as well. The presence and stability of the commons is critical to democracy. We need space for political freedom, places where people can demonstrate, express dissent, and freely voice opinions in public. This right can be fragile and vulnerable; let's not forget that in many places, public space has all but vanished, replaced by private enclaves — places of exclusion, segregation, and political suppression.

Given all of that, Toronto has a very particular public-realm challenge. It involves overcoming the real and perceived prewar city and postwar urban-suburban divide. Central Toronto lives on its historic capital of relatively dense and interconnected prewar neighbourhoods, with their shared public space, but, as David Hulchanski, director of the Centre for Urban and Community Studies at the University of Toronto, points out, through his studies of the census over time, there has been an alarming erosion of city-wide shared neighbourhoods and common ground. Increasingly, income polarization is reflected geographically in Toronto's division into three very separate cities: the growing area of poverty (housing a large population of recent immigrants) in the postwar suburban fringe, a growing high-income enclave in the city centre, and a shrinking middle class in between. This division has resulted in a lack of equity in terms of access to public space and public facilities and overcoming barriers that divide us.

There is another very basic argument for the presence and quality of public space, one where social equity and enlightened self-interest come together. It is the economic counter to the ultimately self-defeating neo-conservative legacy of neglect and withdrawal that leads to private wealth inside gated communities and public squalor without. There is now a broadly shared understanding among many economists that cities, with their ability to attract investment in a diverse creative economy, are the principal generators of wealth. This new paradigm for economic development emphasizes that quality of life and quality of place have a value equal to, if not greater than, traditional factor costs (i.e., land, labour, and capital). Cities and regions that compete with each other primarily on cost are engaged in a losing game — "beggar thy neighbour" policies inevitably lead to a race to the bottom and impoverishment of the public realm and public services.

There is substantial evidence that the presence of attractive and well-maintained parks and open spaces — the commons — creates economic value in surrounding areas that is retained over long periods of time. In a world of intense competition, the quality of place becomes a key consideration in location choices for businesses, institutions, and individuals. We often get to know and experience other cities through their great parks and public spaces, and they become the magnets that attract investment.

170

A generously endowed and welcoming network of public space offers significant benefits to public health, both physically and mentally. We are in the midst of a public health crisis, exacerbated by sedentary lifestyles where an overreliance on the automobile and a tendency to spend long hours in front of screens has produced an epidemic of obesity as well as increases of diabetes and heart disease — especially alarming among children. This, coupled with the inevitable (and perhaps, in some cases, desirable) shrinking of private space as a reflection of economic pressures, puts a premium on public spaces where people of all ages can get out and participate in active pastimes, from simply walking and cycling to a whole range of year-round sports and athletic activities close to where they live and work, making these health-promoting activities part of their daily life routines. Driving to the gym or health club is no substitute.

Increasingly, regional health authorities recognize the relationship between the urban form that enables walking and cycling and public health. Patterns of development that discourage parents from allowing their children to walk to school, or which require the use of a car for every journey, are now proven to be problematic. In Toronto, former medical officer of health David McEwen actively drew attention to the relationship between civic design that promotes active lifestyles, and reduced health care costs. While government policy lags behind the research, more and more members of the design community are acting on the evidence.

A similar correlation holds true for mental health. In October of 2017, I was invited to speak at a conference at the Royal College of Physicians in London entitled "Unleashing Heath by Design," bringing together a mix of design professionals and health practitioners. The issues of mental health related to social isolation and the importance of public space for social connection were considered as significant as those related to physical well-being.

We now have a large, aging population that has grown up with the car as a way of life and can no longer safely drive, and, as a result, now finds itself stranded in places where there are few good options for informal social gathering close to home. An expanded public realm that offers spaces to gather and socialize with other people available close to where Torontonians of all ages, abilities, and incomes live and work is a critical component of a sustainable community.

Paradoxically, just as the understanding of the importance of the public realm has gained traction among designers and decision makers, it has been threatened and undermined by severe funding challenges. Insufficient funding, not commensurate with our growth, is producing chronic underfunding of public services and public spaces. We can see the damage in the deterioration of urban infrastructure and public space around us, as maintenance has been disastrously deferred. This has severely limited the ability of the city to maintain existing public spaces or to create new ones. Toronto is not keeping up. New means and resources to address this growing public space deficit are urgently needed.

The current dearth of accessible (and fundable) public space in the city is forcing planners and community groups to look for opportunities waiting to be exploited. There are a huge number of potential sites. To identify and develop them, we will need to create a big-picture vision for the public realm in Toronto. Unconventional, creative strategies like that used to develop the Bentway can be employed to expand and improve public open space in our city. By transforming our underutilized spaces more creatively, we will create opportunities to link existing and new green spaces into continuous interconnected webs — linear greenways formed not just by conventional parks, but also trails, bridges, and "green streets" of all scales. Our future success depends on us exploiting these arteries and veins, which can be stitched together utilizing our currently unsung hidden-in-plain-sight ravines, hydro corridors, and laneways. This stitching may be the key to our own *genius loci* in the public realm.

We actually possess an extraordinary quantity of latent land resources — more than sufficient to accomplish the goal of "green" connectivity throughout the city. Once we remove the previously defined boundaries that isolate public space as a stand-alone category, there emerge endless opportunities for piggybacking on essential infrastructure including transportation, stormwater management, and flood-proofing systems. By integrating with Toronto's underlying natural systems — the fifty-kilometre Lake Ontario shoreline, the river and creek systems that feed it, our regional watersheds — and reusing and connecting existing spaces to form networks, Toronto can create its own version of cottage country within the city, one that extends right into the heart of existing and newly forming neighbourhoods.

The Meadoway is a remarkable project that helps to accomplish this goal. Occupying a sixteen-kilometre stretch of the Gatineau hydro corridor in Scarborough, it will provide a complete meadowland trail and bike path all the way from the Don River Valley trails to Rouge Park (Canada's largest urban national park), connecting four ravines, fifteen local parks, a number of schools and community centres, and thirty-four neighbourhoods along its route. Once more hidden in plain sight like the Bentway, this thriving green space and connector is currently home to more than one thousand species of flora and fauna.

This initiative has been made possible with $25 million in funding announced from the W. Garfield Weston Foundation, in partnership with the Toronto and Region Conservation Authority and with the involvement of Park People. The conservation authority has also provided funding to transform mowed grass in the hydro corridor into a thriving habitat for butterflies, bees, and other pollinators toward what will ultimately be an $85-million project connecting existing spaces and overcoming a number of physical barriers that isolate neighbourhoods. The Meadoway revitalizes kilometres of mowed hydro corridor with little biodiversity value, but it also ties disparate communities together through green space. When complete, it will be possible to bike from Rouge Park through The Meadoway to the Lower Don Trail and down to the central waterfront — almost entirely through off-road trails.

Similarly, the five-kilometre Green Line on the west side of the city, spanning from Lansdowne Avenue to Spadina Avenue, is another example of a community-driven project being shepherded by Park People. This adaptive reuse of a hydro corridor connecting various green spaces on the west side of Toronto took a major step forward at the outset of 2017, with a budget and design team in place to begin to realize the vision.

It is a matter of identifying these low-hanging fruits, where design can play a key role in unearthing (pun intended) new opportunities. This involves fundamental problem solving with scarce resources by not doing just one thing at a time, but combining multiple objectives for mutual benefit. Climate readiness combined with the creation of public space is a prime example. Corktown Commons, the new park that is the centrepiece of the new West Don Lands neighbourhood (which began life as the Pan Am

Athletes' Village), is the surface of an engineered earth form that provides flood protection for much of downtown Toronto. Sherbourne Common is simultaneously a water filtration plant, landscape, and public art.

Every time a piece of obsolescent twentieth-century infrastructure is retired, new possibilities for an expanded public realm open up. For instance, the city's previously industrial Toronto Harbour has re-emerged as a recreational blue "harbour room," surrounded by new green spaces. Street renewal projects offer similar opportunities for transforming or expanding public spaces. There are currently a number of projects on deck, including an extension to the redesign of Queens Quay; a transformation of Yonge Street, both in the downtown core and North York Centre; and alterations of King Street, John Street, and others. These projects all provide opportunities for expanding the public realm. In fact, the city renews the entire system of rights-of-way periodically, and each rebuilding offers an opportunity for redesign. New transportation initiatives by Metrolinx, the expansion of regional rail, and TTC subway extensions all provide similar occasions for combined budgets to augment and enhance public space.

One of the most significant opportunities for an expanded public realm lies in Toronto's ravines, which, some would argue, are the spiritual heart of our city, penetrating most of our neighbourhoods. These spaces, protected by the Toronto and Region Conservation Authority since the traumatic flooding caused by Hurricane Hazel in 1954, occupy about 17 percent of the city's land mass and are still largely inaccessible. The trails that do exist reveal the incredible beauty of this resource, unique to our city and still largely undervalued.

Toronto has the advantage of actually having a lot of green space in the city's underserved suburban neighbourhoods — much of it thanks to the ravines. The problem is that currently the green space does not meet the community's needs. It is tough to access, and the spaces offer little in the way of programming or amenities. This lack poses both a challenge and an opportunity.

Toronto's vast network of laneways offers another huge potential. There are over 2,400 laneways, which, combined, extend for more than 250 kilometres in length. In terms of area, the laneways occupy over 250 acres, an area more than half the size of High Park. More significantly, this mid-block network penetrates many of the city's neighbourhoods, providing the potential for an intimate network of open public space, pedestrian and cycle routes, and extremely valuable land for housing, studios, workshops, and service spaces. The redevelopment of the laneways is currently being undertaken by the city and community-led initiatives. Ideas are being examined in a series of probes and tests, supported by local neighbourhoods and the volunteer Laneway Project. Each test reflects the distinct character of the surrounding neighbourhood. Rush Lane is one example: famous for its murals and dubbed "graffiti alley," it served as the background for Rick Mercer's TV rants. Reggae Lane in Little Jamaica, which also features murals, captures some of the area's rich musical history.

Putting together all the pieces — laneways, street redesign, ravines, hydro corridors, rail lines, stormwater management systems, flood-proofing plans, and transportation initiatives, along with development-related park contributions and consolidation of major public sites — a vastly expanded public realm can emerge, one that addresses many of the city's current deficiencies. This new realm will be different, both in scale and kind. Rather than discrete and bounded public spaces carved out of a grid of street blocks — parks and squares — this new kind of public space has the potential to become the fully continuous, connective tissue of the urban fabric itself.

The greatest challenge to this kind of holistic thinking and operation are the "siloed" mandates of the many different agencies that provide and maintain the functional pieces of the public realm — streets or parks or hydro corridors or protected natural areas. These agencies must now work collaboratively to bring these components together to form the physical places we experience in the city. This is easier said than done. Jurisdictional jealousies, bureaucratic inertia, and risk aversion are powerful impediments. But the politicians' and staff's will to break through these administrative and legal barriers is growing, thanks to an increased sense of the public's need (and right) to overcome these stumbling blocks, and progress is being made as agencies redefine their mandates and develop collaborative strategies.

New projects and linked networks like the ones described above — the lands along the West Toronto Railpath, the areas surrounding the Bentway, and the nexus of connections through Corktown and the Lower Don linking to the Martin Goodman and Waterfront parks and trails — all reveal this latent potential to expand the public realm. These examples demonstrate that the entire city can become more park-like, green, and connected for people on foot and on bicycle. Fostering residents' ability to move around relatively freely and experience more of the city this way helps to break down the perceived barriers between neighbourhoods and districts. Discrete places are joined; relationships and flows become more continuous.

The elements of the public realm that serve as links between areas play a vital role in helping to make the city feel like a seamless whole. Examples of these important connections can be found everywhere. There is, as mentioned, the Bentway in Toronto; other important structures include the High Line in New York; the Simone de Beauvoir Bridge over the Seine in Paris, which links the new Tolbiac and Bercy neighbourhoods; and the George C. King Bridge across the Bow River in Calgary, which connects the Bridgeland neighbourhood and the new East Village. Another important structure in Toronto is the Humber River Pedestrian Bridge. A wonderfully well-used landmark, it performs a vital role linking South Etobicoke and the Western Beaches across the Humber River and tying together the river valley and waterfront trail systems.

Toronto has developed a number of potent examples of this holistic way of thinking about public space, and a new generation of policies and plans, such as TOcore, which is attempting to set a new course for expanding the public realm in Toronto's core by encouraging groups to pool their efforts. With time, it can be anticipated that the examples of connection that we have today will become the rule. This turn toward interconnected public spaces has profound implications for the practices of architecture, landscape architecture, and civil engineering, among other civic disciplines. In future, projects will no longer be viewed and developed as isolated entities; instead, the contributions that individual buildings and spaces make to the larger urban context, will become central to their design.

Not only is Toronto witnessing a new way of expanding the commons, it is also inventing new forms of co-management and bringing new partners to the table. As we have seen, shared public space or common ground is the lifeblood of a great city. It is far too important to be neglected. Public-private partnerships have become a critically important vehicle for accomplishing what government can no longer manage alone. This redefining of public and private roles has many benefits, but just like government, civil society needs to be accountable in clearly defined roles. Philanthropy should be seen as a complement and a stimulant, not a substitute for government involvement.

The Bentway was intended to be a model demonstrating what kinds of design and programming are possible in reclaimed spaces, but it is also an example of partnership with the city, inspiring others to come forward with innovative projects. What is critical, and this is enshrined in agreements with the city, is that in these partnerships the essential public quality of the space not be compromised in any way and that accountability to the public be preserved.

Expanding this premise of an enlarged commons at a broader scale, Park People is an independent charity that builds strong communities by animating and improving parks, placing them at the heart of life in cities. Originating in Toronto and now operating across Canada, it is an advocacy group representing the roughly 1,600 existing parks in Toronto and promoting the emergence of new forms of community engagement. I have been on the board in the past and my wife, Eti, is currently serving as a board member.

Park People provides leadership in helping to ensure communities have a big vision for parks; working with grassroots organizations, foundations, cities, provinces, and the federal government; acting as a valuable clearing house for ideas bottom up and top down; supporting and connecting existing initiatives; identifying gaps and inventing and fostering new delivery methods for capital investment and programming and maintenance; and developing new stewardship models. Janie Romoff, the general manager of Toronto's Parks, Forestry and Recreation Division, has expressed her appreciation for their work and attends the annual Park Summit to deliver a State of the Parks message.

In conjunction with Park People, Eti and I have recently made a donation to fund a new project called the Public Space Incubator, which will operate over a two-year period to elicit innovative ways of reimagining

Toronto's public spaces based on the premise that we need to creatively make the most of every space in our city to contribute to our quality of life. Toronto is already seeing a growing interest in innovative ways to inhabit and enliven our public space — and find new ones. With Park People, we are looking for people who have bold, creative, and radical ideas for Toronto's parks, plazas, schoolyards, laneways, streets, and other publicly accessible open spaces. Our personal contribution to this effort has been matched by the Balsam Foundation.

By providing access to funding and professional networks, the Public Space Incubator will support tangible pilots that test new, innovative ways to bring underutilized public spaces to life. With a focus on innovation, partnerships, programming, and scalability, the Public Space Incubator will provide ten projects — five in each of 2018 and 2019 — with up to $50,000 in funding. And, as an incubator, it will support successful applicants in implementing projects by connecting them with a network of professionals.

In line with the Incubator's core principles, the selected projects must be innovative, community driven, programmable, catalytic, and scalable. They must take place within publicly accessible outdoor open spaces in the City of Toronto, whether privately or publicly owned. We've created a two-stage application process starting with a letter of intent and then, after an initial selection process, a full application. A jury of outstanding individuals with a wide range of backgrounds has volunteered to assist in the selection process.

The first five projects selected represent a wide range of untapped potentials. Red Embers is a site-specific work by Indigenous artists that activates a walkway though Allan Gardens, one of the city's most historic parks; plazaPOPS is a pop-up plaza in one of the city's lively strip-mall parking lots along Lawrence Avenue in Scarborough; Nicholson Lane Linear Park is a community partnership to transform a laneway into an active public space through lighting, paving, planting, and animation; the Thorncliffe Park Community Café is a project to expand the reach and operation of a food-centred program in R.V. Burgess Park, led by the Thorncliffe Park Women's Committee; and Urban Discovery is a youth-focused train-watching platform and exploratory play space overlooking the city's major rail corridor at Bathurst and Front Streets. We are full of anticipation waiting to see what these will produce. We expect that it will be inspiring.

With the shift to a more expansive sense of the public realm, a new reading of the city is emerging. In the realm of transportation, the city will no longer be orienting itself only or primarily by highways and major arterials; increasingly, green networks and alternative connected networks of common space will serve as guideways throughout the city. This more fluid idea of the cityscape as a landscape, where flows become more organic and seamless, following natural features like watercourses and topography, in some ways gets us back to a pre-colonial sense of the land we inhabit as a shared "commons," a space less hard-edged and bounded by surveyed property divisions and functional categories.

5

The City in Nature

Fifteen minutes by bike from where we live, Eti and I keep a double kayak at the Harbourfront Canoe and Kayak Club on the Toronto Harbour. We have made a mutually beneficial arrangement with the owner, Dave Corrigan, donating it to the club. Dave stores and maintains it; we can use it when we give notice, and he can rent it out at all other times. Whenever we do have time, usually on a weekend when the weather beckons, we set out with a picnic lunch from the Rees Street Slip, paddling in the direction of Toronto Island, circumventing the buoys protecting the Billy Bishop airport runway, and eventually heading for the Eastern Gap, one of the two openings to the inner harbour from the lake, when we are feeling ambitions.

At first, we are in the busiest section of the harbour. We have to time our movement very carefully to dodge the three fast ferries as they travel on fixed routes (with very little ability to manoeuvre) to the ferry terminals at Hanlan's Point, Centre Island, and Ward's Island. Sometimes we have to deal with the choppy wake thrown up by powerboats. As the hard edge of the seawall recedes, delineating the historic piers of a once-active port and now lined with a dense wall of new buildings, we get closer to the continuous band of vegetation ringing the Toronto Islands, and things calm considerably.

Heading east past the remnants of the industrial port lands and passing the mouth of the monumental ship channel that served it, we make our way through the busy traffic in the Eastern Gap and breathe a sigh of relief when we enter a new, expansive, even quieter body of water, the Outer Harbour. Here there are no ferries and fewer powerboats, and, depending on the day, more small sailboats and windsurfers. To the east, there is popular Cherry Beach on the south shore of this harbour, to the west around the bend a sheltered beach on Ward's Island. Sometimes these are our destinations, but mostly we continue across this second harbour, making for a new fringe of green shoreline defining the edge of Tommy Thompson Park, commonly known as the Leslie Street Spit, extending some five kilometres out into Lake Ontario from the foot of Leslie Street.

We usually find a convenient place to pull the kayak up onto a small stretch of beach where we might find a fallen log to sit on to rest and enjoy our lunch, often entirely alone, before continuing our exploration of the openings to inner bays along the shore. At our leisurely pace, it may have taken us fifty minutes to an hour to cross a little over five kilometres of water. We are still in the city, but in an entirely different world. It is sublime.

This is an entirely artificial place. It was never intended to be a park, but it became a magnificent one. We are on the edge of a wild area where a forested landscape has grown up on its own, aided by the wind and stowaway material transported in dump trucks of fill from excavation sites. Habitats of increasingly diverse flora and fauna have miraculously appeared, largely through natural succession, with some more recent delicate assists by the conservation authority. Bird colonies have appeared in profusion, and small mammals have found their way here.

There is a similar story when we arrive by land. Travelling by bike along the Martin Goodman Trail from the west, as we typically do, or from the Eastern Beaches or Leslie Street to the north, we pass the threshold of Leslie Street and Unwin Avenue, beyond which cars are not permitted on the Spit. From that point, the roadway that once served dump-truck traffic carrying excavated material becomes a trail, and alongside it there are now parallel walking paths closer to the shoreline. If arriving by car, there are periodic shuttles that can drop you off at points right out to the tip. Cycling or walking out into Lake Ontario on the narrow roadway or trails that surround the central bays is like entering another world. It is liberating and magical.

We feel an extraordinary sense of contrasting realities. Turning toward the lake, the city almost disappears, dwarfed by the immensity of the horizon across the water. Turning back to the city, a magnificent skyline can be seen through the trees, wild nature in the foreground and dense urbanity in the background radically juxtaposed across the harbour in middle ground.

On our bikes we are irresistibly drawn to make it out to the end. The reward, the world seen from the lighthouse at the tip, is awe inspiring — the boats coming close, the waves pulverizing the residue of bricks and concrete that built the city and now armour the point, the power of wind and waves, the long views and unusual panoramic vista of this vast unfolding scene before us. We have to linger. Where we are resembles nothing else. It speaks to the massive capacity of humans to alter the land, and, at the same time, the immense power of nature to reassert itself in a field of detritus on a barren site. What we are experiencing is nature re-emerging in the heart of the city. It reminds us that we live in nature, a city fused with nature.

How did this extraordinary creation happen? A few short years ago this appendage to the shoreline wasn't here. We would have been in the lake under ten metres of water.

The Spit is a man-made headland, the result of five decades of lake filling by the Toronto Port Authority. It was extended roughly five kilometres in a southwesterly direction into Lake Ontario to form and protect the Outer Harbour, part of a massive engineering plan to expand the capacity of Toronto's Harbour in anticipation of marine traffic via the St. Lawrence Seaway, which opened in 1959. But with the advent of containerization in the 1960s, many cargo ships became too large to make it to Toronto and traffic shifted to East Coast ports. The Outer Harbour was no longer needed.

But the Spit kept growing. It was treated as a useful repository for fill and construction waste from the building of Toronto's subways, office towers, and other large projects. In the late 1970s, dredged material from the nearby Keating Channel was also added to the growing spit, an action seen as a better solution than dumping the polluted material into open water. As the Spit grew, the question then became: What to do with this massive landform?

At the time that the Spit began to develop, I was living in the nearby Eastern Beach neighbourhood and with some of my neighbours began to explore this vast, barren, and windswept finger extending out into the lake. We were captivated by its stark beauty but also noticed an interesting phenomenon: the Spit was beginning to be carpeted by an ever-increasing variety of plants, grown from seeds blown there by the wind. With no human help, it was rapidly becoming green.

Aided by the botanists in our group, I produced a plan drawing showing how this process, led initially by poplars, might proceed to produce a forested tree canopy. I joined my neighbour and colleague Professor Roy Merrens and his students at the York University Department of Geography in 1972 to produce a map called the *People's Guide to the Toronto Waterfront*. The map was intended to entice the adventurous into navigating the vast, unknown territories of the port, highlighting the Spit as a special place being reclaimed by nature.

But others had different ideas, wanting to use the site for active commercial activities. Public discussions on the future of this area, then referred to as the Aquatic Park, were held in June 1974, and proposed uses included mooring for over five hundred boats, along with bicycling, picnicking, and fishing facilities. A master plan was prepared for the Toronto and Region Conservation Authority in the mould of other landfill sites it was developing across the region, and the details were publicized in March 1976. The consultants' report proposed significant development, including expanded marinas (mooring for 1,500 boats), an amphitheatre, a water ski area, and a hotel.

As it turned out, this proposal was the beginning of a lengthy struggle. Perhaps no other piece of land has attracted such passionate defenders, nor had such a lengthy battle waged on its behalf, simply to allow it to grow as nature dictated. Seeing the extraordinary possibilities this area presented where the process of natural succession was occurring, a non-partisan community advocacy group formed in 1977 called Friends of the Spit to allow the Leslie Street Spit to evolve as a Public Urban Wilderness, with the goal that it would remain a car-free environmental resource, entirely public and accessible at no cost. I was an early member. Here was an unforeseen gift of naturalization occurring, offering a chance to return part of Toronto's shoreline to nature and so redress the tremendous loss of the historic marsh and Ashbridges Bay, which had been drained and filled to create the adjacent Port Lands in the early part of the twentieth century.

The Friends' voices were ultimately heard at City Council when city councillor Colin Vaughan pointed out that only twenty acres of the 250 acres under study were to be set aside for naturalized areas. The master plan was heavily criticized by several groups and the powers that be were persuaded in the end to back off this controversial proposal. A new process was launched by the conservation authority in 1984, and in the meantime the Spit was quietly naturalizing, with little interference.

In 1985, the TRCA announced that the northern portion of the Spit would be designated as an environmentally sensitive area and that future plans would accommodate both recreational and naturalist groups. This was a critical about-face for the conservation authority. The Spit was re-designated Tommy Thompson Park, named after a former Toronto Parks commissioner, and henceforth managed by the TRCA. As late as 1973, there had been no formal access to the Spit, although visits could be arranged with the Toronto Harbour Commission. But by the summer of 1974, the Toronto Harbour Commission was providing bus service to the Spit on Sunday afternoons. It is currently open to the public 5:30 a.m. to 9:00 p.m. on weekends and statutory holidays, and from 4:00 p.m. to 9:00 p.m. on weekdays. It is still closed during the day on weekdays owing to the ongoing construction of the Spit, conducted by PortsToronto.

Wildlife has flourished on the Spit, and the area is now a popular bird-watching spot. More than three hundred bird species have been identified there, forty-five of which breed on the headland. Among the birds that may be observed on the headland are the ring-billed gull, the black-crowned night heron, the double-crested cormorant, the common tern, the Caspian tern, and the herring gull. It has been designated an Important Bird Area (IBA) by Nature Canada and Bird Studies Canada, and is the site of a comprehensive bird research station run by the TRCA. The Leslie Street Spit's evolution into an urban wilderness was never in the city's earlier plans. Its protected status was secured by a number of organizations, with the Friends of the Spit at the forefront of advocacy to naturalize the site, and a remarkable resource was preserved.

The Spit is an accidental park; its creation was a gift of nature. The city's mid-course changing of gears speaks to a much greater transformation underway in how we understand our position as urban dwellers within the natural world. In fact, perhaps more rapidly than we realize, we are witnessing a major dissolution of the false conceptual dichotomy that has divided the city from the natural world. Like many powerful and timely impulses, this reconciliation has had many sources: scientific, cultural, and aesthetic. It is a striking example of simultaneous discovery, motivated by a major shift in public perception and a rising sense of crisis as the scientific community calls attention to the appalling degradation and dangerous consequences of thoughtless human development, and we come to understand the undeniable fragility of life on the planet.

The creation of Tommy Thompson Park is an example of the breaking down of barriers in our thinking. Toronto's current attempts to find ways to merge nature and city life mark a dramatic reversal from the traditional belief in our right to dominate nature, exemplified by the cavalier way in which human interventions have destroyed the continuity of natural ecosystems, disrupted hydrology, and contaminated soils. Throughout history, humans in large, agriculture-based civilizations have polluted the atmosphere, cleared the land, levelled forests, scraped away the topsoil, drained wetlands, and channelled rivers at will. Thanks to the explosive population growth and physical abuse that came with the Industrial Revolution and massive resource extraction, very little of the planet remains untouched by these effects. In Toronto, nowhere was this more evident than the place where the Don River was channelized, the wetlands obliterated, and natural shoreline eradicated adjacent to the spit.

Torontonians now find themselves facing the consequences of those actions. We are beginning to realize that unless we are willing to resign ourselves to spoiling our nest to the point of no return, major adjustments are urgently needed. Fortunately, there are signs that our collective view of the natural world is changing. Almost everyone now recognizes that climate change is real, and this realization has called into question a number of our previously held views and current practices. No place on the planet is untouched. Toronto is affected by increasing extreme weather events — flooding, drought, high winds, and extreme temperatures. The city's

Tommy Thompson Park enables hikers, birders, and wanderers of all descriptions, ages, and abilities to experience wild nature and access the lake in a bucolic setting right in the heart of the city.

With no competition from motorized vehicles, the trails out to the end of the Spit are irresistible for cyclists, runners, walkers, and in-line skaters, all able to stretch out in complete ease and comfort.

vulnerability has been revealed. In order to prepare for the effects of climate change, the city has now recognized that every aspect of its planning and building must be adapted. The city's various development codes and norms need to adjust to new realities.

This seismic shift in goals and priorities is also producing a cultural predisposition toward a new form of coexistence, the intertwining of city and nature. It is creating an altered sense of place. And as this altered perspective takes hold, we can look forward to a change in the image and use of urban places and a greater integration with natural settings. The renewed places, built to reflect these approaches, will become more rooted, specific to their geography, with the underlying layers of natural setting revealed and better appreciated. Places like the Spit have extraordinary inherent value as part of an urban ecosystem: they help to make the city less of an "urban heat island" — i.e., an urban area with elevated temperatures — by contributing a counteracting influence to the heat reflected from the large paved areas in the city. The vegetation that flourishes on the Spit and in other natural areas also absorbs carbon, thereby helping to lessen the release of greenhouse gases into the atmosphere; further, it supports diverse habitats, and contribute to human health and well-being.

Many inspired practitioners and writers have anticipated and fostered this change in consciousness regarding nature in the city, and have called attention to the unintended by-products of our harmful practices. These include Ian McHarg in *Design with Nature*, Anne Whiston Spirn in *The Granite Garden*, and Torontonian Michael Hough in *City Form and Natural Process*. Their ideas opened possibilities for a new way of thinking beyond the conventional practice of attempting to mitigate our impact on nature, instead finding opportunities for creative synthesis, working *with* natural processes, acknowledging that humans are part of nature and that nature everywhere on the planet has become a built environment deeply altered by human interaction with it.

As we come to these new perceptions, we've discovered remarkable opportunities to forge new relationships with natural features in cities. As the imperative to modify our self-destructive practices leads us to find more environmentally sustainable forms of development that are attuned to natural processes, cities (soon to house 50 percent of the world's population) are the crucibles where innovative solutions are often found to intractable problems. Pockets of denial notwithstanding, the environmental thrust is gaining traction and broad popular appeal as a common ground that cuts across class, cultural, and political lines and is rapidly pushing all scales and forms of design into new and exciting areas of investigation.

The presence of nature in the city is health-giving physically, producing cleaner air, soil, and water, but also in terms of mental health. Increasingly, medical studies are showing that urban greenery has a tremendously positive impact on the mental health of individuals, reducing stress, anxiety, and depression; diminishing violence and aggression; and fostering community identity. It is increasingly understood that living on a tree-lined street, or within a few minutes' walk of a park, can impact your physical and mental health.

A review of academic studies by Danish researchers for the International Federation of Parks and Recreation Administration found that the "direct health benefits for which we found evidence on positive effects included psychological wellbeing, reduced obesity, reduced stress, self-perceived health, reduced headache, better mental health … reduced cardiovascular symptoms and reduced mortality from respiratory disorders."

A better understanding of the complexities of succession and interdependence in nature can be linked directly to a greater awareness of the parallels that can be drawn between dynamic character of sustainable cities and their diverse and evolving environments, exhibiting a greater mix and complexity of land use, and a broader demographic of people served by full life-cycle housing options. A second and related corollary is that this increased complexity clearly demands new and expanded professional alliances. To create cities that are truly part of nature, using the knowledge we have to work with the natural process while respecting its power, will require radical changes in our current practices. We need to create the incentives and develop new alliances to make the shift.

The stakes are very high. The benefits of these changes will not just affect our personal lives; they will have a very real impact on the survival of spaceship earth. A synthetic way of thinking about how we live, one that recognizes ecosystems' fragility and sees human ecology as an extension of the natural world, must now infuse our attitude toward cities. The ease with which the natural ecosystems of the city can be rehabilitated will vary according to context. Some of the inner suburban areas can, in certain ways, more easily embrace this new urban-nature paradigm, as they are less likely to have culverted their creeks or severed their natural byways. In the denser parts of prewar Toronto, these systems may have to be reclaimed and restored incrementally through a multiphase process of land reclamation, revegetation, and environmental engineering.

Toronto is taking its place among cities across the world that are rediscovering their natural roots and attempting to connect with the great natural features: the waterways, the recharge areas where he watershed replenishes the groundwater (the Oak Ridges Moraine is a significant one in the GTA), the topography, and the vegetation that once defined their geographies. This change will not result in a return to some pre-urban pastoral state, however; instead, a new hybridization will emerge that will allow once desiccated urban deserts to bloom, and will help clean polluted waterways within their urban context. Cities that turned their backs on these features are now discovering that by changing their practices they can become more intensely urban, more compact and walkable, and, at the same time, more green.

Toronto has an extremely rich natural legacy to build upon, with rivers, creeks, and ravines etching the topography as they drain to our fifty kilometres of Lake Ontario shoreline. It is in these green fissures and green-and-blue borders that a new vision of our city can emerge, one where nature has reasserted itself, supported by a new generation of sensitive planning and design. The city's willingness to continue and expand on such nature-oriented changes in design and construction will be the great test of our resilience as stewards of our land. If we rise to the challenge, we will grow greener as we grow denser. The Leslie Street Spit has served as a bellwether, pointing to what Toronto is attempting on a larger scale — searching for a new synthesis, a new reconciliation with nature in our midst.

Adjacent to the Spit lies another area in which a new balance is being struck between the environment constructed by humans and the natural one. The Toronto Port Lands were once one of the largest natural wetlands on the Great Lakes, fed by the lower Don River as it emptied into Toronto's inner harbour. As the city grew in the late nineteenth and early twentieth centuries, the natural landscape was dramatically altered by breakwaters, channels, and other man-made structures created to manage flooding in the area. Most failed or caused additional problems, however, and in 1912 the Toronto Harbour Commission produced a plan to completely fill in the wetland (seen as a swamp) and transform Ashbridges Bay into a massive new seven-hundred-hectare industrial district. In keeping with the thinking of the day, nature was to be eradicated and the land hardened to make way for "progress." The Olmsted Brothers, sons of the great landscape architect Frederick Law Olmsted, participated in the creation of this plan. They had proposed a narrow band of waterfront parks and summer homes on the lakeshore edge, but this was never realized.

To create this new district, the mouth of the Don River was channelized in 1914 at an abrupt right angle into the concrete-lined Keating Channel. Infilling of the surrounding wetlands followed. The filled lands were occupied by some industry, but with the arrival of the Great Depression, they never became the promised economic engine. The *coup de grâce* for the river mouth came with the construction of the cross-waterfront Gardiner Expressway in the 1950s. The Don River became awkwardly entangled in a web of off-ramps, bridges, and abutments, and access to the river was virtually cut off.

By the mid-twentieth century, the industrial uses of the Port Lands were languishing, and a new, community-led vision began to emerge for the naturalization of the abused river mouth. The Task Force to Bring Back the Don was established in 1989 after five hundred people gathered at the Ontario Science Centre to rally in favour of cleaning up the neglected and polluted Don River. Inspiration for the group came from a visioning exercise led by landscape architect Michael Hough who proposed a naturalization and release of the cramped river mouth. This was an entirely different approach, based on the interweaving of nature and the city, solving multiple problems by working with nature, a radical departure from the heavy-handed engineering that had corseted the river in the early decades of the twentieth century.

This new consciousness of the significance of nature on the waterfront was part of a much larger phenomenon. Nearly ten kilometres of Lake Ontario shoreline were taken up with this industrial harbour of piers, slips, rail sidings, and warehouses, directly across from the downtown core of the city. By the mid-twentieth century, much of that industry was departing due to obsolescence, globalization, and the fact that large container ships could no longer navigate the St. Lawrence Seaway. The vast area of port industrial lands was becoming available for other purposes.

The city was gradually beginning to reconceive its lakefront as a place for public use, including recreation, culture, and private development. Efforts to reclaim the post-industrial waterfront were accelerated in 1972, when the Government of Canada acquired one hundred acres of obsolescent industrial property along Queens Quay west of York Street and south of the Gardiner Expressway. This was part of a larger move across Canada that saw similar purchases of waterfront land in Vancouver for Granville Island, the Forks in Winnipeg, the Vieux-Port in Montreal, the Bassin Louise in Quebec City, and the Halifax Waterfront.

The development of Harbourfront has already been discussed. Although the project was a success in many ways — introducing, for example, a variety of highly innovative arts and culture initiatives to the area — with the exception of the Music Garden it offered little in the way of publicly accessible green space on the harbour. This flaw was made worse when a series of unfortunate development deals were made during the recession of the 1980s in an ill-advised effort to make the Harbourfront Corporation self-sufficient. The public reacted strongly to what it saw as loss of public access to the waterfront. The Harbourfront Corporation's role and scope were curtailed, and only Harbourfront Centre, a cultural entity on a ten-acre site, was retained.

The question of how to deal with the remainder of the waterfront remained. A pause in development was called and former mayor David Crombie was asked to head a Royal Commission on the Future of the Toronto Waterfront in 1988. Over a period of six months beginning in January 1989, the Royal Commission held a series of public hearings; more than three hundred groups and individuals came forward with submissions that clearly demonstrated people's profound interest in the future of their waterfront. This extensive process of community engagement and in-depth studies led to the recommendation of a broad-based "ecosystem approach" to the redevelopment of the waterfront, as spelled out in the commission's 1992 report entitled *Regeneration*.

The essential premise of the ecosystem approach was that the city is a natural phenomenon, not separate from nature. Within cities we have vegetation, forests, fields, streams, lakes, rivers, terrain, soils, and wildlife. Hydrology, topography, and climate set the fundamental structure and conditions for human habitation and the building of the city itself. *Regeneration* cites Kevin Lynch, who wrote in *A Theory of Good City Form*, "People and their cities are as much natural phenomena as trees, streams, nests, and deer paths. It is crucial that we come to see ourselves as an integral part of the total living community." The key concept was that only by understanding the city as a part of nature can we deal with the wounds inflicted on it, mend its ways, and design its form so that it functions sustainably to satisfy needs without diminishing opportunities for future generations.

The frame of reference had been dramatically opened up. The challenge was no longer just about a narrow strip of land along Toronto's central harbour and a struggle over the size and shape of individual condominium developments fronting it, but about the integrity of the entire system of watersheds leading to the Lake Ontario shoreline and the creation of a well-endowed, generous, and continuous public realm along the entire length.

A very different approach was needed to guide the opening up of vast territory. A way had to be found to implement significant changes to public and private property to promote public access and overcome major environmental, governmental, and financial obstacles. The non-profit Waterfront Regeneration Trust, established in 1988, has provided guidance in making the transition and reasserting this more publicly oriented agenda.

Its territory broadened as it led the movement to create a continuous waterfront trail for the Canadian Great Lakes and St. Lawrence River, in partnership with 114 and growing community partners, supporting corporations, foundations, and partner organizations.

A great opportunity came with Canada's decision to compete for the 2008 Summer Olympic Games. The reservoir of available waterfront land in the port seemed like an ideal venue for an Olympic Village, or for the

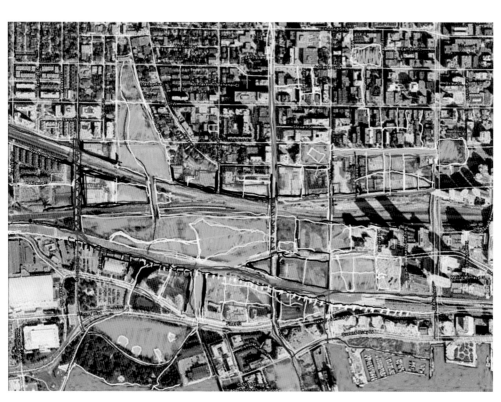

A sketch I prepared to accompany my article in the *Fife and Drum*, published in 2011 by the Friends of Fort, illustrating the potential of the Fort York National Historic Site and the adjoining space under the Gardiner Expressway to become a new central park for the surrounding and rapidly growing high-rise neighbourhoods.

By the mid-twentieth century, economic shifts, demographic pressures, and the "retreat of the industrial glacier" on the city's southern flank opened up a vast terrain of availability for redevelopment that began to propel a major change in the form of the city.

Unquestionably, Toronto is growing vertically, as this image of the new skyline dramatically demonstrates. This raised burning questions around how this growth can be shaped and managed to provide a viable, sustainable, productive, and inclusive city for all.

The Leslie Street Spit was a man-made creation extending five kilometres out into Lake Ontario to frame an outer harbour for Great Lakes shipping that never materialized. It was formed by a combination of excavated material from construction, rubble, and dredging. Seen here in the mid-1970s as it was being created.

Nature took over, populating this barren peninsula with flora and fauna to form an extraordinary green finger, which was defended by citizens and ultimately became the beloved Tommy Thompson Park.

In the early decades of the twentieth century, the Toronto Harbour Commission drained what it saw as a "swamp," filling in the largest wetland in the Great Lakes to form the Port Lands. Seen here in 1988, the industrial area never really fulfilled its promise and remained largely moribund for decades.

A monumental undertaking is currently underway in the Port Lands, relocating and liberating the channelized Don River mouth to provide flood protection through a park-lined river estuary entering the harbour. This will provide essential green space for mixed-use neighbourhood development in a vast new frontier on the waterfront.

The Bentway's opening weekend on January 6–8, 2018, drew close to twenty thousand people in -30°C weather to experience the 220-metre skating trail under the bents.

other competition venues that would have to be created. In 1999 a Toronto Waterfront Revitalization Task Force, chaired by Robert Fung, was established by the prime minister of Canada, the premier of Ontario, and the mayor of Toronto. It was created to propose a mechanism for dealing with the undeveloped, misused, and derelict lands of Toronto's Central Waterfront to create this Olympic venue.

The task force recommended the establishment of what became Waterfront Toronto (initially called the Toronto Waterfront Revitalization Corporation), jointly funded by the three levels of government, to oversee and lead waterfront renewal. In October 2000, the federal government, the province, and the city announced their commitment to spend $1.5 billion to revitalize the Toronto waterfront. Although Canada lost its Olympic bid to China, the recommendation was accepted and the agency was created and funded in 2001. In fact, the consolation prize, not winning the bid, has proven to be a boon to the city in advancing the ecosystem approach to developing the waterfront.

Waterfront Toronto's mandate includes combining investments in its public realm with expenditures on environmental protection, cultural facilities, and recreational opportunities on a vast scale. It must find solutions to a number of fundamental problems: the area's separation from the rest of the city by an elevated expressway and a railroad; the poor quality water along the Toronto shore of Lake Ontario (most of the rest of which is swimmable and fishable); potential flooding from the mouth of the Don River; and widespread contamination of properties formerly in industrial use. These core values and objectives have also been enshrined in the city's official plan for the Central Waterfront, entitled "Making Waves."

To get from words to deeds, an agency like Waterfront Toronto, and the support it receives from all three levels of government, has been essential, because the funds required to fulfill this complex mandate for revitalizing the waterfront far exceed what any private property owner or owners could raise, even if assembling fragmented ownership were feasible.

Waterfront Toronto has been successful in maintaining governmental and public support because of its sustained commitment to lead development with the expansion of the "public realm" and by focused neighbourhood "precinct" planning, organized around a comprehensive public realm framework — streets, parks, beaches, hardscapes, and softscapes — instead of just one-off developments, which had proven to be the Achilles heel of its ill-fated predecessor, the Harbourfront Corporation. Will Fleissig, the then CEO of Waterfront Toronto, said that his ambition was for this new frontier of the waterfront to become every Torontonian's second address.

With Waterfront Toronto in place, the potential was created for bold comprehensive planning of the Mouth of the Don River. On June 28, 2017, Prime Minister Justin Trudeau, Premier Kathleen Wynne, and Mayor John Tory arrived by water taxi across a choppy Lake Ontario to the edge of Polson Quay, where a relocated Don River would enter the Toronto Harbour, to announce a $1.25-billion plan to flood-proof and redevelop Toronto's industrial Port Lands. A crowd of reporters, government officials, and long-term community leaders, including members of the original Task Force to Bring Back the Don, stood listening with obvious satisfaction. This was the culmination of over ten years of hard work.

We were standing in the middle of what was known as the Lower Don Lands, a 125-hectare (308-acre) area that runs east from the Parliament Street Slip to the Don Roadway, and from the rail corridor south to the ship channel. The area forms a critical link between the new waterfront communities that are emerging in the East Bayfront, the West Don Lands, and the industrial areas of the Port Lands. In the early 2000s, addressing this site was the next logical step in revitalizing the larger Port Lands. Its planning needed to address a myriad of requirements and challenges, including flood protection from Don River overflow, which affects a large area; the need for new municipal infrastructure and public transportation; and the delineation of development opportunities and park creation. Various teams were advancing solutions to address each of these issues individually in siloed, functional categories, and a number of environmental assessments had been initiated.

But as these segregated plans emerged, it became clear to Waterfront Toronto and its city partners that the results would be less than satisfactory. A time out was called to reassess. This was a classic problem of organized complexity, the kind of design problem that would require interdisciplinary creativity applied to all of the city's goals simultaneously. With this insight, Waterfront Toronto launched an international design competition in February 2007 to produce an overarching concept that would provide the unifying vision for merging the natural and urban fabric into a green, integrated and sustainable community, and provide common ground for the numerous environmental assessments (EAs) required for the area.

This became Waterfront Toronto's most complex and ambitious project to date. It dictated a new way of working, not dealing with one thing or one issue at a time but a true ecosystem approach. I joined a team that combined the many skill sets and knowledge required for a challenge of this breadth — landscape, architecture, several branches of engineering, hydrology, and ecology, among others — led by landscape architect Michael Van Valkenburgh and his associates, with whom I had collaborated on the Brooklyn Bridge Park. Our working method was of necessity highly collaborative, as breakthrough ideas rapidly emerged from all team members and were integrated in an iterative process involving drawings, computer simulations of river behaviour, and large-scale physical modelling. Critically, the team's detailed attention to soil conditions and remediation, engineering requirements, and landownership issues helped produce a plan that was cost effective and achievable.

Our proposal took the form of an interwoven vision: dramatically shifting the riverbed itself to form a central public space framed by new waterfront neighbourhoods on both banks. In this plan, the river would enter the harbour surrounded by one hundred acres of parkland. That parkland would serve as a flood protection zone and enable the development of new infrastructure, multi-use buildings, habitat restoration, and multi-modal transportation — all tied together to work harmoniously with nature. The plan took a bold, innovative approach to naturalizing the mouth of the Don River and transforming a long-neglected area into sustainable new neighbourhoods.

At its heart was a celebration of the river itself, now seen as the key "asset," no longer a flood-prone liability, whose naturalized mouth provided an iconic identity for the area. Our plan aimed to create a context for addressing urban design, transportation, naturalization, sustainability, and other ecological issues. Our vision was of the Lower Don Lands transformed into a sustainable, "green" urban estuary, a new destination where city, lake, and river interact in a dynamic and balanced relationship. Realigning the river's mouth from the Keating Channel to the place where it enters the harbour in an area of parkland doubling as flood plain, the scheme reasserts the Don River's stifled identity in the city. The formerly hidden river mouth would become the centrepiece of a cluster of new mixed-use neighbourhoods, integrating the natural and wild with urban place making and creating a privileged address for the new waterfront neighbourhoods.

The Keating Channel remains intact in the plan, refurbished as an urban canal with bridges to link the neighbourhoods to the north and south, the combination of river and canal forming an island (to be called Villiers Island). With its edges envisioned as retail- and recreation-oriented water's edge promenades, and with some significant historic structures retained, the Keating Channel has the potential to become an animated destination for city residents and visitors. The Keating Channel and an additional spillway into the ship channel to the south also act as floodways in extreme events.

The parkland along the river integrates with the neighbourhoods that surround it, with perched wetlands on an upper level that also provides generous green space for recreation and the enjoyment of nature. This green space has the capacity to absorb seasonal and major fluctuations in the water level, transforming the necessity for flood protection in this long-neglected area into a thriving, productive part of the city landscape. Our aspiration was to use this competition to create a new local and global model for sustainable city building.

In May 2007, the submission from Michael Van Valkenburgh Associates, Inc. (MVVA), "Port Lands Estuary," was announced as the winning design. The plan has won many awards and was selected as one of the founding projects for the Climate Positive Development Program, an initiative of former U.S. president Bill Clinton's Climate Initiative and the U.S. Green Building Council. It received the 2008 Royal Architectural Institute of Canada's (RAIC) Sustainable Development Award. The award is designed to recognize the role urban design and architectural excellence play in maintaining and enhancing quality of life in Canadian cities. The Keating Channel Precinct, the Lower Don Lands' first planned community, received the Best Futuristic Design Award at the Building Exchange (BEX) 2009 Conference.

As with all waterfront planning initiatives, public consultation has been a key component of Lower Don Lands planning. Due to its complexity and the number of stakeholders involved, the Lower Don Lands integrated planning process has included numerous public meetings as well as a number of workshop sessions after the competition. The City of Toronto, the TTC, and Waterfront Toronto worked to develop a framework, based on the competition scheme, which integrates the project's numerous concurrent required environmental assements (EAs) including the Don Mouth Naturalization and Port Lands Flood Protection Project EA, the various transit EAs, and the Master Servicing EA, with the design of the precinct plan for the Keating Channel neighbourhood.

The Lower Don Lands planning documents went to City Council in summer 2010 and were unanimously approved. But at that point there was a major interruption when newly elected Mayor Rob Ford tried to derail the plan, attempting to drastically reduce parkland as part of a cost-cutting agenda and substitute an alternative plan to turn the lands over to a private developer for a megamall and a luxury yacht club, with the usual accoutrements of Ferris wheel and monorail. He also proposed that Waterfront Toronto be removed from its implementation and oversight role. By that time, according to CEO John Campbell, Waterfront Toronto had spent years designing a plan for the Port Lands and spent close to $20 million in consultations and studies for the area.

Almost immediately the public, major civil society actors, leading urban designers, architects, academics, and all those who had worked on this groundbreaking plan to "bring back the Don" for decades pushed back vigorously. A petition with seven thousand names was presented to city hall by the members of CodeBlueTO, a grassroots coalition protesting the proposed abandonment of the hard-fought vision for the waterfront, and in September 2011 Toronto City Council again voted unanimously to re-affirm the plan and have Waterfront Toronto remain in control of the Port Lands after Mayor Rob Ford's administration ditched its plan to wrestle the area away from the agency. The feeling was clear: the people of Toronto had stated that the waterfront belonged to them.

Zooming out from the Central Waterfront, to view the area from South Etobicoke to the Scarborough Bluffs and beyond, what has been emerging all along the Toronto waterfront is one of the most remarkable transformations of its kind in North America and beyond. The revitalization of a band of strategically located, obsolescent lands is providing notable new and improved places for the public to enjoy — parks and trails, a linked series of neighbourhoods, places to live and work, and places of recreation, of repose, of natural beauty. It is becoming "cottage country" in the heart of the city for the many hundreds of thousands who can't afford Muskoka, or a plane ticket to more exotic resort destinations.

It is also where Toronto is reinventing itself for the twenty-first century as the whole city adjusts to its newly accessible southern face on Lake Ontario. The waterfront is materializing not as a singular project, but as the collective work of generations of Torontonians, supported by the cumulative investments of all three levels of government and the private sector. Its future contours are just starting to be visible as the many pieces fall into place along its length. Links are being established, connecting the new parkland along the Mimico motel strip to Humber Bay and the Western Beaches. Moving to the east, there is the promise of a revived Ontario Place and Exhibition Place joining with Coronation Park, Little Norway Park, the Music Garden, the Queens Quay "Greenway," Sugar Beach, and Sherbourne Common in the heart of the new East Bayfront neighbourhood. The vast area of Lake Ontario Park that frames the outer harbour will link to Asbridges Bay and the historic Eastern Beaches. From there, parkland continues along the shoreline to the Scarborough Bluffs and beyond. In this public vision for a great and generous waterfront, we are witnessing one of the largest such revitalization efforts in the world.

Financial contributions from the three levels of government have been confirmed, and work on the Don River relocation and a $1.25 billion flood-proofing project is already underway. This support has created a rare opportunity to realize the benefits of decades of work at this critical juncture, where once multiple barriers and flood vulnerability inhibited the city's ability to open up the waterfront. Returning to the river to deal with flood-proofing, improve environmental quality, and open up vast stretches of green space for public use is a concept that is travelling beyond the mouth of the river, right up the Don Valley.

The ravines have long been woven into Toronto's mythology, its fiction, and its dreams as a significant (if somewhat hidden) part of its identity. The city is also beginning to appreciate that it has this extremely rich natural legacy to build upon as valuable green space, with rivers, creeks, and ravines etching the city's south-sloping topography as they drain from the Oak Ridges Moraine to Toronto's shoreline.

In some ways, Toronto's decision to integrate itself with the natural environment has been a voluntary one. It can be argued, however, that nature has imposed this decision on it. In 1954, Hurricane Hazel hit Toronto, causing widespread destruction, including a huge amount of flooding along the Humber River. It was the city's great wake-up call. It shattered the hubris that underlay the planning decisions made before it. It made Torontonians acknowledge that Toronto is not a flat city. Prior to the hurricane, the city had been dumping infill in valleys, burying creeks in sewers, and pushing development into the flood plains of the rivers and creeks that flow through it into Lake Ontario. Hurricane Hazel forced the city to acknowledge the 17 percent of the city's land mass occupied by the ravines, and led to the creation of the Toronto and Region Conservation Authority, which was given a mandate to both protect the city from severe weather events and also to provide stewardship for this great natural resource. This acknowledgement of the power of nature, and of our need to make a virtue out of a necessity by augmenting our access to nature, has only increased with time.

The ravines enable Torontonians to escape into wilderness: only a short walk, bike ride, or TTC ride away from almost anywhere in the city. As the city grows denser, these natural assets become increasingly important. In 2013, a new campaign, "Toronto, It's Time to Love the Ravines," was launched by a diverse group of businesses and environmental groups to showcase this most precious resource. As they note in their educational material, the ravines provide 10,500 hectares of recreational space; they also improve air quality, control flood waters, and attract visitors. The campaign aimed to educate Torontonians about the many social, environmental, and economic benefits they deliver, and to inspire residents to celebrate and care for these naturally occurring wild places within the city.

There is no room for complacency. A recent study by University of Toronto researcher Eric Davies warns that an ecological collapse of Toronto's vast ravine system is underway as a result of the widespread presence of invasive species, and notes that key organisms necessary for a healthy forest environment are increasingly missing. The trees, plants, and wildlife that should be present in the city's valleys are disappearing fast. The report recommends that the city move quickly to restore the "ecological integrity" of the ravines and develop a plan to get rid of invasive species and replace them with native plants. It also suggests that a public-private partnership may be a way to accomplish this.

Another major example of our reassessment of priorities is occurring in the Don Valley. Planning for the Don Valley Parkway began in 1954, the year of Metropolitan Toronto's formation; the entire route was completed by the end of 1966. It was a time when moving traffic was the city's highest priority. Construction ran roughshod over the river valley, requiring the removal of several hills, diversion of the Don River, and the clearing of woodland. The area was sliced and diced, and access to this enormous valley for anything other than motorized vehicles was extremely limited.

By the late 1970s, the drive to release the underlying power of this remarkable but abused and largely inaccessible natural setting had gained community support. When I was leading the Urban Design Group at the city in the early 1980s, one of our major accomplishments was opening up a continuous trail through the Don Valley, from the waterfront to Pottery Road and the Brick Works. This was an effort of negotiating access, weaving and stitching together postage stamps of access points and green space to make the whole length of the valley passable for cyclists and pedestrians. It revealed a remarkable hidden landscape in recovery mode that had been all but lost to memory for most Torontonians.

As soon as people were able to penetrate it, the Don Valley began to be appreciated as a park, not just a parkway. Step by step, it is being brought back from oblivion and neglect, once more with civil-society actors in a leading role. In 2017, CEO Geoff Cape of Evergreen announced ambitious plans to rescue, restore, and make accessible the vast areas of land monopolized and trapped by the Don Valley Parkway and the rail corridors. With the Toronto and Region Conservation Authority, Evergreen launched the Don River Valley Park project, a multi-year, public and private fundraising campaign to create a "super park," a massive 480-acre green space running from Evergreen Brick Works south to the mouth of Lake Ontario.

This vast *terra incognita* in the city's midst is being restored step by step to Torontonians as a key part of the city's natural setting. The intuitive connection of the river valley to the harbour and the lake is being revealed and made whole. Bit by bit, this renewed appreciation of the natural setting as a seamless and unbounded whole, as opposed to discrete and isolated pieces, is being extended to all of the watercourses and ravines that feed the Don Valley watershed.

Existing natural areas are being made more accessible, and previously unrecognized natural features are being recognized as a new frontier for the city. There are many opportunities to reuse vast tracts of obsolescent port, industrial, railway, and warehousing lands. In the mid-1990s I first used the phrase *retreat of the industrial glacier* as a metaphor for this process. In many cases, like the Toronto Port Lands, the creation of these zones involved the suppression of nature — an action based on the belief that it was necessary for the city to all but obliterate its presence in order to grow and prosper. Valleys and wetlands were filled in, creeks were buried, the natural vegetation was removed — to make way for progress. As the industrial glacier recedes, it reveals an extraordinary new terrain of possibilities to restore this natural presence.

This heightened consciousness is informing a number of innovative projects where design with nature is replacing the kinds of traditional engineering practices that had formed the hard-edged Keating Channel at the river mouth a century ago. The West Donlands neighbourhood, which served as the Pan Am Athletes' Village in 2015, is a case in point. When planning for this area was initiated in 2005, there was a need to decontaminate the site and provide flood protection from river overflows for a large area of downtown to the west.

The solution developed by Waterfront Toronto and the city was a park on an engineered landform that would simultaneously provide protection from flood waters, remediate contaminated land, filter stormwater, and create a recreational heart for the new neighbourhood. This concept, in which I played a small role, became Corktown Commons, a new eighteen-acre park, designed by Michael Van Valkenburgh Associates, which opened in 2013. With its distinctive, contoured topography and rich native planting, the park has become a highly popular gathering place for the newly forming community. As well as popular water play features and a playground, it boasts a working wetlands that treats stormwater and contains aquatic plants, birds, frogs, ducks, and other wildlife.

A floodgate opening in the landform connects Corktown Commons to the now improved Don Valley trail network I worked on in the 1980s, extending both up the valley and down to the new river mouth. Inland, the "green stitching" continues, and Corktown Commons is linked up to King Street via Underpass Park, which includes another unique children's playground under the off-ramps of the elevated Gardiner Expressway — a means of expanding the web of connections, human and natural, feeding into the river valley.

The transformation of the lower Don Valley is being echoed throughout the region. The provincial Growth Plan has been shaped by the Greenbelt that encircles the Greater Toronto Area (GTA), legislated to protect natural areas and focus growth in the already-built-up portions of the city region. The Greenbelt, established in 2005, adds one million acres of farmland and environmentally sensitive areas to the already protected Niagara Escarpment and Oak Ridges Moraine. It is the largest of its kind, spanning almost two million acres of protected forest, farmlands, and wetlands and has become a world-class model for preservation.

Shortly after the Greenbelt's creation, the Friends of the Greenbelt Foundation was established. Operating independently from the government it coordinates and funds activities that bolster and enhance the Greenbelt. Since 2005, it has invested and leveraged more than $47 million into farming, environmental protection, and tourism projects. These natural systems are all connected. The Greenbelt frames and encircles the

City of Toronto's ravine network, and that relationship, too, has achieved greater recognition. Recently, the province has taken steps to enable cities to designate urban river valleys as integral parts of Ontario's Greenbelt, permanently protecting them and connecting them to a wider network of green space that spans more than 1.8 million acres from the Niagara region to Peterborough.

We see the world differently now. The allure of these natural features is drawing people to them; they offer respite from the increasing pressures of city life. The centrality of these post-industrial places (like the Port Lands) means they have an inherent capacity to produce more "sustainable" development, putting housing closer to workplaces and reducing travel times. For many city dwellers, the "naturalized" public realm becomes the "resort" in situ for leisure in close proximity, a high priority as place becomes the key to value.

The barriers between the natural world and the urban world are blurring. As Betsy Barlow Rogers, the former executive director of New York's Central Park Conservancy, put it: "As the city becomes more park-like, the park becomes more city-like." The green fissures in the fabric of the city have expanded and extended. They now include everything from the greening of rooftops, courtyards, streets and squares, to new parks that follow natural water courses. In many cities, buried rivers that had been drained or placed in pipes are now being "daylighted," both to improve environmental health through habitat renewal and to reveal and celebrate a location's natural history.

Paradoxically, greater urban density often goes hand in hand with the celebration of nature. Surprising as it may seem, city dwellers often have easier access to the natural world, as this process advances, than their suburban counterparts. Rediscovered natural features offer fertile possibilities for expanding and improving the public realm. The walking and cycling trails that provide access to these spaces have gained in popularity, as they wind along creeks and rivers, opening up areas that were formerly *terra incognita*. Old rail lines and abandoned rights-of-way provide new conduits to these once "forbidden" territories. The desire to stroll through the city is ancient, but these green sinews providing continuous links between traditional parks also offer something new, encouraging walking, jogging and cycling in previously undiscovered parts of the city.

There is also the basic link to public health discussed previously. Increasingly, health authorities are recognizing the relationship between sedentary lifestyles and obesity and heart disease, and trumpeting the value of providing people with opportunities to walk and cycle close to where they live. *The Walkable City: Neighbourhood Design and Preferences, Travel Choices and Health*, a report by Toronto Public Health, found a direct correlation between the walkability of a neighbourhood and the body mass levels of its inhabitants. On average, a resident living in a walkable district enjoys a one-point lower body mass index (BMI) compared to those who don't.

Venturing into new territory on these urban trails can be deeply satisfying, a quest that combines discovery and self-discovery. There is the serendipitous pleasure of encountering others en route and people-watching on the fly with the possibility of gregarious encounters. Seen from a fresh perspective, the city reveals itself in new ways. Self-propelled motion at relatively low speeds offers us more than exercise and a chance to commune with strangers; it restores an intuitive understanding of the geography we occupy, one that is not available when driving. It establishes a sense of real distances between things, and of how the parts of a city connect within natural settings.

In October 2017, a new organization called Waterfront for All, which Eti and I are part of, held its first annual summit, inviting organizations and individuals from across the entire fifty kilometres of Toronto's Lake Ontario shoreline. Some four hundred attendees from Long Branch to Port Union gathered to share experiences, goals, and aspirations, and to plan for a new generation of advocacy. Waterfront for All (which is now an umbrella organization representing twenty-nine local organizations) picks up on the still valid nine guiding principles enunciated by the Crombie Commission's Regeneration Report in 1992: Clean, Green, Connected, Open, Accessible, Usable, Diverse, Affordable, and Attractive. Listening to each other present projects across the city, it was fascinating to see how the individual pieces of the puzzle — increased water's edge access, habitat corridors, birdways, vegetation, and wetlands — are starting to overlap and come together to form the armature of a city in nature.

6

Institutions as City Builders

From the south-facing entry of the new home of the Daniels Faculty of Architecture, Landscape, and Design, a long, dramatic vista opens up of Spadina Avenue looking down toward the harbour. It was always there, but rarely seen. The school now occupies the circle in the middle of the avenue known as Spadina Crescent. Until now, this crescent has always had an ambiguous presence as the unfulfilled promise of something special.

It began life as an idiosyncratic punctuation point and touch of gentility, one of a handful of gestures in nineteenth-century Toronto intended to create special moments in the emerging patchwork of north-south and east-west streets stitched together to form the city's quasi-grid. In 1835 its first trace appears on a plan as "Mansfield's Old Gardens," subsequently renamed Spadina Gardens. It then went from a void to a solid in the form of Knox College, a south-facing Gothic revival building that has housed in succession a theological seminary, a military hospital, a penicillin factory, an eye bank, and multiple University of Toronto departments.

In the post–Second World War era, Spadina Crescent was swallowed by encircling transportation infrastructure — streetcars and then heavy volumes of vehicular traffic — becoming largely inaccessible and suffering from benign neglect. Now, however, when the emphasis is shifting from auto-dominance to pedestrian life at street level, a skillful reversal of its isolation is revealing its latent potential. With an inspired act of civic leadership, the reappropriation of this circle by the Daniels Faculty of Architecture, Landscape, and Design has taken it from introversion to generous extroversion, enabling the university to provide an exemplary model of civic invitation to the larger community.

This new building is emblematic of something powerful and different; the university is changing its stance vis-à-vis the city by expanding its mandate from simply providing for its own needs to taking on a role as a vital contributor to the city around it. The institution is coming out of its "ivory tower," moving from self-contained and self-sufficient to interdependent, welcoming, and more inclusive.

A dichotomy — town and gown — is being overcome. This reaching outward has particular significance for Toronto, given its extraordinary diversity, which is nowhere more evident than in the student bodies of colleges and universities. These young people will inherit and shape the city, and their active participation in the enterprise of city building is crucial for success.

The relocated John H. Daniels Faculty of Architecture, Landscape, and Design is now known as One Spadina. It was made possible by a generous gift from John and Myrna Daniels, which enabled the school's dean Richard Sommer to hold a competition for the design and produce its spectacular new home. Nader Tehrani, principal of the internationally acclaimed firm NADAAA, and collaborator Katie Faulkner were chosen to lead the design team, with Toronto's Public Work as landscape architects, ERA Architects as preservation architects, and Adamson Associates as executive architects.

This hugely ambitious project is distinguished not only for the quality of its architecture, but also by its embrace of city building as part of a new generation of exciting institutional buildings and public spaces that are transforming Toronto in this period of astonishing growth. It boldly establishes new relationships with its neighbours on all sides of the circle at this remote corner of the U of T campus. The prominent, south-facing Spadina Avenue axis is celebrated with a raised belvedere and event space. A landscaped promenade circumnavigates the building within the circle.

Five enhanced pedestrian crossings of the traffic "moat" and ample bike parking extend the welcome mat, inviting the public into the circle, and an east–west "passage" through the building on axis with Russell Street.

Open twenty-four hours a day, seven days a week to daily pedestrian use, it will be animated by a café gallery, Flex Hall, labs, printing, lockers, lounge, and administration offices, with permeable edges and alcoves all linked to a generous commons.

The challenges of the site have been seized as an opportunity to re-shape this edge of the campus — changing it from a hard boundary to an interlacing, blurred border, fluid and interpenetrating. The circle's very completeness, disconnection, and inward focus had previously produced a sense of remove and aloofness. The impressive neo-Gothic Knox College building had a clear front and back, but its somewhat rigid, rectilinear symmetry clearly did not address its evolving 360-degree context. The formerly "blind" northern face of the building has been transformed from a back to a new front, reopening the dialogue with the city on all sides. Within the building, strategically placed openings offer glimpses of the city outside, creating the pleasurable sensation of being in a ship moored off the edge of the campus. In combination, these design moves introduce a fine-grained permeability to the site, creating a city-like microcosm within the building.

These extroverted gestures benefit both the city and the university. They speak to a new understanding of the university's place in the city as a steward and active contributor, an enlightened city builder with an expand-ed commitment to the city that hosts it. It is only fitting that the mantle of leadership as an urban design exemplar and catalyst for the western edge of the campus should fall to the Daniels Faculty of Architecture, Landscape, and Design, a school (of which I am an alumnus) originally established in 1890 and which, over the years, has migrated to several makeshift locations around the university before landing in a purpose-built building.

Reflecting the growing interest in design and city building in Toronto, the school's ambition to play an overt leadership role is displayed in its development program. Its new public gallery along the northeastern edge of the site, extending outside the circle to include the historic Borden Buildings, will anchor an emerging "design arts district." Public lectures of international significance, with an emphasis on experimentation and emerging talent, will be presented on subjects such as architecture, land-scape architecture, urban design, visual studies, and other allied design fields. The gallery, the city's only exhibition space exclusively devoted to architecture, landscape, and design, is described by the university as a space that "will host travelling exhibitions from abroad, as well as exhibitions on Toronto's architectural heritage and its contemporary design challenges — generating debate, broadening public interest, and exploring the important ways in which design shapes neighbourhoods, cities, and daily lives."

Heritage preservation is a critical issue in a city that is evolving so rapidly that the few remaining traces of its past lives are at risk. But beyond saving these artefacts, the challenge is how to interact with them, incorporating and acknowledging potent palimpsests and cultural memory in a meaningful layering of past, present, and future. Rising to the challenge, the project carries on a rich architectural conversation across a century and a half. The heritage structure — neo-Gothic, vertical, rectilinear, frontal, heavily grounded, load bearing, with structured, cellular rooms — is in ardent dialogue with the new: fluid, fractal, dynamic shapes, curves and lightness, warped and interpenetrating. At the "joint," the linking elements frame a shared interior passageway. The neo-Gothic spires of the original building, reflecting the nineteenth-century Toronto vernacular, create a foil to the new addition, a large floor plate structure with a glass curtain wall facade, containing studio space that overlooks the courtyard below.

On a technical level, the building is a living lab for the students, encouraging interdisciplinary work on sustainability. Echoes of the site's previous use for medical research (it housed the world-famous Connaught Labs) are still present, but now the building serves as a different kind of city and architectural science lab, introducing a range of new best practices. Its north-facing windows exploit opportunities for natural daylight, producing energy savings; the building incorporates stormwater harvesting for grey water needs and irrigation; it invites active transportation to the site and utilizes white roofs to reduce energy by reflecting rather than absorbing sunlight. Students are engaged in systems such as opportunities for landscape students to carry out green-roof testing, and for building science students a "dashboard" interface to monitor systems performance.

What we see today is the first component of a two-phase project to both renovate and expand the iconic former Knox College structure, transforming the existing building and site into a framework more relevant to the contemporary teachings and aspirations of the Daniels Faculty, while also allowing for the building's evolution into a flexible facility that can respond to changes in pedagogy in years to come. Its large, column-free space, covered by a cantilevered, canopy-like roof, suggests a broad range of ways to expand, contract, and combine programs appropriate to our time.

In the postwar era of urban specialization and separation of functions, the University of Toronto, like many great universities and colleges located in the hearts of cities, seemed detached from its urban setting. As it grew, it sought to maintain a firm campus boundary, expanding west across St. George Street from its historic core to form the West Campus. Typical of the era, the campus was characterized by boxy, stand-alone buildings interlaced with surface parking lots. Lacking city uses inside the campus, it felt sterile and barren in between class changes. Its expansion caused anxiety in the surrounding neighbourhoods, which saw it as an unwelcome intruder, and city planning staff, while acknowledging the university's need for space, were focused on its containment from further expansion.

Now, a number of factors are driving the campus's move to greater integration and mix. There has been a shift away from the isolated campus model, with a cluster of academic buildings occupying a large land area, remote from other uses, to one that is fully integrated in a lively, mixed-use urban setting. There are multiple advantages to this greater integration. It acknowledges that universities and colleges can form mutually beneficial symbiotic relationships with their host cities to make more effective use of limited space and shared resources.

The U of T campus, which had grown up in a setting where there seemed to be ample room to spread out, now finds itself in the middle of a dynamic, highly sought-after urban area that is itself undergoing major vertical expansion and growth on increasingly valuable real estate along the university's primary borders on Bloor Street, Spadina Avenue, College Street, and Queen's Park. The combination of internal pressures to grow and external constraint is pushing toward a more intensive overlapping of campus and city life.

By turning its major limitations as a "hemmed in" campus into an asset, U of T is affirming its unique identity as one of the most urbane campuses in the region, and an integral part of the of the City of Toronto. This change in priorities brings a move to joint planning and stewardship

Spadina Circle, seen here in 1970, was long occupied by the looming presence of the grand Gothic structure of Knox College on the edge of the University of Toronto campus. It was a site of great prominence, and yet it seemed isolated inside its traffic circle, cut off from its surroundings on all sides.

In an act of great civic outreach, the Daniels Faculty of Architecture, Landscape, and Design has established its new faculty at One Spadina, repurposing and adding to this valued piece of the city's architectural heritage while rescuing it from its isolation. Here it is seen from the south, terminating with a grand vista up Spadina Avenue.

With an extensive restoration of the original structure facing south (top) and a skillful addition of new studio space that forms a new city-facing elevation to the north (bottom), the school is inviting the public to cross the "moat" and penetrate the building's interior from all directions.

around a shared vision. The fate of the university is inextricably bound with that of the city, its host.

When universities and colleges compete for resources, students, faculty, and research grants, the quality of life in their urban environments is an essential asset. Cities increasingly view campuses as catalysts for economic development. Combined, these perspectives bring a renewed appreciation for the lively university "quarter" with its surrounding neighbourhoods. The University of Toronto is just such a case.

Not only are the university's external boundaries becoming more fluid, but the city itself is infiltrating the campus as it becomes in turn more penetrable, inviting, and city-like. The transformation of St. George Street (a project which also involved the Matthews as donors) with widened sidewalks, landscaping, bike lanes, attractive contemporary buildings filling in the former gap teeth, and uses that invite the public into the university is further solidifying this sense of seamless interplay of campus and city. Subtly and progressively, the campus becomes the city, the city becomes the campus.

In 1999 I was involved in preparing an Open Space Master Plan for the University of Toronto entitled "Investing in the Landscape" with my previous firm, Urban Strategies. The plan took a broader look at the opportunities for improving and expanding the public realm within the campus, with an eye to better connecting to the larger city. Universities and colleges contribute unique public places in the city, offering relief, repose, and special kinds of public space and amenities not otherwise available. The rich legacy of internal quads and green oases of the historic St. George campus were seen as part of the larger shared commons, not just perceptually and spatially, but also for the programs and activities they could offer to the surrounding non-student population, as well.

For the city, the campus becomes an asset and catalyst for renewal. Key integrating "moves" — joint infrastructure projects like the redesign of St. George Street — lead to reinvestment opportunities, spinoffs, and entrepreneurship. Permeable edges, new links, and connections lead to softened edges where shared neighbourhoods are enhanced by the role and presence of staff, faculty, and students in the community.

In all of my work on master planning for universities and colleges in and around Toronto, this theme of collapsed boundaries has been a constant. Best practices have emerged to promote shared and overlapping use of resources such as access to transit, parking pools, retail, and community facilities.

This allows the university to focus its capital dollars primarily on the academic facilities themselves, reducing the capital and operating costs of the campus. Some "university" facilities can be accommodated in mixed-use buildings through vertical co-development, while others can be owned and operated by third parties, with access agreements for the university, or simply co-located next to the academic facility. In addition to financial benefits, this approach to a campus results in a lighter footprint. Intermixing university facilities with other uses in an urban setting can create a high-quality urban experience that is more consistent with contemporary student expectations and preferences for participating in city life, while relieving the university of a number of traditional responsibilities.

This is inherently a more sustainable form of development, as it uses scarce resources and land to greater advantage to meet the daily needs of the academic community. When the city provides resources, the university or college does not have to — housing, jobs, restaurants, parking, public facilities, recreation. The student quarter can serve a wider, year-round market for the cultural, recreational, and educational facilities (libraries, theatres, fitness centres, swimming pools, eating establishments, bookstores, entertainment) that campuses typically provide and generate around themselves.

In the global knowledge economy, cities need "engines" to create, attract, and retain knowledge workers. A city can provide a mutually beneficial competitive advantage for the university and the city. Increasingly, campus research activities stimulate valuable spinoffs related to their research capabilities. They inspire knowledge-based companies to cluster around the edges of campus. As this shift occurs, universities (along with other urban institutions such as hospitals and museums) are emerging as leaders in the move to more sustainable city-building practices, often drawing on their environmental research capabilities to do so. Access to nearby employment can help prepare students for career opportunities, connecting them to real-life learning experiences, including placements with employers, research opportunities with outstanding faculty members and innovative organizations, and opportunities for business incubation and entrepreneurship.

The sense of an enlarged commons fusing institutions of higher learning and the city also corresponds to an internal shift in the nature of education itself — a much greater emphasis both within and outside buildings on fluid common gathering spaces as valuable places of learning and exchange in their own right — beyond the classroom, the lab, and the traditional library. New models of teaching and learning are changing the nature of academic spaces. Individualized learning, blended instruction, combining classrooms, and online instruction are reshaping academic building requirements.

Circulation spaces, corridors, and entries, once minimized, are now often combined with cafés and seating areas, and are equipped to be used as new and highly productive learning and gathering spaces. In a curious sense we could say that we are coming full circle and returning to informal, peripatetic spaces of learning within the city derived from Aristotle's alleged habit of walking while lecturing in the *peripatoi* (colonnades or covered walkways) of the Lyceum where the members of the Peripatetic School met and conversed.

This trajectory in Toronto is clear, but within the broad spectrum of post-secondary institutions there are both commonalities and differences. Every case has some particular "seed" or circumstance that is the genesis of an integrating idea or concept.

Ryerson University faced a unique challenge. Land-poor, but with an urgent need to expand, Ryerson committed itself to city building in its downtown neighbourhood through innovative partnerships that redefined the shape and character of the university.

Founded in 1851, it had progressed over the years from a provincial normal school (teachers' college) at Church and Gould Streets in a corner of downtown, to a polytechnic institute in 1964, to a full-fledged university with a mandate to grant graduate degrees and engage in advanced research in 1993. In 2006 Ryerson University was experiencing enormous growth and needed to prepare a master plan framework for expansion and renewal for the coming decades.

In an effort led by then President Sheldon Levy, a self-described city builder, a team from KPMB Architects, of which I was part, prepared that framework. With little space to grow, the university looked to the surrounding city (itself undergoing a remarkable period of intensive growth), turning a necessity into a virtue through a strategy of radical mix of campus and city life. It identified major opportunities for growth and transformation through co-development with the private sector including, famously, the Maple Leaf Gardens transformation, in which an iconic hockey temple was remade as a ground level grocery store with academic space for Ryerson, and an upper-level sports facility and hockey rink for university teams. Breaking new ground, the master plan project presented a unique opportunity to engage the city in influencing the future development of a significant surrounding neighbourhood and community in the heart of downtown Toronto. It reinvented the heart of the campus by pedestrianizing Gould Street as its signature public realm; sought partners to increase close-in housing opportunities; and expanded its outreach to the surrounding community while affirming Ryerson's identity as a pre-eminent urban university and making a commitment to design excellence and sustainability.

The framework plan is currently being implemented. There are more projects on deck, each significantly changing the city around it as new partnership opportunities for co-development emerge, combining academic facilities in the lower levels of new buildings with retail below and housing and offices above.

This kind of extroverted strategy, getting more out of scarce land and giving more back to the city, is increasingly being imitated by other institutions.

On March 31, 2015, Ryerson opened its new, iconic Student Learning Centre at the corner of Yonge and Gould Streets (on the former site of retail landmark Sam the Record Man). It had been a fervent desire of President Levy, who championed this project, that Ryerson have a "face on Yonge," Toronto's most emblematic main street. Over a year later I found myself standing at the entrance with newly elected President Mohamed Lachemi and City Councillor Kristyn Wong-Tam for a press event to discuss the university's plans for its Yonge Street "face." The building there would feature a stepped entry that would serve as an urban amphitheatre and great new informal gathering space.

Top and bottom: The corner of Yonge and Gould Streets, here in the 1980s, was long anchored by Sam the Record Man, a large and popular record store on Toronto's most iconic main street. Immediately to the east, Ryerson University was sometimes jokingly referred to as the "university behind Sam's."

216

Top and bottom: In a dramatic move, Ryerson has established its presence on Yonge Street with its inspired new Student Learning Centre, creating a generous invitation to the public both indoors and outdoors and clearly demonstrating the university's commitment to its urban neighbourhood.

Designed by two renowned architectural firms — Snøhetta of Oslo, Norway, and New York City, and Zeidler Partnership Architects of Toronto — the Student Learning Centre boldly marks Ryerson's new place on Yonge Street in a fresh contemporary language, transforming the vibrant intersection of Yonge and Gould Streets. It provides the entire Ryerson community with an outstanding, state-of-the-art environment with a flexible, comfortable, and informal space to gather, study, and share ideas.

This project takes Ryerson a significant way forward in meeting its goal of developing and supporting unique, professionally oriented programs while pursuing its city-oriented master plan. Playing to both the university and the city, the building's generously dimensioned, welcoming, accessible, and digitally connected lobby is available for student activities and public and community events. The Yonge Street frontage features retail at and below grade, providing retail continuity on Yonge.

This project makes clear what President Sheldon Levy meant when he described himself, and by implication Ryerson, as a city builder. It has been a long-standing objective of the city to transform Yonge Street itself, to widen its sidewalks and reshape its environment to respond to the much higher levels of pedestrian activity it accommodates today. An environmental assessment to make that ambition a reality is now underway. Ryerson, along with its neighbours, has put its shoulder to the wheel to support this initiative.

Ryerson is one of an increasing number of institutions all over the city that are becoming extroverted city builders. The walls are coming down.

By contrast, York University began life in the 1960s as a suburban campus with no surrounding city on six hundred donated acres surrounded by farmers' fields, on the edge of the growing metropolitan area. Its development from scratch followed all of the leading planning precepts of the day. With plenty of room, it spread out in splendid isolation. The academic core of the North York Keele campus was surrounded by a ring road giving access to twelve thousand surface parking spaces for daily commuters. Within the encircled core, individual buildings were arranged in a checkerboard of geometric patterns, with the never-fully-realized plan to create a second-level interior walkway system to free up much of the ground plane for vehicular service access.

Over fifty years later, urbanization has caught up with the university; significant growth is occurring around it on all sides in a rapidly emerging part of the city, and the recent extension of the Spadina subway now brackets the campus with three stops at Finch and Keele, the heart of the campus, and Steeles Avenue. In 2009 I was part of a team with the Planning Partnership selected by the York University Development Corporation to update the university's master plan. This was obviously a period of momentous change for York, and there was a need to respond to the combined and overlapping impacts of many internal and external pressures.

These were the planning and design challenges: How to make the transformation from isolated suburban campus to a "campus in the city"? How to leverage the powerful, game-changing potential of the subway extension? How to meet the institution's evolving needs for academic and student facilities, including strengthening undergraduate and graduate programs, increasing science and research-related activity, and realizing the opportunity to create new faculties?

In contrast to the past, when cars and buses provided the only means of accessing the university, it is now possible to travel to York via the subway. Arriving at the campus up the escalator from the new, ultramodern York University subway station is a dramatically changed experience. The long-awaited station at the east end of the Harry Arthurs Common, with its distinctive, low-slung boomerang shape, opened officially on December 17, 2017. It was designed by the team of Arup engineering consultants and Foster + Partners Architects. Natural light flows through a large, sunken, west-facing "window" on the concourse to the platform level below. An artwork titled *Piston Effect* features liquid crystal displays (LCDs) that produce a lighting display that responds to the passage of trains.

The York Common, too, is a work in progress. It has gone through multiple lives. Originally conceived as a formal, auto-oriented drop-off forecourt, it then became a bus loop overwhelmed and isolated by the virtually continuous circulation of the more than 1,400 Toronto Transit Commission (TTC) buses that served the campus every weekday, in addition to hundreds more from other services, including GO Transit, York Region Transit/Viva (YRT), Brampton Transit's Züm, and Greyhound. Over time, new buildings began to fill in the gaps around the edges of the Common, struggling to provide a continuous sense of enclosure. Now with the arrival of the subway, the Common feels quieter and calmer. Fewer buses enter campus. Modifications to the Common's landscape are planned to welcome greater student use as a central public space.

Every aspect of the initial campus design became an opportunity to reappropriate and alter the use and meaning of what was a quintessentially suburban paradigm. The ring road, originally conceived as a vehicular collector for parking lot access, was reconceived in the plan as a circumnavigating, landscaped "greenway" and bike route, now with buildings lining both sides. It is a major component of a new campus identity, helping to minimize the travel time between campus buildings that are challenging for walking but ideal for biking and, ideally, some form of bike share.

Within the academic core, the pattern of service lanes and intermittent, discontinuous walkways had left a legacy of oddly chopped up spaces. Weaving these together into a network of coherent pedestrian routes and grade-level gathering spaces, taking advantage of new building insertions, and filling in missing links became another focus of the master plan. Black Creek Road, which literally had been treated as an undervalued "back" to the campus, became a new front with opportunities for building sites facing the expansive green space of the valley.

The biggest opportunity for making the shift to an urban future, however, lay in incrementally repurposing the vast area of surface parking lots outside the perimeter of the ring road. The modal shift was changing significantly even before the opening of the subway; parking permit sales were down and the university was reducing its role in the parking business. The City of Toronto had already approved secondary plans anticipating significant new mixed-use urban neighbourhoods on the lots surrounding the campus.

Our client, the York University Development Corporation (YUDC), was responsible for shaping, guiding, and managing the development of these lands surrounding the academic core. This significant amount of real estate constitutes an important "endowment legacy" for the university, not only in monetary terms, but also through its potential to significantly alter its context. The campus's greatest weakness — its isolation — now had the potential to become its greatest strength.

In a new assignment, YUDC hired our team to do more detailed precinct planning, working with the university community for the conversion of these perimeter lands. There was a need to flesh out the city's proposed designation of sites for mixed use on these peripheral lands within the larger six-hundred-acre site, to create a plan that included an expanded public street network and public realm. This would constitute a flexible, but secure development framework that would allow for opportunities to emerge over time to "monetize" non-academic real estate. These opportunities in turn would support the university's academic mission in partnership with private-sector providers for student, staff, and faculty housing, and a variety of compatible mixed uses.

Despite some challenges and shaky starts in the redevelopment process, York University continues to evolve in an urban context dramatically altered by new, high-order transit investment. The university is increasingly conscious of its role as a city builder. Given the market demand created by the subway, there is a real opportunity to work with the private sector to create a permeable border for the campus in the form of a mixed-use campus neighbourhood with needed attractive housing, offices, shopping, restaurants, cafés, and a variety of daily life activities. If done well, this highly desirable neighbourhood environment will serve not only students, staff, and faculty, but also the larger population that takes advantage of the academic, cultural, and recreational facilities the campus provides.

This changing relationship between the university and its new immediate neighbours holds great promise for mutual benefit. High-quality development that takes full advantage of the presence of the university community will enhance the quality of life in the vicinity of the university, and so will serve to enhance its ability to compete for resources, students, faculty, staff, and research grants. By enhancing the edges of the York campus extending out to its larger periphery at Keele Street, Steeles Avenue, Finch Avenue, and Jane Street, York will be affirming its altered identity as a major urban university serving the region.

As university and college campuses become more integrated, they take on more influential roles in the economic development of the municipality, region, and province. Partnerships between universities and the private sector to develop business incubators, innovation centres, and research labs encourage collaboration between the university and the surrounding community, and allow businesses and socio-cultural initiatives to grow using the resources and knowledge of the university. This demands a new level of transparency and openness about goals and objectives from both the university and the city.

York University is currently developing a second twenty-first-century campus within the City of Markham's emerging city centre to meet the growing need for higher education in York Region. Their shared goal is to optimize access to transit from the outset and facilitate overlaps and sharing of resources and spaces. This partnership came about through a multi-stage selection process. Initially, York University invited bids from municipalities in the region with urban settings undergoing transformation; there was then a second phase where the Province of Ontario made a final choice based on bids' compatibility with the provincial policies ("Places to Grow" and "Big Move") shaping regional growth.

Working with private-sector partners in Markham, the university planned a new campus, strategically sited within a mixed-use, transit-oriented environment right on the GO system. This location offers many non-academic supporting facilities through the private sector, often with shared use, including housing, parking, retail and amenities, recreation facilities, and public spaces. The university (and the province) will be able to focus its limited capital dollars primarily on the university's academic facilities.

This collaboration is a great demonstration of the value of getting things on the same plan and using the same chess pieces wisely to do more things. It requires getting out of traditional silos to think more broadly and reach across property lines and contract limits to see a bigger picture. Transit investment and changes in mobility are often the key integrating catalyst. That was the case on both York's Keele campus with the subway creating the opportunity to reclaim parking lots, and in Markham with GO and light rail. The moves in terms of that transit investment and development are not always concurrent, however. There is often a time lag, a delayed development call-and-response, a leapfrog process as things evolve. A long-term view is essential. As noted above, the province has now cancelled its financial contribution to this Markham campus as well as a number of others. At this writing, efforts are being made to keep the project alive by seeking alternative sources of funding to make up the difference.

The public realm is the connective tissue that ties the institution and the city together, and therein lies one of the greatest and most poorly understood challenges to combined city building. Capital and operating budgets in institutional settings tend to be building-project–specific, both for provincial formulas and for private philanthropy. We do not typically budget sufficiently for the quality of in-between spaces, the "commons." It takes special skill and inventiveness on the part of administrators and designers to find the needed resources to make those generous, extroverted gestures across boundaries that make for successful shared places. One of the most radical examples of city-campus fusion is George Brown College, which, having no land for a consolidated campus, adopted the strategy of seamless integration from the outset. As a student I had participated with planner Donovan Pinker in 1969 in preparing a study for the college entitled: *The City Is the Campus; Planning the George Brown College of Applied Arts and Technology, City of Toronto.* Making a virtue of a necessity, the college has been nimble and innovative in developing a series of scattered sites throughout the city, and now has three primary locations: the St. James campus, the Casa Loma campus, and the Waterfront campus.

In each case, city sidewalks and open space constitute the campus public realm. The Waterfront campus, for example, takes full advantage of the adjacent Sherbourne Common and the waterfront promenade while providing year-round animation through its student presence. In similar fashion, OCAD University's main campus is located beside the Art Gallery of Ontario and relates strongly to the refurbished Grange Park, with a second, growing south campus a five-minute walk away in the city's Arts and Entertainment District.

Some other brief snapshots of recent Toronto collaborative successes. The new Fort York Library in my neighbourhood, designed by KPMB Architects, opened its doors on May 29, 2014. It was full the day it opened and has been ever since. This small, elegant building is dwarfed by the massive towers surrounding it, but it punches well above its weight. It is a unifying beacon for the larger neighbourhood, occupying a crossroads midway between CityPlace, the Wellington Place neighbourhood, Niagara neighbourhood, Bathurst Quay, and the new Fort York neighbourhood, which has sprung up south of the historic fort.

This popular library provides a welcoming presence on the street and a warm and friendly atmosphere in a bright, well-lit space. New technologies combine with the low-tech and no-tech pleasures of turning pages while sitting in a comfortable chair and watching the passing life of the city outside. It will be the easterly terminus of the Bentway skate trail extension in a new Garrison Creek Park beside the library, where the long-buried creek once emptied into Toronto Harbour.

A second example is one of my favourite new places in the city: Koerner Hall, a brilliant addition to the Royal Conservatory of Music, also by KPMB Architects. The building lovingly embraces the original conservatory building and Philosopher's Walk through the University of Toronto from both outside and within, where the lobbies provide entrancing views and vistas of this green walkway through the campus. Way beyond fulfilling its own program needs, Koerner Hall has taken in the city around it and in return added a new richness to civic life. I believe that there is a particular Toronto design sensibility in the latest generation of institutional projects that is both fresh and contemporary, but at the same time attuned to context and to expanding and enhancing the public realm.

A third is the Art Gallery of Ontario, which, in tandem with its own internal transformation, sponsored and delivered a remarkable transformation of adjoining Grange Park and OCAD University in partnership with the city and the surrounding neighbourhood. This is a clear example of unifying disparate elements and providing the missing connective tissue. Emblematic of the change is Henry Moore's *Large Two Forms* sculpture, which has been relocated to the middle of the renewed park where it has added a whole new life and vitality to the space along with a gracious central lawn and great new playground. What these examples all illustrate is the enormous benefits for the city that can be realized when artificial boundaries are erased and the focus shifts to the seamless places we experience as Torontonians as the city congeals and fills in.

What all of these examples are telling us — the universities and colleges (both urban and suburban), the library, the concert hall, and the art gallery — is that their mandate has expanded to include an embrace of Toronto. This embrace is mutually beneficial, and it helps to change the face of the city in profound ways. While fulfilling their own programmatic missions, these institutions have also become more active participants in the broad coalitions of public interest and communal life around them. Set in the middle of a dynamic, cosmopolitan city, they are inevitably now engaged in city building, giving rise to new, hybrid forms of public life and community and increasingly playing a critical role in Toronto's evolution into a more vibrant, open, and diverse city.

7

Suburbs Become Urban

In 2008 I was invited to speak to a large gathering as part of a community visioning exercise in Mississauga City Hall. Among other things, this planning forum addressed the ways in which the city is coming to the suburbs in Mississauga City Centre, and changing a way of life previously based on the car. Square One, a regional mall created on farmers' fields in the 1960s, with vast surface parking lots, had become the nucleus of the newly forming city centre. The Square One Shopping Centre is the second-largest shopping centre in Canada, as well as the largest shopping centre in Ontario, with over two million square feet of retail space and more than 360 stores and services. On average, the mall serves over twenty-four million customers each year. With its extensive surface parking and excellent highway access, it was, when it was built, the epitome of modern design for a suburban, auto-oriented lifestyle.

But by 2008 the world had changed, and Mississauga, which had been guided by long-term mayor Hazel McCallion into a sprawling, auto-dominated suburban city of over 700,000 residents to the west of Toronto, was now ripe for change. In fact, the mayor herself had seen the need for a radical shift in direction and had embarked on promoting an urban future for the city centre around Square One. This emerging "downtown" was already anchored by the Mississauga Civic Centre (City Hall) with its Celebration Square, a YMCA, the Mississauga Living Arts Centre, and the Mississauga Central Library. Located within the mall grounds was the main terminal of the MiWay (formerly Mississauga Transit) bus network, which opened in 1997.

By 2008 major high-rise residential development had sprung up in this area, and there were many new construction projects on the way. As a result of high downtown land costs, there was a desire for affordable urban convenience; also, demographic shifts and lack of affordable housing in the core had made the suburbs the major new immigrant reception areas. The area surrounding Square One had become the location of choice for many young families. This designated city centre was but one among many such suburban locations, and developers were responding with new, dense, "urban" projects.

I didn't quite know what to expect when the residents, most of whom were living in this newly forming tower neighbourhood surrounding Square One, filed into the hall. They were a young, very diverse group, many of whom were raising families. It became clear that they were looking for ways to improve the livability and convenience of their emerging high-rise neighbourhood. As they told me, it didn't really feel like a neighbourhood at all. Most of the development was isolated from the amenities of the emerging "centre" around the nearby shopping mall, cut off from it by a vast sea of surface parking and heavily trafficked arterials.

The key intersection on the Hurontario Corridor is its crossing at Burnhamthorpe, the major east–west arterial. While surrounded by tall buildings, including the curvaceous "Marilyn Towers," whose landmark design was selected through an international competition, at street level, this is not a welcoming urban place. Here pedestrians attempting to cross the street are faced with roughly fifty metres of road, comprising seven lanes of traffic, plus free-flow right-hand turning lanes.

In some respects, taming these overly wide suburban arterials is one of the last frontiers in building more livable communities. It's necessary to simultaneously shrink the space devoted to cars, and, at the same time, reassemble the aspects of our daily lives that have been fragmented and separated. This means both shortening the distances between things and reducing the need for trips altogether. The endgame is clear, but getting there can be extremely challenging.

The lack of connection between the various elements in the area was frustrating the establishment of a real community. The irony was that, seen from thirty thousand feet, all the elements were present. The density was there in the form of many individual high-rise towers. There was the enormous mall, with its own world of destination shopping and restaurants and cafés; a few isolated office buildings next to parking pads; but these were all disconnected. There was no *there*, there. What was missing was the connective tissue that would make this feel like one place. The great opportunity was to convert the vast parking lots of Square One into viable, mixed-use urban blocks, to fill in the voids and overcome the barriers and so create a walkable, connected downtown neighbourhood.

To address this challenge, I was engaged in the preparation of the Downtown 21 Master Plan on a team led by Glatting Jackson Kercher Anglin. Our mission was to establish a long-range urban vision for the city centre, and in particular to focus on ways to attract employers and jobs and generate strategies for supplying the missing components critically necessary for a thriving and sustainable mixed-use downtown; cheaper land was no longer a sufficient incentive. The team concluded that the best strategy to encourage office employers was to create a true mixed-use urban environment, the antidote to single-use suburban office parks. The goal was to redevelop the area to foster proximity, walkability, and mix that would enable downtown workers to enjoy a higher quality of office life before, during, and after working hours — all without being dependent on their cars. We looked, among other things, to build on the energy of an already popular farmers' market (in the parking lot), giving it greater visibility in an active retail setting. In some ways, this is a return to the past, but in some ways it is a step forward — the ingredients on the ground, in particular the valuable land resource of surface parking, could be used to create a new, vibrant urban environment.

In my introduction to *Walking Home* I describe an imaginary journey from the heart of the prewar city centre out through successive waves of postwar suburban development. During this journey it becomes crystal clear, from observing how the relationships between buildings and streets change, just how much the car increasingly came to occupy the place of privilege. With hindsight it has become obvious that less is more, and the

What was to eventually become Mississauga City Centre began its life as Square One, a regional mall with vast acreages of surface parking surrounded by farmers' fields in a burgeoning suburban municipality on the western border of Toronto.

This area, designated as Mississauga's downtown, has now radically transformed, with a distinctive skyline formed by new residential and commercial towers, a large and growing live-in population, major civic and cultural institutions, a college, light rail transit on the way, and the ongoing conversion of parking lots to form a new pattern of urban blocks.

older prewar downtown neighbourhoods, where there is comparatively less room for cars, have ended up with a distinct advantage. With smaller streets and shorter blocks that are inherently more walkable, they support mixed use including local shopping. They also typically have better access to transit.

The problem is that we can't fit everyone into their inherited prewar neighbourhoods; we need places to grow that have their desirable and sought-after characteristics, both in already-built-up areas, and also in new ones outside the core to address the demand. Because there is only so much of this prewar neighbourhood fabric to go around, the challenge now is to make new, affordable, urban places in the postwar suburbs.

To solve this problem, city planners and transportation departments in suburban areas have had to rethink their current sets of rules and standards in order to "legalize" the qualities that these older neighbourhoods possess. Many of these qualities had been rendered illegal by prescriptive zoning that separated land uses and introduced parking standards and streets devoted to the free movement and storage of automobiles, creating an inhospitable environment for pedestrians.

This new model is posing a new test for a development industry that had become expert in producing one isolated real estate "product" at a time — residential (in homogeneous groupings), retail (in malls or power centres), and office space (in office parks or clusters) — challenging it to break the mould and begin recombining all these uses in new, walkable, mixed-use settings. The developers who rise to the opportunity and embrace this new paradigm are turning out to be the most successful.

There is no doubt that the suburban paradigm is a tough nut to crack, but suburbs like Mississauga can and will evolve. This process of absorption and transformation of suburb into city is not entirely new. The early *faubourgs* outside the walls of European cities were eventually absorbed into the city fabric. A smaller-scale local example is the Beach in the east end of Toronto, which started life as a horse-drawn streetcar suburb and now feels like a central Toronto neighbourhood.

The impetus to make this change in the current hard-wired suburban pattern has to be powerful enough to overcome myriad objections and an extraordinary tangle of intractable rules and rigid zoning regulations. That impetus existed in Mississauga in 2008, and it motivated the Downtown21

Master Plan proposed a way to accomplish that goal. It set out a flexible framework and vision for a vibrant urban downtown with a fine-grained grid of walkable streets, with places to shop, restaurants and outdoor cafés, public squares, parks and outdoor markets, and a range of venues to experience the rich arts and culture that this increasingly socially diverse city has to offer. It outlined a guide for the city to ensure everyone who has a stake in the downtown — residents, landowners, and developers — has their say as the new planning framework for downtown Mississauga is developed. In fact, the vision is rapidly coming to fruition.

Access to the city centre was already improving; not only was there more transit, there was also an expanded network of bike paths. One of the early challenges, however, was to ensure that the proposed introduction of north–south light rail on Hurontario, the main adjacent artery, would actually enter and serve the city centre. Initial plans had called for it to remain on Hurontario, bypassing the heart of the city centre. We proposed a rerouting to provide that essential direct access to transit; in the end, this modification was accepted. With this transit access secured, we developed plans for the larger downtown area, introducing an urban street grid and public realm plan within the parking lots. Unlocking the surface parking lots and dealing with the parking conundrum, breaking the expectation of free parking, was a chicken-and-egg problem. The alternatives had to be in place to allow the shift to happen. With the future prospect of a light rail line entering the city centre connecting to GO stations, employers could provide their employees with a realistic and practical alternative to driving to work every day.

This investment in transit was the key to dealing with the transportation dilemma and unlocking the lands around Square One. For over sixty years, transportation planners have tried to slay the congestion dragon. With ever wider roads, freeways, and management systems, our cities (and suburbs) have been drowning in traffic congestion and its corresponding social, environmental, and economic stresses. Torontonians are only too aware of the damage done by an overreliance on urban expressways, with their high-impact corridors pushed through the hearts of cities, eviscerating neighbourhoods and creating barriers. To the city's everlasting credit and benefit, Toronto mostly escaped that fate, famously rejecting the proposed

Spadina Expressway, Crosstown Expressway, and Scarborough Expressway. It was Mississauga's turn to focus on improved transit alternatives.

With transit as the critical enabling factor, a timely opportunity arose during the preparation of the Downtown21 Master Plan. Sheridan College was looking for a new campus location in Mississauga. It had all but settled on a traditional, stand-alone location with highway access and ample surface parking, but was persuaded in an eleventh-hour reversal to locate in the city centre, where it would have access to transit and could share parking with the shopping centre, as well as have access to the resources provided by the library, YMCA, Living Arts Centre, and other downtown amenities.

This was proof of concept. Hazel McCallion Campus (HMC) opened in 2011. It is home to the Pilon School of Business. In 2017 the college opened a new wing, increasing its enrolment capacity to over 5,500 students, with state-of-the-art classrooms, studios, labs, and production spaces, a Centre for Creative Thinking, and a gallery space to showcase students' creativity and innovation. The college contributes a young population that enlivens the city centre, helping to guarantee the success of the area's increasingly diverse offerings, which include large infusions of new residential and office development within the evolving pattern of urban blocks.

As well as improving the viability of the redesign of the city centre, Mississauga's new light rail transit, which will run on the Hurontario Corridor from Port Credit to north of the city centre, has spurred a much larger suburban transformation in multiple locations. In 2009, following the completion of the design for the Mississauga City Centre, I joined a team with the MMM Group, which had been selected by the City of Mississauga and Metrolinx to prepare anticipatory master plans for the Cooksville and Port Credit Mobility Hubs. These lie at the intersections of the GO commuter rail stations and the light rail on the Hurontario corridor. The goal was to ensure that Metrolinx's expensive investment in transit capacity, increased service with more frequent trains, and, eventually, the electrification of the GO lines would be used to best advantage.

Typically, the extensive lands around GO stations have been used exclusively for park-and-ride surface parking lots. This is clearly a wasteful use of the transit investment and strategic public lands. The development of the two mobility hubs surrounding the Cooksville and Port Credit GO stations, both identified as critical locations to support the objectives set out in Metrolinx's 2008 Regional Transportation Plan for the Greater Toronto Area ("Big Move"), offered a great opportunity to correct the mistakes of the past. They were seen as essential building blocks in the process of a region-wide urban intensification. The objective of these master plans was to work with the city and Metrolinx to ensure the lands surrounding these stations would have compatible development, featuring a robust mix of housing, employment, and community services. They would be transit-oriented "urban villages," built around excellent access to key links in the transportation network.

The elements of the mobility network and land-use patterns are mutually reinforcing. They involve maintaining a larger view that sees connections and capitalizes on opportunities, running the gamut from provincial policy initiatives to municipal planning, public sector infrastructure investment, and private development. In some ways more advanced than other 905 municipalities, Mississauga, now led by Mayor Bonnie Crombie, continues to make advances in shifting to a more urban future. Virtually every part of the 905, the band of suburban municipalities forming Greater Toronto, is emulating this shift to a more sustainable future.

Ten years later, in another location, an opportunity arose to take this challenge head-on and really make a difference. Mel Lastman Square in North York City Centre sits some fifteen kilometres north of Toronto Harbour. At first blush the scene feels dense and urban, lined with tall buildings; but a closer look reveals an area with a confusing sense of unfulfilled promise. The six-lane stretch of Yonge Street in front of the square feels highway-like, hard to cross and inhospitable; there are some doors on the street, but animation and street life are overwhelmed by the traffic. Today this is an area in the throes of a radical, multi-stage transition. Some blocks are now lined with restaurants and shops that are busy late into the evening hours, there is a big city skyline, and the basic ingredients of city life are present, but at street level the signals are mixed, and the sense of place is weak and contradictory.

Yonge Street, Toronto's famously longest street at fifty-six kilometres, makes its way all the way from Queens Quay north to Barrie on Lake Simcoe. Along its route, it is the main street for a series of villages and towns. The stretch around North York City Centre, known as Willowdale, began life as a "postal village," a label assigned by the post office to small rural postal depots in the mid-nineteenth century, and early traces of that village can be seen in some spots on the street in the form of one- and two-storey commercial structures typical of small-town Ontario and small postwar strip plazas.

Today, in one of the quickest inventions from ground up of a dense urban place in the entire Toronto region, one can now find in that area a generation of massive condo and office towers. These were built from the 1980s on, when the area was chosen by North York mayor Mel Lastman to be developed as a central business district.

North York City Centre stretches out as a narrow spine of these tall towers for roughly two kilometres north of Highway 401 between Sheppard and Finch. It is cordoned off by Doris Avenue and Beecroft Road, which form a ring-road system that separates it from lower-density neighbourhoods to the east and west. To support his vision for the area, the mayor persuaded the TTC to construct a subway station, in its heart, flanked by Sheppard-Yonge and Finch stations located at the south and north ends of the area. North York Centre station was completed in 1987. But despite the fact that the area is now accessible by subway, the car still rules in North York, and as high-density commercial and residential development rapidly advanced, the roadway was widened and the space for pedestrian life pushed back.

Following the amalgamation of North York into the City of Toronto in 1998, North York City Centre became the largest of four central business districts in the city outside the downtown core. Like Mississauga City Centre, it has many of the institutional accoutrements of a downtown district — there is the North York Civic Centre (former North York City Hall), fronted by its civic plaza Mel Lastman Square; the North York Central Library; the Toronto Centre for the Arts; Earl Haig Secondary School; and the Gibson House Museum — but here too any sense of a coherent urban fabric is lacking.

Toronto's "second downtown" on Yonge Street between Sheppard and Finch has the potential to be a vibrant, mixed-use community thanks to its density, but it is not fulfilling that potential. From end to end, this section of the city centre should be a leisurely thirty-minute walk; but it is one that few would take now. The area still feels like a kind of halfway house between auto-dominated suburb and city. The explosion of condos, malls, office buildings, theatres, and numerous new businesses still seems somewhat random; each element seems unsure whether to prioritize its internal parking structures or the street and sidewalk. There are now upwards of a hundred thousand people living within walking distance of this stretch of Yonge Street (and they do walk), but with the exception of a few stretches, it is not really a place that feels comfortable for people on foot.

A rare opportunity has developed to finally address this ambivalence and radically transform the character of Yonge Street and North York City Centre. To repair its aging utility infrastructure, this stretch of Yonge Street needs to be rebuilt in its entirety. This is a $50 million project and a generational opportunity to make a positive change. A choice has to be made about how to do this — put the street back together in its present form, or use the opportunity to create a new kind of contemporary main street for North York City Centre. This dilemma has led to an environmental assessment and an invitation to the public, championed by local city councillor John Filion, to reflect on the future of the street and the neighbourhood, entitled "REimagine Yonge." I was part of the consultant team undertaking this study, led by the engineering firm WSP.

A two-year public process began in 2016. It involved detailed study and analysis of transportation by all modes, taking account of local context, impacts on adjoining properties, and services and utilities. Findings were reviewed, and input sought in an extensive series of community meetings, workshops, and guided walks on the street. Eventually, as required by the environmental assessment, a series of options for the redesign of the street were identified in ascending ambition, ranging from: Do Nothing (status quo), Enhance, and Modify to Transform (reapportioning the space in the right-of-way).

Ultimately, the consultant team and city staff recommended the "Transform Yonge" option to expand the sidewalk width from just south of Sheppard Avenue to just north of Finch Avenue. The additional sidewalk width would allow adequate space for pedestrians, trees and landscaping, a bicycle lane, and outdoor seating for restaurants. The extra space would be created by removing two of the six lanes of traffic. This recommendation was made carefully with an eye not only to the city we have today, but where we are heading in the future as we move away from auto dependence.

This section of Yonge Street should be a place where people like to comfortably shop, meet, and gather. The six lanes of fast-moving traffic that obstruct community enjoyment are an impediment, but the study revealed that even with today's volume, the traffic impacts of the preferred option would be minimal and the gains enormous for other users of the street. The reduction in lanes would, among other things, make Yonge Street much safer and easier to cross for vulnerable populations: seniors, children, and people with limited mobility.

Experience shows that enhanced sidewalks and bicycle lanes will attract more pedestrians and cyclists, who will support local business. It seemed clear that if North York City Centre is to mature into an interesting, vibrant hub consisting of more than a cluster of high-rise condos, its central public space would need to be transformed. Despite this area's importance and the huge amounts of revenue it already produces for the city, it has underperformed, particularly in terms of generating employment. Lacking a clear identity thanks in part to its place next to a six-lane, highway-like artery, the area also suffers from poor planning and questionable developer deals. This was the once-in-fifty-year chance to make the shift. To fail to do so would be an egregious missed opportunity.

The population in this area has been evolving and becoming more diverse, reflecting the city's larger trends. Whereas in the late eighties and early nineties, newcomers to the area were mostly empty nesters moving into the new residential buildings, in the past twenty years, most purchasers and renters have been much younger. Here, as in Mississauga City Centre, many are raising families. Increasingly, the area will become populated by residents who do not own a car, preferring instead to walk, cycle, take transit, rent a car share, or summon an Uber. That trend will continue with the coming of automated vehicles.

Even Toronto's neighbouring municipalities, such as those to the north in York Region, are moving to a reduction to four lanes. Almost all of the rest of Yonge Street, all the way from the foot of Yonge Street at Toronto

Harbour up to North York City Centre, is only four lanes, with the sole exception being the section close to the 401 that handles traffic entering and exiting the highway. It made little sense to have this one section of Yonge at the north end of the city continue to be the only stretch with six lanes.

While we are making these kinds of positive transformations in numerous locations in the downtown core, we have very few, if any, examples in the inner suburbs. This was a rare opportunity to make an enormous difference for a population that deserves better. Not surprisingly, the recommendation to go with the "Transform Yonge Option" garnered broad support from the deputy city manager, the general manager of transportation services, the city's chief planners, past and present, and many of Toronto's best urban thinkers, along with strong endorsements from the surrounding neighbourhood and a series of city-wide organizations dedicated to community health and the quality of the public realm.

A supporting letter to the mayor and City Council from the Ontario Association of Architects eloquently made the case:

> Option 1 [Transform] is a cost-effective option that focuses on narrowing the divide between the east and west sides of Yonge Street in favour of wider sidewalks that enhance pedestrian use and enjoyment of the public space of the street. It also creates space for active transportation options that are suitable now and in the future. This serves to make this important section of Yonge Street into more of a "Complete Street," fostering a healthier, more engaged community.
>
> As we REimagine Yonge Street, consideration should be given to the current realities of how the urban environment is used, as well as long-term trends and the evolution of how we use our public streets, where and how we work and how we live in our neighbourhoods.
>
> Yonge Street cannot reach its full potential to support and enhance the community life depending on it until it has been REimagined as a street that is lived in and on, rather than as a highway whose primary purpose is increasing traffic flow.

Unfortunately, however, at the time of this writing, we have a hung jury. In February 2018 the city's Public Works and Infrastructure Committee rejected the staff recommendation, and in a surprise move supported an alternative plan (not one of the identified alternatives) proposed at the last minute by a councillor from another ward, which would keep the six lanes of traffic intact and move bike lanes to an unsatisfactory location on a parallel street, only recently rebuilt, at a great additional cost of some $20 million. Yonge's sidewalks would continue to underserve the population in the area, missing the opportunity to make any significant change in the status quo.

This matter went to the full Council in March 2018 and resulted in a tense debate lasting almost an entire day. In the end there was a stalemate and the matter was deferred. It is to be hoped that there will be another opportunity to move forward and not miss this unique window for change. To be clear, this debate is not just about removing two lanes of traffic for several blocks on Yonge Street, or relocating cycle lanes. In fact, it is a referendum about the future of Toronto and the kind of city we want to be. What it demonstrated was how deeply car culture is entrenched in the minds of some in our suburban areas, and how challenging imagining another way of living can be.

On April 23, 2018, at 1:26 p.m. on a sunny Monday afternoon, a deranged individual drove a white rental van onto to the sidewalk at Yonge and Finch and then drove south, mounting the sidewalks at high speed for two kilometres (eerily matching the exact Transform Yonge length), mowing down pedestrians, killing ten and injuring sixteen more. The city was devastated by this senseless act, and reactions of sympathy and support immediately poured in from around the world. Toronto's sense of security, like that of many other cities that have suffered from similar events, had been shattered. This happened as I was writing this chapter. Two days later I was asked to do a radio interview on Radio Canada about the ways urban design might help to counter this kind of attack. This is a profoundly difficult question. It seemed that the desired answer was that we should somehow armour our streets with barriers to prevent this from happening, or defend against it.

I was reminded of 9/11 and its aftermath, when I feared that New Yorkers, and people in other cities, would react to the tragedy by retreating from public life and public space. In fact, the opposite happened. New Yorkers defiantly reasserted their solidarity, strength, and desire to come together in public spaces as the city continued to expand its public realm. As this situation unfolded in Toronto, the very same thing was happening. There was an extraordinary outpouring of acts of kindness and strength, and spontaneous public gatherings. The tragedy revealed Torontonians to be open and generous, deeply respectful and caring of each other. The heroism of the officer who apprehended the suspect, managing to do so without firing a shot, and his modesty afterward became a fitting symbol of a more enlightened approach to law enforcement.

What emerged immediately in one of the most culturally diverse neighbourhoods in Toronto was the intense desire of residents, workers in the area, and the whole city to come together on the street to console, comfort, and support the victims, their families, and each other. A number of makeshift memorials appeared, adorned with bouquets of flowers, hundreds of candles, and notes on communal bristol boards expressing heartfelt sentiments in more than a dozen languages. Suddenly, the oft-repeated statistics of our cultural mix became urgently real and on full display. It was clear how precious these sidewalks were to the life of the individuals in this neighbourhood — all ages and occupations, all origins. A now-ironic phrase from a puritanical past, "Toronto the Good," took on new meaning to describe this powerful shared feeling in the face of this indescribable horror.

While some measures can be taken in some places, the truth is that there is no foolproof defence against such acts. There is no way to harden all "soft" targets. We cannot line all of our sidewalks with impregnable barriers, and even if we could, the crowds crossing in crosswalks would still be vulnerable. While it can never offer a full defence against these outliers who intend to harm, our most significant "armouring" and protection lies in the strength and cohesiveness of society and its ability to connect more of us to each other, to know each other. This only reinforces the need for shared public space, where we can meet in the open and in the light. There is a lesson to be taken from this terrible event about how to make our streets safer:

we must focus on the ongoing project of transforming the rights-of-way for shared use by pedestrians, cyclists, transit users, and drivers. In this way we can create safe spaces for us to be together. Our goal to eliminate collisions, with their unbearable toll of casualties — Vision Zero — is what we should continue to focus on as our highest priority.

It just might be that the horrendous act that took place on April 23 will serve as the catalyst to break through the political gridlock in North York City Centre and, pushing aside faint-hearted excuses, help to produce something special on Yonge Street. I hope it will be possible to create something new here that showcases our rich street life along with our extraordinary diversity: a pedestrian-friendly street, more welcoming, slower-paced, and a true destination, rather than just a pass-through for commuters in cars.

That future dream remains yet to be fulfilled. At present, things are at a standstill. To understand why this is the case it is necessary to go back to the meeting in March 2018, when City Council, lurching forward and then backward, decided against the plan recommended by the environmental assessment after intensive study and community input. The transformation of streets — anything do with traffic — had become a third rail in Toronto. Recall 1997, when by fiat and in the face of overwhelming public referenda rejecting the idea, the provincial government of the day forced the amalgamation of the City of Toronto with the postwar suburbs of Metropolitan Toronto: Scarborough, North York, Etobicoke, York, and East York to form the so-called "megacity" of Toronto. As we have seen, amalgamation fostered "them and us" attitudes. This was fodder for wedge politics, even if it led people to act against their own interests, harming the most vulnerable and handicapping the city as a whole.

Much but certainly not all of this perceived divide had to do with a fraught argument about the role of the car (the first pronouncement of the newly elected Mayor Rob Ford was about "ending the war on the car"), and the defence of a way of life built around it with obstinate resistance to developing any serious alternatives for how we move in the city. LRT (light rail), which Mayor Ford insisted on derisively calling "streetcars," was demonized because it meant giving up space in driving lanes.

This created a situation in which decisions like the one in North York were being made by forty-four councillors for the entire city of 2.8 million people occupying an area of 630 square kilometres, the majority of which was built around a car-oriented paradigm. The ability to make locally specific decisions around the sensitive issue of cars and traffic was complicated by the symbolic freight each decision carried for the city as a whole.

The "subways, subways, subways" mantra Mayor Ford espoused was only really ever about resisting surface transit and preserving unencumbered space for drivers on wide arteries, seen as a God-given entitlement even though it favoured the few over the many. At the same time, for those suburban residents who bought into the slogan, it was a poignant plea for respect. The problem was it was a promise that could never deliver. It ended up robbing the postwar suburbs of exactly what they needed most: access to viable transit sooner.

Case in point: the proposed Scarborough subway extension insisted upon by Rob Ford, who intimidated others to fall in line. It will end up costing well over $3 billion of city, provincial, and federal tax dollars on a subway that will take much longer to build, and serve far fewer people with less effective service, than the previously approved (and derailed) light rail transit plan. That's one and a half times what the province is planning to spend annually on the entire regional network comprising the "Big Move," serving a vastly larger population. It's a "trophy subway," a luxury that no other self-respecting city would allow itself. Other elected officials' submissive approval of this illogical plan can only be understood as an act of pandering.

It's all too easy for politicians to feed the polarization that exists around the inevitable and desirable transformation of both downtown and suburb, exaggerating differences, describing areas of our city in mutually exclusive terms, creating and fostering a "them and us" attitude for the purposes of wedge politics. It rallies a "base" and appeals to our tribal instincts. It can be used to demonize opponents and delegitimize and vilify the "other." The media, unfortunately, relishes controversy, all too eagerly jumps on this bandwagon, and amplifies negative messaging, sometimes even inadvertently promoting this sense of division. In the end, however, the impulse to sort citizens into types in this way is destructive and unhelpful. It gives rise to false dichotomies and distorts our collective understanding of the real challenges that require thoughtful responses. It gets in the way of problem solving and the kind of lateral thinking that thrives on creative tension and respectful disagreements. We freeze up and lose our ability to see the bigger picture and appreciate the commonalities that bind us together in the evolving urban space we share.

Another example of the dangers of this polarization was the decision City Council made in December 2016 about a portion of our aging mid-twentieth-century infrastructure, the eastern portion of the elevated Gardiner Expressway. This stretch of the Gardiner is falling apart, and the question was whether the section between York Street and the Don River should be kept and rebuilt, or whether it should be dismantled. The section east of the river was dismantled almost a decade ago, and few lamented its passing. City planning staff and Waterfront Toronto staff both argued, based on detailed technical studies, that it should be dismantled and replaced with a surface boulevard. About a hundred cities around the world have made the decision to take down or scale back inner-city expressways like the Gardiner, realizing they are mid-twentieth-century infrastructures that no longer make a positive contribution to city life. That money goes instead toward transit alternatives. In the end, however, it was a step too far for our Council, and they voted to rebuild the Gardiner (admittedly in a better location away from the water's edge), essentially performing the same highway function for an additional cost estimated at $2.3 billion.

This is the backdrop that made the Council decision in March of 2018 so difficult and why the North York plan had become a hostage of a cultural divide. Getting beyond this kind of stalemate is a crucial rite of passage for Toronto, one that will call upon all of our collective ingenuity and reserves of good will to finally debunk the debilitating myth that we are somehow stymied as a city divided along an urban-suburban fault line, as if these were fixed categories with defined borders.

Toronto's suburbs are not, in fact, monolithic. They are remarkable for their diversity, creative energy, and entrepreneurial talent. Tapping this energy through local initiatives in various places throughout the GTHA, transformative intensification projects are starting to appear at different scales, like acupuncture points that change the flow of energy in the city. They involve revisiting underutilized sites, tower locations, transit stations, malls, obsolescent industrial sites, big box stores, low-density main street strips, plazas, and parking lots. Piece by piece, these pressure points are adding up.

One of the most ubiquitous and fertile opportunities in our suburbs comes from a particular Toronto pattern of development that occurred from 1950 to 1970 in the form of clusters of high-rise apartment slabs widely dispersed throughout the region. Following the familiar postwar prescription calling for separation of land uses, they were exclusively residential. They depended on auto access from highways and major arterials, and, while roughly modelled on the modernist "towers in the park" ideal, they more often ended up as "towers in the surface parking lot." For the most part, their initial intended clientele was upwardly mobile young professionals. In fact, things turned out very differently.

Today nearly two thousand such apartment towers in the Greater Toronto Area provide shelter to nearly one million people, one of the largest pools of such housing in the developed world. Largely in the inner suburbs, these towers comprise roughly 20 percent of Toronto's total housing supply. They have become the default stock of more affordable rental housing for new immigrant populations, often in multi-generational families with lots of children. The buildings are severely challenged in many ways, with aging structures, some in dire need of repair and others requiring significant upgrading. Many have single-glazed windows, making them energy guzzlers. Based on the assumption that everyone has a car (no longer true), they have often ended up as socially marginalized vertical dormitory neighbourhoods with poor access to transit and community amenities.

Thorncliffe Park is a prime example. This densely populated, extremely diverse neighbourhood with a vast majority of new-immigrant tenants in the former Borough of East York has a residential section consisting chiefly of thirty-four high-rise and low-rise apartment buildings grouped in and around an oval. It was originally designed for 12,500 residents; today with a very different population, it houses thirty thousand, and its residents rely heavily on public transit by local bus. Socially it has a vibrant local community, and there are many community-based initiatives in Thorncliffe. Among them is one of Toronto's oldest community gardens, which provides garden plots to approximately one hundred local residents and their families on a non-profit basis and donates fresh produce to local community agencies such as the Scott Mission. The local elementary school, Thorncliffe Park Public School, has grown to over two thousand students since 2003 and is the largest elementary school in North America.

Every problem comes with opportunities. The city now recognizes that it is necessary for this important building stock to evolve if it is to be able to meet new community needs in areas like Thorncliffe Park. A "Tower Renewal Program" has been developed, inspired by a graduate thesis at the University of Toronto by Graeme Stewart and launched in 2007 by Graeme Stewart and Michael McClelland of ERA Architects. It has been picked up and further developed through the consulting firms ERA and SVN Architects + Planners in their co-sponsored Centre for Urban Growth and Renewal and by an office of the City of Toronto.

These "tower" buildings generally have a solid structural frame and ample space surrounding them for a reworking of the ground plane, including low- and mid-rise infill development. Taking advantage of this latent potential for change, the Tower Renewal vision has a number of planks, including an energy retrofit of existing buildings, improved livability for residents and their surrounding communities through increased social and economic opportunities within their neighbourhoods, better use of the green space around these towers through mixed-use infill development and improved transit connections to and from these neighbourhoods. The Tower Renewal Partnership is working with a broad range of partners, including the Toronto Atmospheric Fund, United Way Toronto, and developers. Their aim is to generate strategies to implement the transformation of these isolated areas into dynamic, integrated, and low-carbon hubs in suburbs across the city.

In recent years, I have found myself increasingly involved in projects that exploit the intersection of suburban potential for change and strategic interventions. Main and Danforth, in the city's east end, sits right at the threshold of the pre- and postwar cities. To the west, established neighbour-hoods line the Danforth to make a main street; to the east, we see the beginnings of big-box power centres, and the Danforth becomes an increasingly auto-dominated suburban arterial. At the intersection of Main and Danforth are a TTC subway station and a GO station less than three hundred metres apart and yet completely disconnected; an internalized high-rise complex, Main Square, which has become an immigrant reception hub; and vast parking lots around low-rise, single-use shopping complexes ripe for renewal. I was first contacted by a newly forming community group to support their effort to secure a public space at the southeast corner (slated for another tower), and to provide advice as they considered how they could influence the changes that would inevitably come to the area.

An impromptu "pop-up" gathering at a street festival on the corner of Main and Danforth led to discussions with many interested individuals from the neighbourhood. I eventually approached the Toronto chapter of the Urban Land Institute (ULI), an international body representing progressive developers with an interest in city building, to suggest they make this dynamic area the subject of an intensive workshop program as part of their 2018 Urban Leadership Program. That program invites a diverse group of mid-career city building professionals to tackle difficult and unresolved planning problems. They rose to the challenge.

The goal was to develop a vision and framework plan for the area, including the adjacent Shoppers World Plaza at Danforth and Victoria Park. It involved debriefings and walking tours with community leaders and local residents, the local councillor, city planning staff, and other interested parties, gaining insights on key neighbourhood concerns, as well as the opportunities for future development. The area, for example, had a unique connection to the Bangladeshi community, among others. The key was guiding foreseeable "urbanization" in a form that would produce multiple benefits for both existing residents and new arrivals. These would include an expanded public realm, good transit access, and a sustainable mix of uses. Exercises like this are a great way to broaden our vision of the possibilities and unearth the potential for multi-party collaboration.

Another key threshold from city to suburb in Toronto is the intersection of Old Weston Road and St. Clair Avenue West, near a former stockyards. I am currently working there with a consortium of developers, DiamondCorp and Kilmer, on an infill project for a vacant mid-block site that integrates a mix of mid-rise and low-rise residential components, including a cluster of housing units dedicated to Habitat for Humanity scaled to fit within the existing block context. The plan ties its immediate context together with a number of pedestrian routes, with links to the linear park along the hydro corridor, and sets the stage for the future development of additional sites within the block. This site, adjacent to a new proposed RER (Regional Express Rail) Station, is one of many such inner-suburb sites calling for intensification in areas that need revitalization.

I have also worked on a plan for the development of a vacant forty-acre site situated at Highways 400 and 401 near Black Creek Road and Jane Street, occupied by a Leon's Furniture warehouse. The Leon family wants to turn these single-use lands into a mixed-use neighbourhood, a true live-work-shop-play community. This development would help with the problem of Toronto's housing shortage and increase new-economy employment opportunities in northwest Toronto's economically challenged Etobicoke York area (heavily populated by recent immigrants), while also delivering critically needed community amenities and improving access to transit.

The vision for this strategically located site is to create a tech hub focused on digital and health care jobs, because of the site's urban location and the Leons' close working relationship with related employers. A number of additional benefits will result from this development: community amenity space, parks and open spaces, and affordable housing. More low-hanging fruit. The impediment that needs to be overcome here is simply an outmoded restriction on mixed use that prevents the useful repurposing of these underperforming lands.

Finally, in the Town of Milton in the 905 area surrounding Toronto, I worked with the York Trafalgar Corporation on a Secondary Plan for one of the last remaining "super-block" sites in the GTHA with excellent 400 series highway access. This area is also poised for new transportation infrastructure, including a new GO station able to serve a major mixed-use development along a nine-kilometre-long stretch of the Trafalgar Corridor. The Trafalgar Corridor today is adjacent to a major green corridor and endowed with a wealth of cultural and natural landscapes. It is one of the last large remaining infill sites in a void that will make contiguous the urban areas of Milton, Oakville, and Mississauga. What was a circumstantial gap in the twentieth-century-era suburban development around it, now offers a unique opportunity to realize the shared goal of the town, the region, and the major landowner to accommodate significant new uses in a more sustainable form.

This corridor also offers a rare chance to break the traditional, auto-oriented suburban mould at a very large scale as we make the paradigm shift in the GTHA to city building inspired by best practices in sustainable development, enduring urban design, mobility integration, and active and healthy living to create a new model for "complete community." In the case of the Milton project, this aspiration is very real because of a convergence of the need for meaningful change, in the right place and at the right time, nurtured by an alignment of planning policy, infrastructure investments, and shifting market forces.

What we are witnessing in all these cases and many others are parallel transformations within the larger city region as we simultaneously grow inward and upward and aim to reduce our continued outward sprawl. Provincial policies, the Growth Plan, "Big Move," and the Greenbelt are providing a framework which is attempting to direct our anticipated growth: a virtual doubling of our population in the GTHA in the next five decades. Within that time frame, the inner suburbs of the City of Toronto and their 905 cousins will have an enormous role to play as they absorb a significant share of that increased population. This process is messy, sporadic, and uneven, and poses many challenges; but it is probably inevitable.

The mistake that many political decision makers and planners make is failing to grasp the fourth dimension, which is the play of time. The present is not an immutable end state. All urban places, city and suburb, are perpetually unfinished and go through waves of change as layers accumulate. In the coming decades, we will get denser, more diverse, and less car dependent in all our parts. The overemphasis on accommodating the private automobile as the major form of movement in cities across North America has now been acknowledged by most city builders to have been a mistake. We will also change as we invest in transit and shift to the active transportation forms, walking and cycling.

The dysfunctional conception of a city divided against itself does not really fit who we are in Toronto. Still, this mythological characterization has taken hold in many quarters. It is perpetuated daily in the press and risks becoming a self-fulfilling prophecy if we don't challenge it. To get over this hump we need good listeners, not dogmatic shouters; generous, empathetic leaders, not mean-spirited ones; healers that bring us together across the perceived divides, not demagogues who drive wedges and poke at sores. The city, the big city, is not a zero-sum game. We need to get beyond the culture of winners and losers, of gloating triumphalism and resentful victimhood.

A majority of Torontonians now live in our first-ring suburbs, but they are in the same boat as those living in the city centre. Everyone will have to alter their living arrangements and shift to a more sustainable way of life. The fantasy that there will be a technological fix that will allow the current, sprawling, auto-based, high-energy-consuming way of life to proceed unchanged is just that: a fantasy. The way out of our dilemma starts with the unequivocal acknowledgement that we face common challenges. From that acknowledgment flows the understanding that both city and suburb have similar needs to rebalance how we build and how we move. We will all have to summon the leadership, the will, and the resources to make hard decisions about changing course.

If there is the will and the means to make changes, it is physically possible, if admittedly difficult, to convert suburbs to a more sustainable form. The major impediments are cultural resistance to change, a fragmented pattern of ownership, and an extraordinary tangle of intractable zoning regulations. The real challenges emerge whenever we move from large-scale policy to actual change on the ground. It is then that the tensions are revealed in a kind of ongoing tug-of-war like the one that occurred on Yonge Street in North York City Centre. To get to greater density, mix, and overlap; to increase walkability, and make cycling more safe; to overcome barriers and divides, all require a profound change of the postwar canvas. It is far easier in the prewar, pre-auto city, where distances, road widths, and adjacencies lend themselves readily to reappropriation.

On the other hand, the more generous suburban spaces — including wide rights-of-way, surface parking lots, and low-intensity land coverage — can be an advantage when introducing new uses and redesigning streets. Wide suburban roads have the potential to be transformed into multi-purpose urban streets, the arterials converted into boulevards shared with transit and cycle lanes. In fact, the groundwork is already laid for all this, and pioneering examples exist and are emerging in many cities, including our own region.

When the dust settles we will ideally be a multi-centred or, to use a more arcane term, poly-nucleated, transit-wired city region, with people living and working in centres throughout the region instead of converging radially on a single major downtown. We will export growth from an over-heated downtown core to places where there is more room to absorb it, and greater need for the energy it will provide. This pattern of growth will use our infrastructure and human capital more effectively and help to address social and economic inequities.

Opportunities for strategic insertions of new urbanity in suburban locations are proliferating, and as they arise, the entire city region is being reshaped. When viewed from space, our municipal boundaries disappear; we are increasingly one contiguous place that fuses traditional city and suburb. To accommodate our continued population growth sustainably, we will have to exploit the full range of opportunities that our already built-up areas present, such as those described above, where we have significant room to grow and sink capital investment in infrastructure. To help understand and nurture this ongoing evolution, we need to articulate an understandable, shared, big vision for the whole — one that delivers this evolution and its benefits to the entire city region.

8

New Frontier on the Waterfront

Standing at the head of the Parliament Slip on Toronto Harbour, one can feel a strong sense of colliding worlds and impending change. The deck has been cleared for something new. The broad expanse of Queens Quay Boulevard arrives from the west with extra-wide traffic lanes designed for truck traffic in a port long since departed. The boulevard bends diagonally up to meet north–south Parliament Street, crossing the wide span of Lakeshore Boulevard under the looming deck of the Gardiner Expressway before diving through a narrow, punched opening in the railway embankment to reach the popular Distillery District, with its pedestrian streets and mix of new and recycled buildings on the right, and the St. Lawrence neighbourhood, housing ten thousand residents in Toronto's first major mixed-income neighbourhood on the left. Running alongside Queens Quay in this stretch there is a temporary version of the heavily used Martin Goodman multi-use trail, heading east along the shoreline into the Port Lands.

Growing numbers of pedestrians and cyclists pass by on their way along the waterfront or make their way up into the city, facing impatient drivers at the ill-defined intersection. We are only eleven minutes from Union Station by bike and twenty-five minutes on foot at a strategic point on the threshold of the vast new territory of the Port Lands, where the $1.2 billion river relocation and flood-proofing project is underway.

The site of Quayside at the head of the Parliament Slip is currently a bleak, formerly industrial landscape at the east end of the harbour awaiting a bold new future as part of Waterfront Toronto's ongoing program of waterfront revitalization, with Sidewalk Labs as a partner.

A preliminary overview of the Quayside Site Plan showing a combination of mixed-use mass timber structures on several blocks along the north side of Queens Quay, new public spaces framing the Parliament Slip, and a new bridge connection to Promontory Park on Villiers Island.

Within the immediate surroundings, low-scale warehouses and plentiful surface parking fill the lands backing onto the expressway to the north; on the dockside there are some boats up on blocks being repaired. To the east the now empty monumental silos of Victory Soya Mills, built in 1943 to store soya beans, recall another era as the last soldiers standing in a field that has been flattened into a giant parking lot. Looking south across the water, the Parliament Slip aligns with the Eastern Gap leading to the Outer Harbour and the open water of Lake Ontario. To the south is the Keating Channel that will frame the north side of the new Villiers Island, to be formed by the relocation of the Don River mouth. Marching along the harbour from the east, on the waterside, the new buildings of the East Bayfront Precinct rise up at the western edge of the slip. These worlds all converge at this pinch point, the gateway to the new frontier where the city is reinventing itself.

It feels provisional, in a state of suspended animation, awaiting what comes next. There were plans, but a new opportunity has arisen that may change everything. On October 17, 2017, Sidewalk Labs, a unit of Google's parent company, Alphabet, announced a deal with Waterfront Toronto to develop a new kind of neighbourhood on Toronto's waterfront. It would be devoted to urban innovation, demonstrating how data-driven technology could improve the quality of city life, making it more affordable, productive, and environmentally sustainable. The idea was to initiate a partnership in which Sidewalk Labs would invest US$50 million in a year-long exploratory planning and design process for this twelve-acre site at the head of the Parliament Slip, called Quayside. Concepts developed here could then ultimately apply to a much larger area.

The goal was to create a district that would serve as a test bed to "bridge the urbanist-technologist divide," and be a leading North American example of the much-talked-about smart city, an urban district built around this fusion. The announcement was attended by Prime Minister Justin Trudeau, Ontario premier Kathleen Wynne, Toronto mayor John Tory, and Alphabet executive chairman Eric Schmidt. Many of the leaders of the Sidewalk team came out of the administration of former New York mayor Michael Bloomberg. Dan Doctoroff, the project CEO, was NYC's deputy mayor. The announcement generated much excitement and curiosity, but also caution, and raised important policy questions for government and the public about privacy and governance. What would a private-public relationship look like? Sidewalk spoke of an "urban innovation institute" that would bring together academics, Sidewalk staff, and outside developers to delve into these and other critical issues.

I became involved in Sidewalk Labs in 2015 — before there was any idea of the project coming to Toronto. I was invited to a series of brainstorming sessions in New York City hosted by Dan Doctoroff and his colleagues, which brought together an international group of prominent urbanists and leaders from the tech world. The premise was to identify the major challenges facing cities and explore what technology could, or should, contribute to their solution and the improvement of life in the city.

There was much enthusiasm about the possibilities during these initial conversations, but it was also, not surprisingly, tempered by healthy skepticism from some around the table about a number of sensitive issues, including privacy concerns around data: who it belongs to and how it is used. How would the data about the performance of urban systems, intended to guide their operations, be used and kept? How would access to that data be managed, and by whom, in a public–private partnership? While I shared the sense of positive anticipation, one of my particular concerns was, and still is, what these technologies do and don't do for human interaction.

Technology is already infusing everything in our lives, changing how we communicate, altering the nature of our human contacts, shaping the daily choices we make, automating our jobs through AI (artificial intelligence), and impacting issues of social equity, helping to determine who advances and who is left behind. How do we respond by consciously making critical choices for the city in the face of these pressures through the lens of a human-centred urbanism? In collaborations like this one, do we risk becoming the passive recipients of a form of "tech solutionism," granted the same air of inevitability that we gave to the embrace of automobile "technology" in the postwar era?

The questions for me often come down to how a human-centred urbanism could be aided by technology, not be subverted by it. Could we assess potential solutions against human values and decide when to say no, or no, not exactly; to bend, inflect, and choose? As ideas emerged in the debate, it was clear that there were great potential rewards, but also risks and tensions around the possibilities for dehumanizing relationships. Mobility is a good example. How could we ensure that the arrival of autonomous vehicles would not be an invitation to more sprawl and isolation? How could we blend the capacity of this technology with public transit, active transportation, and face-to-face human interaction?

Current advances in technology will inevitably play a critical part in the evolution of our cities. How they are absorbed and what impacts they have are open questions. We have good examples and uncomfortable ones. The uncritical embrace of the car after the Second World War and the ways in which we reshaped the urban world around its needs is a powerful cautionary example of the unintended consequences of the misuse of technology. People didn't anticipate the extent to which car dependence would separate us spatially and socially and produce massive congestion and environmental degradation. They also didn't consider the impact of a sedentary lifestyle on our health. These hard lessons teach us that, going forward, we need to be more selective in the use of technology.

As we recover from that excess (and the good news is that we are recovering), we now have a new and pressing set of challenges in the digital arena. The growing popularity of e-commerce is an example. The technology to replace in-person retail shopping clearly already exists. People can sit at home and order almost all the goods and services they need without leaving their living rooms. Taken to an extreme, this practice could eliminate all human interaction around the shared social experience of "Main Street." But is the consumption of goods and services the sole purpose for the existence of our shopping streets, with their places to walk and sit and gather, their shops, cafés, and restaurants? Or do they have another function, having to do with being together and interacting in public spaces? How do we take advantage of the convenience provided by seductive new technologies without isolating ourselves?

The outcomes of our decisions depend on how we frame our intentions. Here is a tale of two cafés, a really small but instructive example. It is a case of alone together or together together. One is a typical Starbucks. A row of customers is sitting against the wall at a row of tiny tables; everyone is immersed in a laptop or smartphone; no one is talking to anyone else in the room. The other is a small café and bakery in my neighbourhood called Forno Cultura. The owner and creator, Andrea Mastrandrea, studied architecture; for his café space he installed a thin, foot-wide tabletop with stools on both sides where customers sit side by side and facing each other. Behind them is a glass wall looking into the bakery where the breads and pastries are prepared. And in front is the counter loaded with delicious treats, leading to the cashier. There is technology in the room supporting all the operations of the café, but no one is buried in screens at the table and it is very easy to strike up an impromptu conversation; in fact, the space subtly invites us to do so.

The challenge lies in using technology to bring us closer together, not divide and fragment us; to enrich our lives, not make us obsolete; to invent new work rather than just destroy old. We need to consciously decide when the best solutions are no tech, low tech, or high tech, and use all three appropriately by always asking how the technology affects human relations. In a complex, evolving world of Uber and Lyft, Airbnb and driverless vehicles, there are conscious choices to be made and the stakes for the city couldn't be higher. How can we use these advances in technology to our benefit as we face the major urban challenges before us, without getting drawn into unintended and undesirable consequences? Will the outcomes produce authentic neighbourhoods, or a tech nightmare?

I am fascinated now by how new technologies, rather than letting people retreat into isolated virtual worlds, can complement face-to-face meetings among self-organizing groups of individuals, encouraging the discovery of unknown places. An amazing Jane's Walk that took place in May of 2016 entitled "Toronto to Calcutta — A Tale of Two Cities" used an online connection to link simultaneous walks led by Rahul Nargas in Toronto and Iftekhar Ahsan in Calcutta. The walk went through the "Ward" in Toronto and a similar neighbourhood in Calcutta, comparing similarities between the two as "cities of arrival" whose multicultural composition shaped them and sets them apart. A brilliant use of technology enabled physical and virtual, historical and cross-cultural exchange halfway across the world in real time, reinforcing our common humanity.

I was very attracted to the idea that under the right circumstances, Sidewalk Labs' project could make a vital contribution to the debate about the next phase of the city's evolution, capitalizing on the city's inherent capacity as a problem solver and crucible for innovation, addressing the multiple challenges related to all aspects of achieving a sustainable future. Given the inevitability of the infusion of technology into our lives and into the city, I was drawn to the opportunity to be involved with Sidewalk Labs, inside the tent, with people who share many of the goals I espouse, to test and balance ideas and concepts, looking at options and consequences and making informed judgments.

I saw Sidewalk Labs as a valuable icebreaker, creating the time space to do what was needed anyway, suspending conventional assumptions and current practices and using the opportunity to test and experiment with new ideas and in a highly public and transparent way with added resources. To do this it was necessary to move from the abstract and theoretical concepts we were discussing to test these ideas on the ground, not singly or one a time but together in synthetic combinations. What kind of place would that produce? What might it look and feel like? How would it function? As the ideas for Sidewalk Labs gestated and took shape in our internal meetings in New York, it became clear that what was needed was an urban test bed — a place to proactively try out these concepts in a real place, not an artificial tabula rasa. In other words, a partner city with complexity, context, many actors, its own momentum, and real city characteristics.

An overarching theme throughout this book has been about overcoming the barriers and perceived dichotomies that affect where we live and work, how we move in the city, how we respond to the natural environment in the city, or our own diversity as an urban society, reaching for greater prosperity, equity, and sustainability. The Sidewalk Labs project would be an opportunity to address those combined goals, bringing the positive aspects of technology to bear.

There were hundreds of possible candidates, including large greenfield sites and vacant brownfield sites in the heart of a number of cities. The goal was to see how technology could engage the contemporary city and leverage its assets and momentum, including its human capital and talent pool. A number of locations were considered; not surprisingly, I advocated for Toronto.

Toronto particularly stood out as an ideal location for Sidewalk Labs for a number of reasons. A critical deciding factor was an approach to immigration that has produced unequalled diversity, a spirit of openness, and a growing tech sector. One hundred and forty languages are spoken in Toronto, the majority of its residents were born outside of Canada, and, most importantly, talent from around the world is welcome. The city's population is growing at a rapid pace. It is the fourth-largest city in North America. A portion of its waterfront is one of North America's largest areas of underdeveloped land, which provides a remarkable opportunity to test new ideas and innovations.

And with three levels of government committed to Waterfront Toronto's unfolding redevelopment plans for eight hundred acres of east downtown land, our city seemed like an ideal place to test new ways to address the major challenges of urban living, such as high housing costs, commute times, social inequality, climate change, as well as enhancing all-season use of public space by improving the local microclimate.

When Waterfront Toronto issued an RFP for an L-shaped twelve-acre site at the Parliament Slip called Quayside, the opportunity presented itself. Rather than seeking a developer in the traditional way, Waterfront Toronto was seeking an "innovation and funding partner" for this site at a pivotal gateway to the Port Lands. With Waterfront Toronto's decision to select Sidewalk Labs through a competitive bidding process, a period of deep-dive discovery is underway as a joint effort to explore what a new kind of "technology assisted," mixed-use, complete community on Toronto's eastern waterfront might look and feel like.

One of the great attractions of this project for me was to see what technology can contribute to city building through geospatial monitoring tools and with feedback loops (on such things as variable flows of traffic, cyclists, and pedestrians) to improve how we deal with "organized complexity," coping with the broad set of interrelated factors involved in sustainable city building. During the Lower Don Lands competition, we were asked to include everything required to make this district viable — flood proofing, park creation, decontamination of the land, a complete new urban infrastructure with new transportation, housing for about twenty-five thousand people, and workspaces for about ten thousand employees, plus a whole range of shopping, schools, libraries, daycare, and cultural amenities.

To respond to this multi-faceted challenge, our design team included an extraordinary range of disciplines in addition to the core group of landscape architects, urban designers, ecologists, hydrologists, and engineers, all key components of city building. The complexity of this problem-solving process made me more aware than ever of the need to integrate different kinds of information. For large, complex teams engaged in iterative problem solving, where a great range of variables are in play and decisions are informed by data but also team interaction to interpret the data, technology is an enormous aid.

When I started my work as an urban designer, our ability just to correlate all the information about the physical context of projects, never mind other kinds of information, was pretty limited and the effort extremely laborious. Interestingly, there had been an earlier period in the nineteenth century and early twentieth century when we had insurance atlases, Sanborn Maps in the United States and Goad's Atlases in Canada. These highly detailed maps were painstakingly drawn on linen in ink and conveyed an enormous amount of information. Because they were created by insurers that were concerned with fire, they pretty well detailed everything pertaining to that kind of risk, including the materials each building was made of and the locations of all the standpipes for fighting fires.

Then we went through a long period in the mid-twentieth century when such information became siloed and fragmented. We lacked comprehensive "surveys" of cities with that breadth of information. It really wasn't until a couple of decades ago that the technology emerged to grant us a complex depiction of cities by superimposing multiple lenses, and, in particular, to see the play of time. This essential ability to work in the fourth dimension allows us to see how things have evolved historically and how they will continue to evolve through time.

Because the issues confronting the city are so complex, we need to work in a highly iterative way with many actors with different kinds of expertise. Successful outcomes involve coming at city building from these different standpoints, layering inputs. It is not just about two or three variables; it requires taking a whole range of ingredients all at once and trying to understand where optimum solutions lie. Technology is not a panacea, but it is a critical enabler. It does not provide the answers, but improves our ability to see critical relationships and lateral solutions we might otherwise miss.

As our desire to collaborate increases, we need to develop the tools and the ability to have real-time feedback about factors informing the intersecting rings of environment, society, and economics. We also need new ways to bring the public into the picture as decisions are made in a democratic setting, engaging an enlarged array of stakeholders and the general public. That requires transparency and the ability to simulate and assess outcomes. In a kind of generational reversal of competence, it is increasingly young people who are most adept at using technology to visualize and test these outcomes and find new ways to present information.

The virtual world helps to guide us in the real, giving us the ability to visualize the impacts of various options. With the power of these new tools we will be better able to create the comprehensive, interactive mapping of information that is indispensable for collaborative urban design and planning. The key is the ability to better understand interrelationships and bring forward lateral solutions for areas of the city, for example, correlating land use with mobility, energy consumption, and waste disposal and treatment, not dealing with one variable at a time but facilitating "integrative design." Our increased ability to overlap such information about the life and functions of the city extends from the neighbourhood to the whole city region. The Île-de-France, the region surrounding Paris, and Metro Portland, Oregon, have both been leaders in providing this kind of multi-layered data as open online resources. Toronto has many sources of this kind of information, but it is still hard to make connections.

While nothing has been determined, some of the ambitions for buildings, streets, and urban infrastructure that could be explored in this urban test bed — which range from familiar ideas to radical departures — include (but are by no means limited to) the following areas. In the transportation world, we monitor vehicular traffic much more than any other mode of transportation. We measure practically everything about cars' behaviour, but we are really lagging on the pedestrian, public transit, and cycling aspects of movement. A big process of catch-up is required to develop tools for measuring the behaviour of pedestrians, cyclists, transit riders, and so on in ways that are as sophisticated as those used for traffic engineering. Then we need to develop equally sophisticated interactive models that involve all modes.

Movement is just one area where this ability to have meaningful feedback applies. The improved ability to use sensors and algorithms to monitor phenomena applies to many other areas. For example, in waterways, sensors can collect real-time information about water quality in areas of reclamation. This kind of feedback allows for the testing of hypotheses and interactive variables. What might change in one area mean in another? The ability to see these connections allows for solutions that might otherwise not occur.

Used judiciously, technology can address many pressing needs, including promoting the enjoyment of and appreciation for the city's many diverse neighbourhoods by better informing us about the city's plethora of historic, cultural, and retail destinations. Technology could give us improved pedestrian environments, enhanced wayfaring, increased safety of movement, and new opportunities for animation of the public realm. The goal is to create a convenient, comfortable, information- and activity-rich environment that attracts and supports residents, businesses, and visitors. On a personal level, as you move around the city under the guidance of a handheld device (assuming you are not completely captive to it, and are still in the moment) you are also getting information and feedback from the environment. Virtual and physical realities are becoming more and more interactive. There is the real physical environment that you're seeing, touching, smelling; and then there is all the embedded information about it that you're receiving that can be made available if we choose to access it.

Back to Quayside with these new possibilities in mind. As stated above, Sidewalk Labs has committed to spending an unprecedented US$50 million on an intensive exploration of the possibility of bringing innovative technology to bear on some of the biggest challenges Toronto is facing. Their process has included meeting with citizens, governments, universities, and others about what the Sidewalk Toronto project should be. The goal is to come up with a model that Waterfront Toronto, the city, and Sidewalk Labs will find worthy to continue through a partnership that could also have implications for the rest of the Port Lands. This will not be a stand-alone effort. Sidewalk Labs says it would have an "insatiable" appetite for partnerships with other companies, including local tech start-ups, as well as universities and others on the build-out with the goal of serving as an "enabling catalyst" for innovation.

This, in my view, is why the Sidewalk Labs project is worth the risk for Toronto. We are in the throes of an astonishing growth spurt. Our systems are strained; established ways of doing basic things are under stress and are failing to meet needs today, let alone address the challenges of tomorrow. We need breakthroughs, and we need places to experiment and innovate and overcome traditional silos. But as we know, change is hard. Regulatory structures and operating mechanisms that may have served us well in the past are now impediments. We have a need to test them against new realities; to modify, innovate, and introduce creative tension between what is and what could be; and to ask the what-if questions in fundamental ways. The Sidewalk Labs partnership may just provide the catalyst, R & D resources, and the time and space we urgently need to help us make the leap in critical areas.

While nothing has yet been approved, numerous ambitious plans and ideas have been put forward for buildings, streets, and urban infrastructure; they range from familiar ideas to radical departures. The Quayside site can serve as a place for "kicking the tires" of many of these new ideas and concepts, which include but are by no means limited to the following interwoven themes. While most of these innovations probably exist in some form somewhere already, the Quayside site has the potential to combine all of them in one place.

For a start, there is a plan to create, aided by cutting-edge technology, "radical mixed-use" developments. Elements would include housing for all ages and incomes with spaces for a broad range of businesses — including offices, workshops, studios, stores, and cultural spaces — in a more malleable, fungible building fabric than we are accustomed to. Aided by a performance-based form of regulation that would serve to loosen up familiar, defined land-use restrictions, smart buildings could monitor temperature, light, sound, structural integrity, and other characteristics in ways that would allow for dynamic new forms of occupation within buildings and neighbourhoods. With the ability to make adjustments, housing, working, and retail spaces can be made more affordable and environmentally friendly; also, there will be an opportunity to expand the flexibility and capacity of buildings over time.

Inspired by the adaptability of the traditional industrial loft, Sidewalk Labs aims to reinvent how buildings are constructed and subdivided. Like the robust, highly adaptable, and still useful warehouse loft buildings of the Kings built a century ago, these new buildings would have a strong structure, but their interiors would be outfitted with standardized building components, allowing "ongoing and frequent interior changes."

Sidewalk Toronto will pilot the use of construction techniques like mass timber construction, using a renewable Canadian resource and new types of wood technology that allow for safe construction of large and tall buildings, which can be quickly modified for a variety of uses. These structures could be fabricated in the area, prototyping the use of new materials. Picking up on a long-standing ambition in the world of construction, Sidewalk Toronto would establish a program of modular construction, creating sections in a controlled factory setting for rapid on-site assembly.

The potential is to enable the construction of "whole neighbourhoods of lower-cost, quicker-to-build housing," possibly with a nearby manufacturing plant for local production of the modular units. These would form buildings that could be serially occupied by an evolving mix of offices, retail, and residences, including small-scale start-ups and makerspaces. Along with innovations in construction, innovations in regulation and financing will be pursued to identify areas that need to be changed or modified to allow for desirable outcomes that current regulations never anticipated.

One of the project's greatest opportunities lies in the enriching of the "commons," the indispensable shared public realm in a dense, compact, and diverse city. Making it the vital heart of the neighbourhood, more responsive, seasonally adaptable, enriched with both temporary and permanent expressions of art and culture, multivalent and welcoming to all is a key objective. This in turn combines with the idea of a true "community hub" where a full array of public services, from daycare to school, library, community centre, and health care delivery can be integrated into the building fabric in new and flexible ways in this expanded commons.

With more people living in the downtown core, the city needs to explore more transportation options as adjuncts to existing public transit, as well as active transportation to make getting around safer, more affordable, and more convenient than relying on private motor vehicles. This could be an opportunity to expand that range of mobility options while supporting current transit plans; privileging walking and cycling, and exploring innovative solutions like sensor-operated traffic lights that can track volumes to make cycling safer and more convenient but also exploring the operation of self-driving fleets and buses.

With changes like these in place, parking as we have known it becomes a moving target. Through an app developed by Sidewalk Labs, it could "pilot a program that keeps parking prices high, but offers discounts to people who are coming from areas, or at times, when transit options are limited. Technology will enable pricing to vary in real time based on transit availability."

Sidewalk envisages a heavily pedestrianized district with a range of street types and scales that privilege the pedestrian and an intimate human scale. Street design itself is a fertile field for innovation. Distribution of users within the right-of-way, new materials, and technology that enables the street itself to physically and operationally sense and adapt to different conditions and levels of use can be introduced. Animation of the street as a social space can be activated by more dynamic retail, including pop-ups that would come and go within indoor and outdoor spaces.

Improving the microclimate of the public realm of streets, parks, and squares in an expanded, highly walkable, and universally accessible commons is another key ambition. Weather mitigation can be achieved by careful arrangements of buildings and adaptable canopies and windbreaks and, possibly, heated surfaces that significantly expand the times when it is comfortable to be outdoors in Toronto's climate, and also encourage year-round cycling and walking.

We still live in a world where we have large, cumbersome garbage trucks taking up the streets in our cities. Recycling is also taking up a lot of space, and it can be quite inefficient. Major advances have already been made in the introduction of underground vacuum systems and industrial robots that manage the collection of trash and recyclables in a number of selected waste streams. Although these are not yet in Toronto they have been developed in Scandinavia and are now in over a hundred cities around the world. Sidewalk Toronto offers an opportunity to introduce these alternative means of collecting and sorting waste using new technologies that can improve cleanliness and pest control and eliminate the need for large bins on the street and large storage rooms and loading docks in buildings.

These and many other ideas are not technological gimmicks. They go to the heart of how we will live together in the city. Combined in a test bed area like Quayside, their cumulative impact can be vastly greater than if they are scattered throughout the city. But ultimately, these technologies are scalable and exportable, and will have application in the Port Lands, throughout the urban region, and around the world as we learn to use and manage the array of new means available to us as we move toward a more sustainable urban future. They also have the potential to produce cost savings by being more nimble and adaptable, and thus increasing affordability.

Operating at the neighbourhood scale, in between the individual "smart building" and a broad policy framework aimed at the entire city, Quayside provides an opportunity to innovate and a sufficiently concentrated focus to implement meaningful change. It has the potential to demonstrate what a digitally enabled, mixed-use precinct that combines the latest technologies with strongly held community values for an inclusive, equitable, and prosperous city can look and behave like. But to be truly meaningful and viable, many of its innovations will need to be scalable and extend beyond the boundaries of the twelve-acre site.

There are, of course, many very big questions and challenges to be addressed during this exploratory period, including legitimate concerns around privacy, data security, the use of data and trust. Sidewalk Labs and Waterfront Toronto have given assurances that security and privacy protection will be baked into the new infrastructure with the creation of an independent data trust. But ultimately, with many eyes on the project, the city and civil society will weigh in to negotiate the rules of engagement. At this point, this is clearly a work in progress, and many legitimate questions and concerns have yet to be fully addressed.

Furthermore, when a company such as Sidewalk Labs develops a device or process for use in a city, who owns the intellectual property? And what access will competitors or start-ups have to the platform? Sidewalk says it wants to make its "digital layers" widely accessible, describing themselves as an urban innovation platform "whose role is to create the conditions for others to innovate on top of it." And in fact, that's what great cities have always done: a street grid is, after all, a low-tech shared platform. The critical ingredient is a credible process that satisfies the concerns of the community and elected officials as it takes appropriate advantage of the historic opportunity represented by the Sidewalk initiative.

What can Toronto learn from this experience, and how can that knowledge be applied? As other cities have demonstrated, we are part of a great collective learning curve as we innovate in different ways in response to the arrival (or onslaught) of technology. Every city — small, medium, large, and extra large — now has to articulate its aspirations and proactively consider how these inevitable technological advances are impacting its territory and quality of life. The advances are forcing us to rethink how we do everything from organizing municipal services to engaging the public in decision making and implementing new projects, to take a few examples. It is critical at this point for Torontonians to get involved in these conversations. With Sidewalk Labs, we have a rare opportunity to imagine, discuss, debate, and evaluate how our future will look and how technologies will shape it. This may be Toronto's turn to take the lead.

In February 2018, I was invited to be one of the keynote speakers at the Future Cities Forum in Ottawa co-hosted by the National Capital Commission's Urbanism Lab, the Artengine arts and technology collective, and Impact Hub Ottawa. We were asked to share our perspectives on what our future cities will look like, as new technologies take more and more space in our daily lives. In the conversational scrums that took place afterward, it was clear that the young audience felt a mixture of great excitement, anticipation, and some apprehension. At the time of this writing, the draft Master Innovation and Development Plan (MIDP) that Sidewalk must bring forward for consideration has not yet been submitted. It will be carefully scrutinized and will go through the same rigorous process of public consultation that Toronto is known for, and Waterfront Toronto and the city have demonstrated elsewhere on the waterfront. Its primary focus will be the twelve-acre Quayside site as a test bed where Sidewalk would be the actual developer. It will also propose a role within the larger Port Lands, like assisting in the financing of transit, enabling things to happen that would otherwise likely not be possible. This new form of partnership raises many new critical questions that will need to be addressed but also has many benefits. The review of the MIDP will result in a decision as to whether to proceed. The jury is out.

PART TWO A NEW CITY

9

The Threads Come Together

In the preceding chapters, I explored a number of places in Toronto where significant aspirational transformation is occurring. The examples I chose are in many cases icebreakers, testing the waters and charting new directions. While they were described under different headings, in reality, those separations are artificial. These projects spill into and reinforce one another. Neighbourhoods coalescing and shifts in mobility; common ground enlarging and connecting; a new urban cohabitation with the natural world; key institutions opening themselves to the city; suburbs becoming more city-like and opening a new frontier on the waterfront: the places described are all examples of interconnected mutually supportive change.

As we move on all these fronts simultaneously, the city evolves, and the threads of change interweave, redefining our experience of place and the territories we inhabit, from the intimate scale of our dwellings to the block, the neighbourhood, the city, and, ultimately, the entire city region. We forge new relationships as thresholds of ease or difficulty in navigating the city alter our sense of the possible. As these exceptions accumulate and multiply, they gradually become the rule. They inspire imitators and set off chain reactions. They form "innovation hubs" and encourage the spaces in between them to fill with connecting "spokes," redrawing our mental maps and our grasp of Toronto as a whole, connected place.

It all adds up. The city feels different. Changes in degree become changes in kind. Sometimes it takes several attempts to get innovations over the bar, building on the shoulders of others who came before, but ideally they form virtuous circles of positive change, ideally supporting the shared goal of a "city for all." The success of these initiatives matters so much because cities have a critical job to do in a world where we are beset by forces that challenge us and impulses that pull us apart and imperil our shared future. It is important to remember and learn from sobering experiences elsewhere. Back to those children in the swimming pool in Regent Park on a winter's day, many of them newly minted Torontonians. Our shared collective project comes with great possibilities, but also major obligations. What kind of city and world will we pass on to them?

Let's presume that we summon the resources and the will to embrace a destiny that has been thrust upon us. Shaped by core values of a human-centred, inclusive urbanism, what might Toronto be like if our best tendencies prevail? By making a very slight interpolation (not some distant sci-fi projection) from current trends, we find ourselves in a different city. It is not the product of one silver bullet, or two, but an interweaving of all of these place-changing elements across the city region. Much is familiar, much is recycled and hybridized. This new twenty-first-century city of Toronto is both visionary and rooted in practicality, combining emerging technologies with some very old low-tech and no-tech solutions. It is not a facsimile of any other time or place. Let's step into this future, Toronto.

Toronto's population has continued to grow and become even more diverse as the city welcomes new arrivals from all over the world. To accommodate this growth, we have built our own version of mixed-use, mixed-income, denser, more compact, walkable neighbourhoods in a variety of scales and forms throughout the entire city region. Acknowledging that the polarizing forces of economic segregation were threatening the viability of our city, we have figured out ways to finance and build a full range of housing, designed for all income levels. Situated in integrated neighbourhoods throughout the city centre and inner suburbs, this housing has been built using a range of public and private solutions, which, combined, have unleashed the capacity of our development industry to respond to this critical challenge.

We are living in denser, more walkable neighbourhoods, concentrating on opportunities to introduce that missing middle scale that had proven so elusive. We have inserted new mid-rise development throughout the city in previously fallow lands and along our main streets. A push to do this has been driven by a generational shift in a search for convenience — and we're also finding collective solutions more effectively, supplying in shared ways what would otherwise have to be provided individually, such as trading a yard for a balcony or rooftop garden, using smaller appliances, and generally living with less stuff.

Selecting a place to live used to be about the size of the unit and amenities in the apartment or townhouse complex, or the long view on the horizon. Today it is about the neighbourhood, celebrating life outside the front door. A whole new set of criteria came to the fore. It often starts with the most basic of needs: food. Where is the grocery store? What shopping is available within easy walking distance? Is there a market? Is health care available? Where is the nearest hardware store? Where can you go to the movies or hear live music or see a play? Or get your hair cut? Are there convenient and appealing neighbourhood restaurants and cafés?

And for families with kids: Where are the daycares, schools, community centres, and playgrounds? Are the streets safe and comfortable, and are there enough people around during the day to provide casual surveillance? What nearby places can you walk, take transit, or cycle to? Where is the transit? How frequent is the service and where does it take you? Can you get to the train station or the airport? Is there car share and bike share available? This dramatic change in priorities reflects a profound cultural change.

As a result of the greater mix and proximity of daily life activities — living, working, shopping, culture, recreation, and leisure; increased walkability, cycling, and transit — we have a healthier population, back on its feet with a noticeable reduction in obesity and chronic disease. Lively neighbourhoods also offer greater opportunities for neighbourliness and an antidote to social isolation for those who need and seek it — and an increasing number of people do.

Early moves toward intensification had begun with young singles and couples and empty nesters who were the pioneers in newly forming neighbourhoods — the "poplars" in a natural succession — but they were soon followed by young families, as the first arrivals had kids, and then the large cohort of baby boomers arrived to extend their independence at that inevitable moment when the car keys had to be taken away. Accommodating the full life cycle, our neighbourhoods are now home to people of all incomes, capacities, and stages in life, with a major commitment to affordable housing, making mixed-income communities a reality throughout the region. And residential buildings themselves are providing more of the things needed to serve this diverse population beyond the individual units — things like bicycle storage, courtyard, play space, gardens, green roofs, and terraces. There are many places to open a business or a home office successfully. These local places of business provide a daytime population that can support local retail and services.

This shift gained momentum as we moved to more sustainable ways of living, with many collateral benefits including greater stimulation and sociability, rediscovering the joys of city life in the most diverse city on the planet, rubbing elbows with the world at close quarters. Many of our neighbourhoods have taken on distinct personalities and identities building on their unique "stories," the legacy of the people who inhabited them, the buildings and spaces and narrative of local history that makes them special. They have been energized by the presence of community-facing institutions of all kinds — colleges and universities, theatres, museums, galleries, and performance venues, which have opened themselves to the city surrounding them, embracing their role as city builders and adding resources and richness to community life.

A critical mass was needed to make walking, cycling, and transit viable and allow neighbourhood street retail to function. But it was not just density in the abstract that mattered. It was how we made neighbourhoods dense and compact that was critically important — the way buildings shaped public spaces and what happened along the sidewalks to enhance the experience and make us more likely to take that walk. The older prewar neighbourhoods initially had a distinct advantage. With smaller streets and shorter blocks that encouraged shared use like local shopping, they were inherently more walkable; they also typically had better access to transit. But today there are many new places in the city that have these desirable characteristics.

To enable all these changes, the city has radically revised the inhibiting rules and standards to promote intensification. At the same time the city has "legalized" the characteristics of proximity and intricacy that these older neighbourhoods possessed and which had been rendered illegal in new areas by prescriptive zoning that separated land uses, and road designs that created streets that were devoted to the free movement of automobiles but inhospitable to pedestrians. The development industry has risen to the occasion and embraced the opportunity to develop in a new way, reflecting this new paradigm of "complete neighbourhoods."

To accommodate our rapidly growing population, we have colonized obsolescent industrial lands and cleaned and remediated their polluted soils, introducing new neighbourhoods with greater social and cultural diversity, housing vast numbers of new residents and employees in new mixed-use settings throughout the region. We have densified our arterial main streets and interstitial spaces, including opportunities for living and working on our 250 kilometres of laneways. Our suburbs have also begun to thicken, diversify, and densify, developing active and dynamic city centres with their own distinct identities.

This consolidation and "infilling" has also given birth to lower-impact lifestyles. We have moved a long way toward zero-carbon-footprint communities, or even "net plus," by creating energy from our waste and from renewable sources where we live and work. We now have many buildings that put energy back into the grid. There are new integrated approaches to stormwater and waste water management, making our waterways healthier, cleaner, and more often swimmable.

All of the innovations described above, and others, have broken down traditional barriers among places of living, workplaces, retail and hospitality, transportation, leisure activities, and education and learning. In many areas we have integrated physical experience with data-driven services and smart technologies, blending physical and virtual infrastructure. Project Sidewalk at Quayside on the waterfront offered us many opportunities to deeply explore this emerging new territory for city building in one focused area, and provided many valuable lessons. We have embraced the sharing economy and work differently, with room for large- and small-scale enterprise, combining start-ups and scale-ups and many kinds of new partnerships.

These woven threads build on trends already in evidence, responding to need and desire. There is an element of recall, something revived from an earlier past, and yet something entirely new and liberating. The urban environment has become multi-functional and more intuitive, intimate and user friendly, with a greater sense of conviviality. The city is experienced viscerally through body and mind and all the senses; it looks and feels different. The boundaries have blurred, and hybrid spaces where many things can happen have emerged.

Combined with openness to change and experimentation, we have created the conditions for a vital and performing city, and at times a spontaneous city. But perhaps what is most strikingly different is the impact of the extensive new "glue" filling in the previous gaps and voids with new, extroverted buildings, which add life and people to the street. The city has become more continuously walkable again, changing our perceptions of distance and time.

Many of us occasionally use the next version of personal mobility devices, but we probably don't own those vehicles and are getting around by using a greater variety of modes, plan including our feet. Commuter and intercity rail are on the rise with the "Big Move" plan introducing regional RER expansion with all-day electrified service. SmartTrack and RER have established a vast network of new stations across the region, serving many destinations including our grand regional hub, Union Station, a magnificent beaux arts structure built in 1920, with its refurbished grand interior hall and monumental colonnade on Front Street. It is much more intensively used, its concourses expanded, and new uses integrated both inside and outside on the plaza.

The stations that were once the objects of our architectural affection and places of grandeur and pride with flourishes of richer materials have made a comeback to occupy a new place of respect and care. The trains offer convenient, comfortable service across a vast city region with frequent, all-day headways. The Presto system (or its successor) has been fully integrated with affordable transfers to all modes of transit throughout the region, all tracked easily on our hand-held devices. Trains are outfitted with convenient bike racks to continue the journey; bike share is available at the stations, along with buses and automated jitneys for the last leg of the journey.

The new stations have become the anchors of compact, walkable urban villages and community hubs throughout the region. Surface parking lots have virtually disappeared, making room for renovated and new buildings housing a clustering of shops for all daily needs, plus a full gamut of housing, services, and new employment opportunities for reverse commuters from the city core.

We have taken up the subway challenge, and our once-meagre subway network has now expanded and filled in the gaps. The relief line is finally in operation, taking pressure off the overloaded Yonge line, but also allowing for convenient and well-designed transfers to the RER, with full fare integration, at locations like Bloor and Dundas in the west and Main Street in the east. Like the rail stations, there has been a new attention to detail and creature comfort in the subway stations. The new stations, seamlessly integrated with dense clusters of development that envelop them, have resumed their function as city builders.

As an essential complement to heavy rail and subways, the LRT network has also been expanded, transporting people on an expanded web of routes to key locations throughout the city region, picking up a thread from a once dense "street railway" network that blanketed early twentieth-century Toronto with city-shaping streetcars.

The natural companions of the legacy streetcar were the many continuous main streets, lined with neighbourhood shopping, readily accessible on the journey home. But with greater intensity in the city, legacy streetcars in mixed traffic, in our narrow twenty-metre rights-of-way like King Street, had become immobilized in rush hour traffic. The King Street pilot demonstrated a way of unlocking this jam by restricting auto access. That initial experiment led to many other applications on other lines.

A new generation of LRTs has been extended throughout the region in separated rights-of-way, providing greater reliability. These new LRTs are good at travelling mid-range distances; they offer conveniently located stops within walkable neighbourhoods, and give riders the opportunity to experience the city at another rhythm. The shared street takes into account the needs of pedestrians and cyclists. In the LRT car, low floors, the ability to get on and off along the way for a single fare, seamless transfers, and very frequent headways (minutes apart) make this a highly efficient and accessible way to accomplish many things in a short period of time. Queens Quay provided an early example of how this can be achieved through skillful design, and its lessons have been broadly applied.

In lower density areas and along the city's main streets, the LRT has become an important complement to the higher-order transit alternatives of heavy rail and the subway, cost effective and flexible and a positive contributor to the feeling and appearance of the street. The multicar articulated vehicles are comfortable and highly sociable, enabling us to still enjoy a view of the city around us. Side-loaded versions occupying one side of the street right-of-way, like Queens Quay, have made the experience of getting on and off easier and safer.

Even the basic bus, that utilitarian workhorse of the transportation system, has evolved. Its design has progressed; it provides more information to passengers and greater comfort. It now comes in all sizes, from the standard bus to small-scale vehicles that can be hailed anywhere along fixed routes. Driverless versions have also appeared.

Cycling is now accounting for an ever-greater share of trips as land uses become more mixed and the need for longer trips decreases. The multiple benefits are compelling: ease, simplicity, health and exercise as part of daily routines, and the sheer pleasure of moving feely, mind and body synchronized, seeing life around us from the slightly elevated vantage point of the bike seat. Who would have imagined a few short years ago that the bike would make such a comeback. The increase in use had been phenomenal in the early years of the twenty-first century, but now the infrastructure is there to support it.

Bike sharing is ubiquitous and has taken many forms. Bikes of all kinds and for all uses — from bike trucks, to electric assist bikes, tandems, and cargo bikes to transport kids — have all appeared in profusion. Facing this enormous demand in the city core but also in the formerly auto-oriented suburbs, and thus needing to improve safety, the city has created complete integrated networks of protected bike lanes, no longer just narrow, striped areas on the road but grade-separated with buffers. Once more, Queens Quay was a leading example.

Walking is, of course, the most basic form of movement; at some point we are all pedestrians. But we two-legged creatures gave up this faculty when we began jumping in and out of cars, and compromised our health and well-being as we transformed the urban world to minimize walking. Toronto has now remade itself as a capital of walking, making foot traffic comfortable, convenient, and stimulating. After numerous temporary pilots clearly demonstrated the benefits of widened sidewalks and pedestrian-emphasis streets, many of these, including Yonge Street, John Street, and King Street, have become permanent, along with many others throughout the city, and many entirely pedestrian districts have appeared.

These "complete streets" have become places of real conviviality, combining daily activities like shopping with increased opportunities for face-to-face contact and interaction in our remarkably mixed city. We have also made sure that these pedestrian spaces are fully accessible and welcoming to people of all abilities. We have once more become used to walking kilometres for sheer pleasure criss-crossing Toronto just to see what there is to see and experience as the city fills in, as the "no man's lands" disappear and there is so much more to see and do in every neighbourhood.

The car, that wonderful twentieth-century invention, is still with us. It is still useful for some trips and always popular with collectors and hobbyists, but it is just not that central to our lives any more. Most of us no longer feel any need to own one, even if we use a car occasionally to transport things or for trips out of the city. We are in a period of rapid "de-motorization," which has become more common for each succeeding generation in twenty-first-century Toronto.

With the advent of automated vehicles, the car has become one of a number of smart devices, a service we can call up when we need it. This in turn has liberated many who were not able to drive themselves. As this change has occurred, the attrition of private automobile use has provided a host of new design opportunities and challenges from all the above- and below-grade space in the form of garages it has liberated.

Making more room for nature in the heart of our city has shown us that we can become better stewards of our land. The experience on the Leslie Street Spit proved that the city and nature (even when artificially created) are indissoluble, compatible, and mutually reinforcing. From the lake to the watersheds that define our geography to the byways of city itself, into buildings and even onto roofs, we are seeing the benefits. We are continuing to grow greener as we grow denser. We have made significant inroads in urban agriculture throughout the city in interstitial spaces and on rooftops.

The augmented presence of nature in the city has proven to be the great form changer. It has softened the hard lines of the gridded, rectilinear city with the reassertion of the more organic forms of Toronto's great natural features — the lakefront, our river valleys and ravines. These green spaces have become among our most cherished and prominent public gathering places with a rich variety of amenities, interconnected throughout the entire city by extensive networks of linked trails.

We are sharing more common ground, living with less personal space, but compensated with a much greater variety and generosity of public spaces. Toronto has continued to reclaim many spaces that were off limits or simply undervalued, like the Bentway. This phenomenon expanded dramatically and the city is now traversed and punctuated by extensive green and sociable networks. These new forms of public space, often with shared community management and stewardship, have provided the impetus for an expanded commitment to civic life.

Two compelling major demonstrations of the potential for utilizing found space have been realized, despite early doubts. The announcement in 2017 by Mayor John Tory and Councillor Joe Cressy to pursue a major twenty-one-acre urban park above the open rail corridor from Bathurst Street to Blue Jays Way had garnered considerable excitement both in the community and among design professionals. It was a creative and timely response to the great need, both locally and city-wide, for additional park space given the extraordinary growth in population already experienced by that time. It has now been skillfully implemented in a form that provides an iconic park and at the same time vital connections between a number of dense new neighbourhoods on both sides of the rail corridor, turning what was once a barrier into a magnificent new highly accessible "common ground" serving all Torontonians.

The second dramatic demonstration of this potential was the consolidated "Lakefront Park" created by fusing the 270-acre combined sites of Exhibition Place and Ontario Place. The large surface parking lots on both sides of Lakeshore Boulevard have been replaced by a grand new public gathering place on the water, including recreation, entertainment, major annual events, theatres, marinas, art galleries, outdoor restaurants, a revived amphitheatre, and restoration of the pods and the IMAX Dome. This magnificent new park extends the emerald arm across the waterfront from Humber Bay to Coronation Park. It is easily accessible via the new waterfront LRT and all-day GO service.

With a great new land bridge over Lakeshore Boulevard, the consolidated Lakefront Park, with its protected waterways and naturalized landscape, traversed by the Martin Goodman Trail, has become a jewel on the Toronto waterfront, serving Torontonians but also drawing visitors from around the world and contributing to a powerful new image for the city. The province made a great start on this in 2017 with the wonderful new addition of Trillium Park at the east end of Ontario Place, and work is now largely complete on the rest of the site.

Toronto is now traversed by extensive green and sociable networks as one of the legacies of a post-industrial age. This has increased physical and psychological access to the city, offering a new form of democratic public space in a powerful reversal of the postwar retreat from life in public spaces. These linear networks have proven to be a low-cost, high-impact solution addressing many needs and offering multiple benefits: health, active transportation, reconnection with the restorative powers of nature in the city, connecting us with each other, providing common ground in a form that is free. These spaces have also been a spur to economic development and a stimulus to ecotourism.

Unlike the more formal public spaces of previous eras, the new generation of public spaces conveys a very different feeling. Often opportunistic, they have been improvised and contain many episodic surprises. The new sensibilities in play for the public realm, like the city itself, tend to be multivalent and overlapping, linear and organic, weaving through the city and intertwined with natural and infrastructural systems. The new green sinews penetrate and open up the city in areas that were formerly *terra incognita*. Unlike the city's grand and formal front-of-the-house spaces, these new spaces provide a unique vantage point and back-of-house experience that is in tune with the complex, overlapping, multi-layered condition of contemporary life.

This twenty-first-century version of the mind-and-body sensorial experience echoes the allure of the untravelled road, but in another form. Venturing into uncharted territory is deeply satisfying psychologically, combining discovery and self-discovery.

For many, the pretext for getting outdoors is to stretch our bodies and enjoy the health benefits of exercise, increased cardiovascular stimulation, and movement of our limbs outside the gym or fitness centre. But outdoor experience is much more than exercise. Moving self-propelled at relatively low speeds restores the intuitive geographic understanding of spatial relationships that the car had weakened — a feel for the real distances between things, a sense that it's all connected. The kinetic feeling in navigating these networks is exhilarating. The city is revealing itself in new ways. More than exercise, it offers a chance to commune with our neighbours.

Is this description of a future Toronto too idealistic? Perhaps. It would be foolhardy not to acknowledge that the way to get from A to B is inevitably messy and contested, with many twists and turns. The churn is chaotic, but I am convinced that there is an underlying positive forward motion. This is a decisive moment for our city and many of the conditions for this transformation are already present. The fusion of these trends, all ongoing works in progress — the renewing and reshaping of whole city districts as well as individual buildings and landscapes, the availability of more and better ways of navigating the city, and the filling of strategic vacuums — are all on the horizon now. This is really not so big a leap; no part of this vision is beyond our grasp and capacity, and every aspect is already starting to appear in some form and in some places. Their great power lies in their purposeful combination as we go forward.

There is an intense chicken-and-egg relationship between the form of the city and the lives we live, the ways in which we relate to each other, our propensity to do or not do things. The shift in our mores as the city evolves is every bit as significant as the changes we make to the physical environment. One of the things we pick up on immediately when we watch films from earlier decades set in cities is how different everything looks:

the buildings, the cars, the lack of cell phones or computers on every desk. But along with the physical differences is how differently people relate to each other — the way they talk, body language, dress — male-female relationships, or how minorities are portrayed. As the city evolves, all of these patterns, behaviours, and expectations are evolving too.

So let's return momentarily to this possible future. There is an evolving DNA informed by the weight of our collective memory of what was, what is, and what waits on the horizon, shaping our ways of being denizens of the city, our expectations of each other. In recent decades we were living in a world where we had the luxury of spreading out. As we found ourselves sharing spaces in more compact neighbourhoods, a combination of urban newcomers — often young people living on their own for the first time and from an increasingly polyglot mix of cultures with as many ideas as to what constitutes acceptable behaviour — found themselves thrown together in close quarters.

With the switch to denser, apartment-style living, chance encounters multiplied and that meant becoming more conscious about how we interact, sharing public space and negotiating a whole new set of relationships as part of city life. We needed to find new ways of interacting. In this period of transition, frustrating situations came to light as we bumped into each other, in some cases literally. Whether it was conflicts among drivers, cyclists, and pedestrians; or dog walkers and young families with kids in parks; or fighting over closing hours for local pubs and restaurant terraces in residential neighbourhoods; or making room for seniors in transit vehicles; or knowing how to use hand-held devices in public, we no longer had the luxury of avoiding friction by using space as a buffer, doing our own things but barely touching each other.

Living in a big city doesn't take away the human need to trust that our fellow citizens will show some level of respect, to feel welcome and safe, to take pride in and ownership of our surroundings. We do this wonderfully in times of great adversity, and come to each other's aid in crises, but what about the rest of the time? We use the term *civility,* from the Latin *civilis* (meaning *proper to a citizen*), to describe how we believe people should behave in relation to others. As we changed our living patterns, we also needed to become more mindful of others and our impacts.

Over time, every city develops its unspoken codes, along with the more formal written laws and regulations that shape the course of daily life and frame the ways people experience each other as fellow citizens and members of society and make life bearable, even pleasurable. All things being equal, the real measures of successful urbanity may be in the demonstrations of mutual respect, the degree to which we are comfortable with each other, the room we make for children and seniors, the tolerance and even embrace of our differences, and the accumulation of small acts of kindness. Our interactions can be gruff, teasing, and humorous, or inquisitive and friendly; they can involve some measure of risk but still speak to some sense of fellow feeling and connection to our shared sense of place.

Torontonians have been making this profound shift in how we live together in our city, and the conflicts described above were in many cases enviable problems of urban success experienced as growing pains. We have demonstrated considerable capacity to adjust. For proof that such adaptation was possible, we had only to look at things like the changing attitudes to smoking in public, the success of "poop and scoop," garbage recycling, and the move to universal access.

It was a matter of seeing the greater good rather than a zero-sum game. It took education, both formal and informal, and understanding as we redesigned the city's spaces for twenty-first-century use. Here are several prime examples of conflicts that played themselves out in Toronto as we struggled to navigate the transition to becoming true urbanites in an inclusive city. They all involved noticing and being more mindful of others and our impacts on them, and recalibrating our expectations.

Perhaps the most obvious one had to do with cars and sharing the roads among pedestrians, cyclists, transit users, and drivers. Impatient drivers had become more aggressive as more and more pedestrians and cyclists claimed their rightful place in the right-of-way. Uncertainty was a major problem; improvising doesn't work well when there are no shared expectations. Drivers simply had to get used to slowing down and occupying less space. Cyclists, when there are many and they had a safe place to ride, tended to be much more considerate. Peer pressure and follow-the-leader patterns kicked in while waiting at lights, queuing at intersections, and staying off sidewalks. Pedestrians too, clearly the most vulnerable travellers, also had to become more mindful. Walking while absorbed in hand-held devices, oblivious to others and bumping into people who are sharing the space while texting, was not okay.

We also had to get better at sharing space in transit vehicles — street-cars, buses, and subways — accommodating seniors, parents with strollers, and those who are physically challenged, voluntarily helping people on and off when help seems needed, giving directions to strangers when they seem to be lost. This was particularly stressful until relief was provided by new lines. In all these cases, small gestures of kindness and consideration became the measures of a civilized city. The eight-year-old and the eighty-year-old both feeling safe and comfortable is the litmus test — 8 80 Cities had it right.

With more people came more dogs, and their owners became very assertive about claiming space in parks and open spaces for off-leash dog runs, or simply let their dogs loose in parks without such facilities. There was an incredible proliferation of dog ownership, especially among young people, and often more than one dog per household. In my neighbourhood it was estimated that over 50 percent of new units produce a dog. Dog walking and dog playing (often with ball-throwing devices for greater distance) began to place an extraordinary demand on parks while also creating a whole new form of socializing, which occurs several times a day.

But this demand was increasing at the same time that other park uses were also growing, and young families wanted to be in the same parks with their kids, who were often fearful around large dogs running freely. This was leading to unfortunate animosity as each side jealously guarded its prerogatives and protected its turf. A fair negotiation of the rules and a protocol for the sharing of spaces was clearly needed. In many places, clearly defined on-leash and off-leash areas were successfully established, but sometimes there was just not enough room for all those who wanted to use park space. Help came in the form of buildings designed to provide their own internal dog runs, often on rooftops; and eventually the amount of green space grew and become better connected and more accessible. But in the meantime, forbearance, acknowledging the needs of the other, and a willingness to compromise were needed, along with enforcement of necessary rules.

Another set of issues arose inside buildings as we lived in closer quarters: controlling noise levels and keeping the buildings clean and well maintained. And unanticipated challenges, like excessive subletting of units for Airbnb with a steady flow of transients in buildings not designed for this kind of use, required new regulations. Similarly, restaurants, cafés, and clubs within and next to residences, especially those with outdoor patios, while enlivening their neighbourhoods, raised legitimate concerns. Controlling the level of the music on patios and termination times, avoiding closing-time rowdiness and antisocial behaviour like throwing beer bottles and cigarette butts — in short, respecting the presence of others — became the necessary preconditions that made sharing the neighbourhood space possible and agreeable. It was part of life in the big city, but as more things were introduced to the mix, it became increasingly necessary to imagine their impacts, and new rules and expectations had to be negotiated.

The ways in which this all got worked out were particular to Toronto, and drew on our local politics, culture and traditions, and unique diversity. These were used as assets and catalysts as we figured out ways to work things out together. In Toronto's case, these urban growing pains were compounded by the fact that we were forging a new urban society out of a collection of many cultures all thrown together, with as many different cultural practices, customs, and social habits.

To make this connection, we needed to step out of our personal spaces and actually acknowledge each other, not avert our eyes. This may seem antiquated in a world of ubiquitous hand-held devices and the temptation to tune out face-to-face contact, but it was critically important to see each other and make eye contact as we recognized each other's presence and needs.

The critical ingredient, and perhaps our greatest asset, was a wellspring of mutual respect. Back in 2018, while standing in the crowd at the memorial in Willowdale, I had a powerful sense of something special and rare — and it didn't feel like it was just for the moment. There was a palpable fellow feeling of compassion and good will emanating from this group of individuals from the entire world assembled together in Mel Lastman Square and spilling out onto the sidewalk and adjoining roof terraces. It felt like we all belonged to something bigger than ourselves as Torontonians, without giving up our individual identities in any way. We were not family, or clans, or tribes, but citizens in a complex, diverse, and inclusive city with a sense that we were stronger and better off by being together.

To realize this optimistic vision of a future Toronto, one that capitalizes on this special advantage, growing denser, more prosperous, and more equitable together, will mean overcoming a number of critical challenges that will test our mettle.

10

Unleashing the Power of the City

Back to the present. On the one hand, there has never been such broad understanding of the importance of city building. At a very high level we get it. Politicians, city staff, agencies, the general public, and business people including many developers are convinced of the value of integrated place making, incorporating the full range of ingredients that go into making successful urban places. On the other hand, every discussion of Toronto's future tends to end up with a review of a familiar set of daunting challenges. Some of these, like housing affordability and runaway congestion, are problems of success in a period of extraordinary growth. The city is now playing catch up, having to make major investments in affordable housing and public services both hard and soft to accommodate the major increases and changing needs of our population. We have accumulated a serious infrastructure deficit and we have failed for decades to make essential investments in public transit. Our narrow sidewalks and poorly designed streets are jammed and uncomfortable. Many of our public spaces are meagre and poorly equipped and maintained. So how can we ensure that our city will be truly equitable and inclusive in the face of its newfound popularity?

This intimidating list could be cause for despair. But in discussions amongst those attending to the current state of the city and its future, there is usually a fierce affirmation that despite all these challenges, Toronto is a remarkable city; its population is engaged, resourceful, talented, and doing all kinds of extraordinary things, and we are for the most part grateful to be here. Our biggest test as a city lies in bridging the gap between imperfect reality and aspiration, putting our better understanding of what the city is capable of into practice.

It is increasingly clear that we can no longer afford to solve one problem at a time, in isolation from other issues. The key to unlocking our true potential as a city is convergence, moving away from compartmentalizing things; blending public and private initiatives; working across disciplinary lines. While it is undoubtedly true that Toronto (and other Canadian cities) are underfunded net exporters of wealth and, at the same time, short-changed on the resources they should be getting back from senior levels of government, that is not the whole story. There are many things that we can do better ourselves, using the assets and resources we do have to greater advantage, and that is what I want to focus on in this chapter. We need to better exploit the inherent capacity of the city to solve multiple problems laterally, not one at a time, embracing Jane Jacobs's profound insight that cities are not mechanical constructs, but phenomena of "organized complexity" better understood by analogy with natural habitats where everything is connected to everything else.

We have discovered that only by making the city dense, walkable, and compact can we reduce our heavy environmental footprint and address the devastating progress of climate change. We know that social inclusion and a sense of belonging for our entire population contributes to productivity, competitiveness, and sustainability. When we make expensive investments in transit infrastructure, we have to also make the corridors and stops into active "hubs," not just by issuing planning permissions, but by creating proactive initiatives to get more people living and working there; otherwise these investments will underperform. We need to use our existing civic buildings and spaces more effectively. For example, creating shared-use "community schools," available outside of school hours for evening classes and community recreation, allows for better use of scarce building resources that otherwise sit empty for long periods of time.

Only by aligning priorities, embracing the perspective of convergence, and pulling issues out of their assigned silos does it become possible to achieve multiple goals. Cross-sector collaboration and strategic partnerships are essential if we are to expand affordable housing options for a diverse population, reinvent our economic base, and retool our infrastructure to improve mobility.

We intuitively understand that these major challenges are interconnected. But while this new way of seeing the city is widely shared in many quarters — citizens, professionals, decision makers — there is a serious time lag between this intellectual realization and the implementation of this new way of thinking. Our inherited civic machinery often still functions as if these challenges occupied separate spheres both inside and outside of city hall.

City government is still, for the most part, organized into functional silos. Planners deal with land use, transportation engineers with moving vehicles, designers with buildings and landscapes, municipal engineers with the arrangement of services, and so on. Even though our thinking has changed radically, the traditional departmental structure set up to deal with specific problems in isolation too often remains intact. This structure is in basic conflict with how city building actually works. It is challenging to accomplish innovative city building projects if forced to feed them into these bureaucratic stovepipes.

To use a medical analogy, we have lots of specialists but few GPs looking at the whole person. We have an assembly line mentality that focuses on discrete products. We still have a legacy of practices that fosters fragmentation: looking at finances with limited objectives and short-term horizons, outmoded planning tools that cannot integrate dynamic processes, and public policies that operate at cross purposes.

Here is a telling example of planning policy and fiscal policy at complete odds. It concerns the building known as 401 Richmond Street. This celebrated landmark project rehabilitated a large, formerly industrial building and brought together a vast array of non-profits, cultural organizations, artists, galleries, bookstores, and cafés in a highly synergistic and renowned cluster just off Spadina Avenue in the heart of King and Spadina, the former warehouse district — a planning success by any standard.

But the future of this award-winning project was threatened when a property tax bill arrived in December 2016. It became clear that the application of market value assessment by MPAC, the Municipal Property

Assessment Corporation, (based on the assumption that the "highest and best" use for this property was the erection of a forty-storey condo in its place, like those on neighbouring sites) would produce an extraordinary tax burden that would make this whole enterprise unviable. This caused a public outcry and sent city and provincial politicians scrambling to lay blame and find solutions.

What this situation revealed was a problem of disconnects. When there is an across-the-board assessment of properties by the criterion of highest and best use (the most profitable), that is, when pure financial terms are the only ones taken into consideration, properties with cultural uses are not able to compete and would be exiled, undermining the city's planning objectives. Fiscal tools and planning tools were not being seen or used in unison. Eventually, both levels of government worked to find a fix and came up with a special category of cultural use projects eligible for a tax break.

Unfortunately, this is not an isolated incident. The 401 Richmond case is one example of how the law of unintended consequences is affecting the thousands of small, independent retail businesses that make Toronto's neighbourhoods vibrant, and how provincial tax policies may be killing the goose that lays the golden egg.

And here is another example. The public sector has created a self-imposed impediment to integrated transit-oriented development: the system that Metrolinx and Infrastructure Ontario use for the selection of private sector bidders to finance, design, build, and operate transit lines and stations. To mitigate cost overruns and pass potential financial risk on to the private sector, the system requires carefully defined project delineations with inviolable contract limits. These have had the unfortunate and perhaps unintended consequence of making it very difficult, if not impossible, to fully integrate the design of stations with surrounding "transit hubs" (a key planning objective), or leverage opportunities for stations to be built right into adjoining buildings as part of a development itself. Decades ago, the TTC managed to integrate development with all of its subway stations on the downtown loop of the Yonge-University subway line. The new rules, however, designed to control the limits of the contract, had the consequence of reducing opportunities for better integration of city-building activities surrounding a capital project. They have inhibited exactly the kind of integrated place-making that is desirable for city building. The good news is that this problem has now been acknowledged and the rules are changing to encourage integrated development.

Once we accept cities as dynamic, constantly evolving organisms, it becomes clear that we need more supple ways of working, harnessing our new understanding of city dynamics and using contemporary interactive tools. This change is a little like the one required to get from classical scores to the improvisational qualities of jazz. It requires a cognitive leap from the ways things are currently done, a disruptive shift that leads to new ways of solving problems and organizing systems.

Toronto's challenge is to create integrated solutions at the intersection of economy, community, and environment. We need a whole new way of working holistically, inside and outside government, that skillfully weaves together targeted public-sector and private-sector efforts to advance larger, shared visions for the city through policies that shape and guide decisions; programs to implement change through allocation of resources; plans that apply new thinking; projects, concrete manifestations of change, and, increasingly, pilots to test the waters.

I want to focus on an area that I believe can have the greatest impact on the city. It is about who is at the table. Jane Jacobs famously said, "Cities have the capability of providing something for everybody, only because, and only when, they are created by everybody." For city building to succeed in Toronto, it has to be done in a highly transparent environment that provides affected communities a place at the table. There are many opportunities to embrace this city's active and engaged civil society. Inclusive planning and execution of projects will enable us to tap all the available resources, including the skills, in-kind services, and volunteer efforts of previously marginalized citizens. The result is a more motivated, inventive, and agile team approach.

In many ways the people of the city have been way ahead of the city's government in staking out new territory. These civic actors can dramatically enhance the capacity of city; we need to go beyond the idea that government should do it alone, and open the doors to city hall in bold new ways. A greater integration of bottom-up and top-down involvement will not only enable us to do more with less, but will also greatly enhance our capacity for honest discussions of hard issues and thoughtful risk-taking on seemingly intractable issues. Virtually all of the transformations described in previous chapters have involved innovative new forms of partnership.

As part of this renewed way of operating, we need to draw on the knowledge and experience of Toronto's highly motivated and skilled civic entrepreneurs and civic innovators: powerful and effective umbrella groups like Waterfront for All, Park People, 8 80 Cities, CivicAction, Greening Greater Toronto, People Plan Toronto, coalitions of neighbourhood and citizens' groups, BIAs, and institutional civic actors like the Canadian Urban Institute, the Ryerson City Building Institute, and the School of Cities at U of T, among many others. We need to bring more of the energy and inventiveness of civil society into the public sphere. We need to be more resourceful and imaginative. Where public resources fall short, we need to enter into partnerships — for example, in the improvement and care of parks and public spaces — to fill the gaps. In the past, city hall's response to these ideas has at times been lukewarm. It is now time for that to change.

Private companies and professionals are moving away from compartmentalization. Increasingly, work is being done across disciplinary lines, and projects are being connected within a much larger, more dynamic city-building enterprise. The Lower Don Lands planning effort is an example of this new kind of linkage, led by Waterfront Toronto with the support of the city, which simultaneously tackled flood proofing, land reclamation, urban redevelopment, the extension of transportation networks and municipal infrastructure, and parks creation. These diverse goals could only be successfully addressed through comprehensive design that drew on cross-disciplinary problem solving.

We need to learn to speak each other's languages, learn to function as team players and synthesizers with allied professionals. The nature of such teamwork demands an extended dialogue. New, less hierarchical approaches to problem solving have emerged. Easy-to-use communications technology now facilitate rapid information sharing, allowing for the layering of many complex variables from various disciplines. A greater number and variety of kinds of knowledge and skill sets are being added to the creative process, helping to expand our understanding of situations of increasing complexity. Increasingly, successful problem solving requires contributions from various engineering specialties — civil, municipal, transportation, marine; economists and market specialists in different sectors, including community development; environmental scientists, ecologists, hydrologists; sociologists, community service providers; artists and arts organizations, among others. This broad fusion of expertise and knowledge is not compromising — it enables richer and better outcomes.

Echoing these changes in the professional world, there needs to be a parallel move toward integration at city hall within and among departments and agencies. We need a retooled civil service for a new era, one that embraces teamwork and breaks down its internal silos. Cross-functional teams will help to incentivize interdisciplinary teamwork. The city's response to the Bentway, which combined staff from a half a dozen departments within the city, was a model of such teamwork.

To deal more effectively with the tsunami of development applications Toronto is now receiving, the city must change its response to be more flexible and strategic. It must more proactively identify and address both problems and opportunities and become more engaged with outside actors and the private sector in ways both informal and formal. It needs to be more open to cross-disciplinary thinking, more involved in long-range strategic thinking, while at the same time more open to immediate actions and catalytic projects. This requires a continual balancing of the city's "guardian" and "entrepreneurial" roles, drawing on the enterprise of the private sector while defending the public interest, seeking mutually reinforcing wins that straddle this divide.

To be fair to city staff, the city's ability to argue in favour of the public interest has been significantly hobbled in the past. One of the underlying problems bedevilling planning in Toronto has been the city's long-standing subjugation to the Ontario Municipal Board. This controversial, unelected body operated as an adjudicative tribunal, set up by the province to hear applications and appeals on municipal and planning disputes. It was criticized for its overly broad powers and willingness on occasion to override the wishes of cities who wished to control development. Fortunately for Toronto and the other municipalities in Ontario, the OMB was replaced by the Local Planning Appeal Tribunal on April 3, 2018. The new body has more limited powers and a reduced scope. It is just beginning to function, and it will be important to see how things actually change.

The highly problematic OMB was a symbol of the impotence and perceived immaturity of the City of Toronto when it came to charting its own course. The OMB distorted the planning process in Toronto — misallocating resources, sapping energy, and frequently producing poor outcomes. Enormous amounts of money were spent, not on better design or planning, but on legalistic gladiatorial exercises. Developers seeking approval for projects that were in conflict with the city's planning regulations quickly came to recognize that it was expedient to have lawyer-led teams. Legal manipulation came to be of paramount importance; architecture and landscape were downplayed and design fees shortchanged. Communities pleading their position before the board typically suffered from highly inequitable treatment, since they usually had less access to resources and power. This arrangement produced great uncertainty for city planners and great cynicism amongst those citizens with an interest in planning and architecture.

Seeing every application as a potential appeal to this body was paralyzing for the city, and led to an enormous and unhelpful diversion of staff resources and attention. In the adversarial atmosphere of an OMB hearing, the so-called "objective" quantifiable issues took precedence over the qualitative. In a strange anomaly, city and community witnesses were not allowed to talk about design, which was seen as subjective (as evidenced in the decisions), when in fact design was precisely what people wanted to talk about — not in abstracted, technical terms, but in terms of its impact on actual places. The province has now given Toronto an opportunity to wean itself from this embarrassing subservience. We need to take advantage of it to change the planning agenda, from litigious skirmishes with unpredictable outcomes to proactively guiding change.

The new Local Planning Appeal Tribunal (LPAT) came into effect on April 4, 2018. In theory the legislation that created this body includes reforms that, according to the government's description, will reduce the number of appeals by limiting what can be brought before the new tribunal; reduce the length and cost of hearings and create a more level playing field for all participants by introducing timelines and requiring the new tribunal to look for ways, like mediation, to settle major land use planning appeals that could avoid the hearing process altogether; eliminate lengthy and often confrontational examinations and cross-examinations of witnesses by parties and their lawyers at the oral hearings of major land use planning appeals; establish a Local Planning Appeal Support Centre, a new provincial agency, which will provide citizens with information about the land use planning appeal process, legal and planning advice, and, in certain cases, may provide legal representation in proceedings before the tribunal and give more weight to key decisions made by municipal officials who have been elected to serve in the interests of the communities they represent.

One of the ways the OMB had shaped the city's development style was to encourage a checklist approach to standards and rules that could be defended. These were broken down within functional categories — urban design guidelines, heritage prescriptions, park space standards, servicing and loading dock standards — often advanced independently by different staff units. In many cases the application of these prescriptive templates didn't fit well on actual sites and was internally inconsistent or conflicting. Now that the arbitrary power of the OMB to approve outlandish height and density in inappropriate locations has been reduced, we can hope to enter a new era where the city can be more creative and look at place-based design more holistically.

As the legislation was being prepared, I joined developer and former lawyer Steve Diamond, former Toronto chief planner Paul Bedford, and former OMB chair Peter Howden in making some proposals to the government that would have strengthened the planning function at the city level in conjunction with the replacement of the OMB. Among other things, we advocated establishing autonomous local area planning advisory committees (PACs) with a range of skill sets and expertise to make recommendations to City Council on all site-specific development applications and site-specific official plan amendments. While Council would still have had the final say, these PACs would have introduced independent, non-political voices into the process to offset parochial ward politics, which sometimes proves resistant to desirable changes. This proposal was not incorporated. It remains to be seen how city staff will take advantage of this new situation to modify their modus operandi.

As is the case in the consulting world, the city needs "places of convergence" in city hall where insights can be pooled, and ways to visualize and represent overlapping constraints and opportunities. When there is an opportunity to pitch new ideas in a collaborative environment, we expand the collective "brain" of the team and, in a sense, simulate the complexity of real-world conditions. The expanded team works together from start to finish — building the entire car together, as it were, rather than by the fragmented method of the assembly line. My teams have often discovered that the solution to a problem in one area actually resides in another. Some would argue that the city lacks the time or the resources to build this kind of collaboration into city hall, but the opposite is actually true. It is a much quicker and more efficient way to resolve differences and solve problems.

Lest this seem impossible, it is interesting to see what the dynamic, contemporary city of Helsinki has done to reshape its municipal structure through a radical overhaul begun over a year ago and led by Mayor Jan Vapaavuori. Like Toronto, Helsinki is in the midst of a truly remarkable stage of urban evolution as the city's population grows at an accelerating rate. The overt goal of the Helsinki City Strategy is to make it the world's most functional city. Helsinki is already highly functional in many respects; it ranks highly in a number of international surveys of quality of life, education, the environment, and safety. But Helsinki's policy-makers and leaders did not rest on their laurels. They have embraced the role of cities in solving major global challenges, and understand the need to be solution oriented and agile in the search for answers to the challenges of social segregation, climate change, public participation, and digitalization.

Helsinki was facing a set of challenges similar to Toronto's, like runaway congestion and housing affordability, problems of success in a period of extraordinary growth. In Helsinki, the city politicians recognized that the established civic machinery often still functioned as if these interrelated problems occupied separate spheres, both inside and outside of city hall. Clearly, a new way of working was needed. The Helsinki City Council made a bold decision at its meeting on June 22, 2016, creating a new City of Helsinki governance system. Some thirty former city departments have been abolished and replaced by four integrated divisions: Education, Urban Environment, Culture and Leisure, and Social Services and Health Care.

Helsinki's new structure was organized around today's priorities, and created fully integrated teams to improve outcomes and get more out of limited resources while making city government more accountable, accessible, and transparent. Senior city staff reported to me that the change seems to be working, and the early results are truly impressive, including facilitating the creation of new mixed-use, mixed-income neighbourhoods with an abundance of well-maintained public space and amenities. While the reform has not been painless, the need was obvious, and they are excited about the results. Obviously, we in Toronto can't simply cut and paste the Helsinki reform onto our city, but there is a great deal Toronto could learn from what Helsinki is doing.

Building on my early experiences working, with others, on a smaller-scale convergence model in Toronto, I helped to set up a Saint Paul design centre when I worked with the City of Saint Paul, Minnesota. With its own director and a small staff, the design centre had a core membership of individuals who worked within city hall as "city designers" in various capacities, plus a larger ancillary group of staff from the county and other agencies. This design centre continues to provide a forum where design and city-building concepts are explored together by city planners and architects in Planning and Economic Development, landscape architects in the Parks Department, Building Department officials, and transportation and civil engineers in Public Works.

It is now also clear that shared and holistic city teamwork needs to extend well beyond project implementation into the ongoing stewardship of built projects, including the maintenance, programming, and operation of public space. Here, too, we have a problem of silos. In the aftermath of Toronto's amalgamation, the city's Parks, Forestry and Recreation Division adopted a "flying squad" model in which city crews and contractors rotate in and out of parks to perform a single, narrowly defined task, like cutting the grass. With this system, workers often do not appear in the same park twice, and no one person has a sense of the whole park or its local community. There is evidence to suggest that moving from the current "flying squad" model to a "zone-based" model, one with local on-site park managers who have a deeper, more visible presence in parks, would result in parks that are better maintained.

The situation is even more complicated when a type of public space needs care that does not fall into a conventional category. In Wellington Place, the forty-five-metre right-of-way Wellington Street forms a "linear park" within the street right-of-way, but since it is not a typical, discrete park with its own piece of property, the division of Parks, Forestry and Recreation will not look after it. Nor does it fall under the usual mandate of Transportation Services. As a result, it is orphaned and neglected, relying on the haphazard efforts of adjoining property owners. This is a real problem as we look to create more and more of this kind of in-between linking public space.

Toronto does have some great exceptions to the rule. In parks like the Toronto Music Garden, Grange Park, and Corktown Common, assigned gardeners take special care and receive special training for these signature spaces. In these cases, there is a holistic view of a place. Toronto parks are incredibly important in the life of communities, and local park employees and supervisors serve as ambassadors, often the first point of contact that residents have when they want to do something in their park — host an event, for example. Making their presence more visible and adding a community-engagement role to their duties would be highly beneficial. Park People originally proposed this in its Parks Platform for the 2014 election, and it still has merit.

Toronto also needs to open the doors at city hall wider and make the post-amalgamation mega-bureaucracy more responsive to citizens. In many ways, the forced and contested amalgamation of 1998, which pleased almost no one, is the root cause of much of Toronto's discontent. There are times when it is important to recognize that a fundamental error has been made and this one needs to be revisited if the city is to progress. Torontonians need a governance structure that is both broader, to strengthen the regional GTHA level overview, and more fine-grained , to break the "megacity" down into more autonomous and knowable units, ones with more decision-making authority. The remedy may not be a straight reversal of amalgamation. Bridges have been burned, and the expense would be unbearable. But there are many ways to achieve a balancing of scales. Much bigger cities than Toronto have figured out ways to decentralize many of their functions while at the same time maintaining a mastery of their metropolitan dimension. New York City, for example, functions well with its fifty-nine community boards, made up of paid staff and citizen representatives. Toronto needs to find its own version.

The whole and the parts play complementary roles in a multicentred region, and each part needs to be respected for its difference and its contribution to the overall diversity of the region. To get beyond the false and manufactured dichotomies that have been exploited to divide us — suburban versus downtown — it is necessary to address the underlying disparities that have fostered the perceived gulf between the city's constituent parts, and articulate an integrated vision for a sustainable city region and its neighbourhoods, one supported by a politics of inclusion inside and outside the current city limits. Many constructive ideas have been put forward, such as creating a mixed municipal governance structure that combines the existing system, with a councillor elected for each ward, with at-large councillors who bring a city-wide perspective to council and foster greater cross-municipal boundary collaboration. This, of course, has now been made more complication by the dramatic reduction in the number of Toronto city councillors.

As we enlarge the table to include more actors in city building, we also need to find new ways of working with the real city — not an imagined, more orderly surrogate. Our large and complex city is by its nature highly diverse and eclectic, and should be allowed to continue that way. Its contrasting layers and idiosyncrasies — its stitched together, improvised street grid; its radical juxtaposition of buildings of different ages, sizes, shapes, styles, and uses; its accumulation of formal and informal public spaces — are part of its identity, part of its charm. The city does not lend itself well to standardization. There should be less preoccupation with "harmonization" or trying to find one-size-fits-all solutions for the entire city, a tendency that came with amalgamation.

We need a different set of planning tools, those often described as "strategic planning," "action strategies," "open-ended frameworks," or, a term I like, "unofficial plans," terms which express a more forward-looking, innovative, entrepreneurial, and flexible approach. These frameworks are no longer just about the regulation of the height, use, and density of development projects. They are rooted in guiding principles, not formulaic prescriptions, using simple tools like built-form envelopes (three dimensional volumes that designers can fill in different ways) that refer to scales, relationship to streets and sidewalks, expanding the vocabulary of public spaces, adding life and vitality to the first ten metres above sidewalk level, identifying on-site and neighbourhood contributions to larger city initiatives such as TOcore.

It's all about relationships, rather than perscription. We can describe these desired relationships — but then leave a lot more room for design creativity to achieve the desired outcomes. Most importantly, every project has to be looked at *sui generis* to assess its unique opportunities, not just through the lens of predetermined formulae. This involves making trade-offs and compromises among competing objectives for heritage, parks, urban design, planning, and transportation to ensure that the whole is greater than its component parts.

The critical leap we have to make is the acceptance of a certain level of indeterminacy. The planning and design of cities will be increasingly about the anticipation and guidance of long-term transformations without fixed destinations, mediating between values, goals, and actual outcomes. Consistent with this open-ended stance, the true test for urban design is to achieve coherence and build relationships, but still leave ample room for the emergence of new ideas, market and social innovations, not overly predetermining outcomes but allowing for added levels of creativity in the translation.

Rigid city plans and traditional zoning ordinances do not hold up well when market forces, changing programs, new needs, and a highly diverse context come into play. We need to make room for innovation, hybridization, organic growth, change, and surprise. This open-endedness is challenging to the kind of planning that aspires to an illusory end-state predictability, but need to enlarge the current gene pool of built form solutions for densification including the many versions of the "missing middle" density in places where it is most needed. It is about an understanding of the play of time, and reaping the benefits of a guided incrementalism.

Combining the talents and resources of the public, not for profit, and private sectors. Allowing things to evolve and self-organize. Seen in this liberating light, the city is a serial creation; one thing leads to another and you don't quite know where it's going to go, but there is room for unexpected things to happen. The planning framework has to be open-ended enough to allow for desirable modifications as opportunities arise, with clear principles and goals but room for flexibility in the interpretation.

Neighbourhood building is a dialectical process of call-and-response and the framework needs to be a living tool responsive to feedback loops as needs evolve. As development proceeds there are incremental investments in public space, providing more neighbourhood amenities, playgrounds, daycare, recreation, and so on to keep up with the pace of population growth.

The city will always have to be responsible for certain things, like the coherence, adequacy, and longevity of the public realm and infrastructure, against more temporal and changeable forms of use and occupancy. But I think the big lesson for everyone involved — including the city — is that we don't have to know everything in advance, we don't have to be able to quantify and locate everything to know exactly how much of this, that, or the other use will be there. In a climate that allows for testing and experimentation, there has to be room for the formal and the informal, the permanent and the temporary in the form of pop-ups and pilots as new ideas emerge and are tested out. Those responsible have to be able to respond and make judgments as opportunities come forward to the different kind of changes that are occurring and be flexible in welcoming desirable change even when unanticipated.

Recently, I worked with the City of Edmonton on the creation of a "Connectivity Framework" to track and guide the evolution of this rapidly growing city. At this stage in Edmonton's evolution, things are moving much too fast for the old paradigm to cope effectively. The goal of the framework is to get Edmonton from a "good city to a great city," developing a dynamic two- and three-dimensional tool that provides an overview of all downtown plans in time and space. This digital framework depicts the downtown both as it is and how it is evolving, adding a historical dimension. At once we can examine how historic forces like the river and the removal of rail yards, as well as new interventions, can be harnessed to help shape the mono-functional central business district into a mixed and vibrant lived-in downtown. This tool shows catalytic projects underway and engagingly displays the achievement of the city's transformational goals.

The framework provides an ability to get all layers "on the same page," much like a Google map with its zoom feature; it has the ability to delve down into individual project areas in more detail. It can harness the city's GIS capabilities to see how the downtown is evolving as a dynamic set of relationships and possibilities, many of which are mutually reinforcing one another, including land uses, modal shifts, changing demographics, and economic metrics.

Framework tools like this one can be extremely useful in simulating outcomes and doing anticipatory planning for communities faced with an endless stream of one-at-a-time development applications, each proposing to go higher and larger, but without a clear sense of their cumulative impact. It can enable an informed conversation about change that brings together communities, developers, designers, and city planners. The key is to be involved at the early stages and develop a proactive stance. Every area has some opportunities for change. It is important to identify and define them, whether they are former industrial sites, under-built commercial properties, or infill sites.

We need qualitative, place-related descriptions of a shared community vision supported by principles and illustrations to map out and anticipate public realm opportunities; housing needs, community services, and amenities for anticipated population increases; economic opportunities for jobs; shopping and mixed use; transportation by all modes, traffic calming, public transit, routes, shelters, parking; and built form, including relationships to public spaces and heritage resources. We now have dynamic tools that can depict these elements in real time and space to inform the dialogue beyond the dry and inaccessible language of traditional planning regulations.

Periodically, a paradigm shift leaves us with a legacy of unhelpful regulations or practices that hold us back. We are now in such a moment. To get the most out of what we already have we need to make creative use of surplus lands, vacant buildings, and underutilized rights-of-way, as the Bentway and the other examples in the chapter on the expansion of the commons demonstrated. But to tap this potential we must give ourselves permission by removing some self-imposed barriers in the form of unhelpful rules and procedures that prevent us from using our land resources more effectively. I have begun to call this process "subtractive urbanism."

It is all too easy, as new issues arise, to keep adding new layers of regulation, new agencies, new secretariats, rather than taking a hard look at the ones we already have. Paradoxically, in many cases we can accomplish more by just subtracting old strictures that are no longer useful and are getting in the way of creative solutions.

There are many examples of such beneficial subtraction. Berlin removed its wall and reunited the city. New York City unearthed one of its most successful public spaces by simply removing traffic on Broadway from 23rd Street to Columbus Circle, radically changing the character of midtown Manhattan. By subtracting cars, Bogotá's weekly ciclovías reclaimed over 120 kilometres of car-free streets, now used weekly by approximately two million people (about 30 percent of the population).

As we saw, just such an opportunity arose in Toronto in 1997 when Mayor Barbara Hall launched the Kings Initiative in Toronto by "deregulating"— relaxing planning and zoning requirements — on four hundred acres in two former industrial areas along King Street east and west of downtown. There were no extraordinary costs involved in the development of the new planning strategy in the Kings Initiative. Staff costs were absorbed into departmental budgets, and there were no consulting costs, as external experts provided pro bono advice. As development occurred, Community Improvement Plans provided a basis for staff to negotiate with property owners to achieve needed improvements to the public realm (e.g., street lighting, pedestrian crossings, sidewalks, boulevards, parks, and open spaces) as the areas were transformed from industrial to mixed-use neighbourhoods. All that was required to allow all of this to happen was to take an inhibiting set of regulations off the books.

In like manner, removing prohibitions on laneway housing and secondary suites in existing neighbourhoods increases the housing stock at no public cost. Park(ing) Day temporarily turns parking spaces into mini parks, removing prohibitions in Toronto on kids playing street hockey, providing needed play space. Removing unnecessary fees for the public's use of parks for events enhances their use. In other words, less becomes more, liberating city life through activities, plans, projects, and untapped resources with little expenditure.

There are many more areas where we could apply sunset provisions to arcane restrictions and unblock enormous potential for good things to happen in the GTHA. We currently have a similar opportunity to release an enormous latent potential for both housing and jobs through a relaxation of counterproductive policies which are inhibiting desirable forms of mixed use in many strategic areas where we are making major transit investments throughout the region.

This will involve unlocking much of the so-called Employment Lands. Unfortunately, our provincial and municipal policy frameworks have not quite caught up with the changing nature of work and the value of mixed use. There is a striking internal contradiction in the latest version of the provincial Growth Plan, "Places to Grow 2017," which prohibits living at many of the existing and proposed transit stations on the GO and proposed regional express rail (RER) network.

Here is the contradiction. On the one hand, Section 1.2.1 of the Growth Plan guides "how land is developed, resources are managed and protected," and public dollars are invested based on integrating principles such as "the achievement of complete communities that are designed to support healthy and active living and meet people's needs for daily living throughout an entire lifetime, prioritize intensification and higher densities to make efficient use of land and infrastructure and support transit viability … and support a range and mix of housing options, including second units and affordable housing, to serve all sizes, incomes, and ages of households."

On the other hand, in the same document, Section 2.2.5 isolates "employment" as a stand-alone category and makes no mention of mixed use, combining living and working, as a key driver of contemporary life.

In fact, it largely reverts to an earlier view of segregated land use planning through protected "Employment Lands" that specifically prohibit mixed use: "Municipalities will plan for all employment areas within settlement areas, with the exception of any prime employment areas, by: a) prohibiting residential uses and limiting other sensitive land uses that are not ancillary to the primary employment use."

The problem is that, not surprisingly, many of these designated Employment Lands hug the railways where they were once served by sidings. These former rail sidings are precisely where the new and existing transit lines and stations are located. While there is undoubtedly a need to "provide certainty for traditional industries, including resource-based sectors," the reality is that most forms of contemporary employment are entirely compatible with and thrive in integrated mixed-use communities.

But by protecting the areas surrounding GO stations for traditional forms of employment, the new forms of employment that gravitate to mixed-use areas, forming vibrant neighbourhoods, are discouraged with a doubly painful opportunity cost. There is now very little need or desire to build the stand-alone office parks typical of a previous era, and most significantly the opportunity is forgone to build thousands of units of housing throughout the region in locations where it would be most desirable, contributing to inherent distributed affordability. The default is often warehouse and logistics buildings, producing very few jobs in valuable locations that will increasingly be served by all-day GO and RER transit service with more frequent, but poorly utilized service.

Zeroing in on a couple of examples makes this problem even more obvious. The sixty-acre East Harbour site (formerly the Unilever soap factory) at the mouth of the Don River, a major gateway to the Port Lands, is a candidate for a major transit nexus with a new RER station and an extension of light rail linking Riverdale to the waterfront. It is also slated for redevelopment. But this former industrial site is designated as Employment Lands, which prohibits mixed use. Reflecting that prohibition, current plans call for one of the largest redevelopment projects in the region to offer over eleven million square feet of office space and zero residences. The closest international parallels, which were actually recently presented at an Urban

Land Institute gathering at the same Unilever site, are Canary Wharf in London and Hudson Yards in Manhattan. Both, of course, are intensively mixed-use developments, combining living and working for the reasons cited above. The contrast was striking.

In fact, what may be replicated on the Unilever site are the conditions Toronto experienced two generations ago when the major bank towers were being constructed at King and Bay in what was then conceived as a monolithic CBD (central business district). The homogeneous sterility of this area, empty after 5:00 p.m., led the City of Toronto to create a new Central Area Plan, which brought residential use into the core. This pioneering, made-in-Toronto mixed-use policy initiative (combined with the Kings described above) has brought in 240,000 residents, a population that is expected to double by 2041, the vast majority of whom get to work by walking, cycling, and using transit.

A more typical example of the conundrum in the GTHA can be found at St. Clair Avenue West and Old Weston Road, where a new RER station is being created, interfacing with light rail. Once more, for historical reasons relating to former industrial use, the majority of the lands surrounding this transit hub are designated Employment Lands. And once more, mixed use is largely prohibited despite landowners who would like to combine forces to leverage the transit investment with a combination of living and working in a compact, transit-oriented, walk-in form.

The claim that a province-wide one-size-fits-all Employment Lands policy is necessary to prevent encroachment by residential development is vastly overblown. It ignores the obvious need to distinguish among different situations related to employment, given that most employment is attracted to mixed-use areas. It also fails to recognize that we have the regulatory tools to achieve a desired balance of uses, as we demonstrated in the past with the Central Area Plan and in other situations where the market required some guidance. Jobs of the future are more than a desk or a workspace and a parking space. They should be part of a community — but we are standing in the way.

These contradictions arise from juggling one ball at a time. It is common practice elsewhere to require "Station Area Plans," requiring vibrant, sustainable communities with a diverse mix of land uses at various densities to be developed within a ten- to fifteen-minute walk from transit stations. We have myriad opportunities in the Greater Toronto and Hamilton Area to do this, as well, as we make this next round of hard-won investment in our expanded transit network. It's time to stop holding ourselves back through self-imposed policy restrictions and get on with adding needed housing and job opportunities well-served by transit by allowing employment to go where it wants to go throughout our rapidly growing, multi-centred region.

11

The Chance to Be Our Best Selves

Toronto, of course, does not exist in a vacuum. It is buffeted by big outside forces. Its course corrections reflect paradigm shifts in the general culture, as well as changing federal and provincial governments with differing urban agendas and differing policies, plans, and programs, and targeted investments. In addition to the more formal "planning" policies and frameworks imposed on the city by higher levels of government, institutions like the now defunct Ontario Municipal Board have also had a powerful influence in shaping Toronto. Likewise, "invisible hands" like MPAC (the provincial Municipal Property Assessment Corporation) have forced changes through the unintended consequences of market value assessment, a practice that is sometimes at odds with adopted planning policies.

To navigate these complex waters, political leadership is essential: to provide focus, interpret events, identify opportunities, set goals, and frame visions for collective action. These are moving targets — inevitably, social, economic, and technical changes will occur — and a continual resetting of priorities and reallocation of resources is necessary to achieve them. A key task of that political leadership is the mobilization of forces in all sectors in and out of city hall to deal with our major challenges. There is a need for longevity — always thinking beyond one administration to draw on and integrate what has already been achieved while pursuing new short-, medium-, and long-term initiatives. Our politicians have to inspire and lift our sights, articulating Toronto's vision for the future in a rapidly evolving context, dealing with hard truths and not pandering to counterproductive biases. The "Vision Thing" may seem overdone, but it is extremely important. It sets the stage for a proactive stance, anticipating change and getting ahead of the curve. Defining the terms of the city's relationship with the private sector will be essential as new resources are brought to the table.

We need to keep strenuously pursuing senior levels of government for reliable, long-term funding commitments even as we optimize our own resources. City regions are playing vital new roles in anchoring their nation-states; for Canada, investing in cities is perhaps the most important thing the country can do to ensure its future success and competitiveness on the world stage. Particular cities have distinguished themselves at critical times in their evolution by being able to rise to the challenge, using their ongoing efforts in city building (in the broadest sense of the word) to great strategic advantage. I am convinced that this is such a critical time for Toronto. Ready or not, the city now has a major voice on the world stage and many are watching how it handles the challenges and opportunities that have been thrust upon it.

An honest assessment would suggest that Toronto is succeeding spectacularly in some ways as it goes through a metamorphosis of extraordinary proportions, surpassing Chicago to become the fourth largest city in North America. This city has never been stronger or more dynamic. Public agencies like Waterfront Toronto and the public library system; institutions like our world-renowned universities, colleges, hospitals, and museums; organizations like CivicAction, Park People, Artscape, and the Centre for Social Innovation; our dynamic arts and culture sector in visual arts, theatre, music, and film; our tech and design sectors; our progressive developers (yes, there are some) are all thriving and winning praise and acknowledgement around the globe. As a result, the city is now finding itself consistently in the top tier of urban centres in various international ratings.

However, Toronto is experiencing major growing pains as it goes through this extraordinary transformation. The city has failed for decades to make the serious investments in public transit and hard and soft services that are urgently needed to accommodate growth. But what if addressing this gap becomes our opportunity to make the inevitable shift from an unsustainable way of life to a more sustainable one? What if this could be the driving force for the city to fully appreciate how everything is connected, that it is not about addressing a single issue — jobs, housing, mobility, climate change, or public health — but how it does everything. What if the city embraced the new paradigm for sustainable economic development that emphasizes quality of life and "place"? What if that big picture could be seen more clearly? What if there was a larger, more inclusive vision for the city?

For this vision to take root, Toronto will have to overcome the divides and wounds of amalgamation and become one city. It will need a broader, more inclusive vision that resonates with both downtowners and suburbanites. It will need bold initiatives that move into the realm of creative city building. Toronto desperately needs the resources to deal with infrastructure deficits and help make the shift to more sustainable (and economical) ways of living. Investment in the future is essential if Toronto is to meet the needs of a rapidly growing city with the most diverse population in the world. It needs to solidify the ties that bind its citizens and address growing disparities. Torontonians have to view the city as an increasingly seamless whole, not an uncomfortable collection of opposing "nations." To do this, an engaged civil society is needed, and a range of city builders must come forward to successfully create complete communities in both older and newer neighbourhoods, acknowledging that one size does not fit all. It is necessary to stop squirming over taxes, acknowledge the costs that must be paid for Toronto to become the city it aspires to be, and decide how to share that burden equitably.

Torontonians need to play chords, not single notes focusing on our shared quality of life, and avoid the race to the bottom that focuses on low wages and taxes. There are, in fact, immense savings to be realized when everything is connected, when strategies for jobs, housing, and mobility are intimately linked. Every chess piece we play contributes to the larger game, and single moves can address multiple problems.

Making the city a shared project and pooling scarce resources will provide greater benefits. Viewing individual decisions in the context of a larger plan will result in better, more informed judgments when challenges arise, such as what to do with the Gardiner Expressway or the island airport, how to accelerate investment in mobility alternatives, or how to accommodate intensification. We will see that it is possible to grow greener while getting denser and become more prosperous while getting less polarized. We will become a humane and equitable city, known not only for its remarkable ability to absorb people from around the globe but also for the opportunities it offers to all its citizens, not just a privileged few. We will restore a measure of civility to our public discourse, avoiding the knee-jerk rushes to judgment that reduce complex issues to sound bites. We will tap the extraordinary energy and resourcefulness of civil society and its intuitive understanding of what makes a great city, with the knowledge that "world-class" is not just about home runs but many singles, doubles, and triples as we make the shift together to a more sustainable and prosperous future.

It feels risky to write this kind of optimistic book in a moment of great turbulence. There may well be a "dark age ahead" as suggested by the title of Jane Jacobs's last book. Her point, in fact, was lest we do certain things it could happen, a view I share. So much is at stake and success is certainly not inevitable. The city, after all, is a never-finished human creation, formed and reformed by the choices of millions of relatively autonomous actors. We will need to tap the full potential of the city as the most extraordinary of human inventions for its ability to take on new challenges and tensions and work things out as new ideas emerge, new technologies arrive and are absorbed, and new people come on the scene, bringing fresh ideas and perceptions. It is the city that provides the political, professional, economic, social, and intellectual space for these interactions, reconciling many false dichotomies and divides.

Ultimately, this book is aspirational, and as much about advocacy, a call for action, as it is an accounting of examples of success. It is about a great promise that I believe is in the cards for a reborn Toronto. But the fulfillment of that promise depends on the choices we make. What comes next is up to us.

Afterword

It is a tall order, living up to this moment in our history.

In reflecting on and reading about the Toronto of the 1960s and '70s, I sometimes find myself envious of the malleability that existed in those years: the city's *contemporary* story was yet to be written; the authors were undetermined. As Ken Greenberg observes, it was a time when there were more unknowns than knowns, a time when a generation of city builders — conventional and not — were about to emerge to co-create that story.

I now see that malleability is directly connected to the agency that Torontonians feel. Seeing it as a place they can individually shape is a direct outcome of feeling *they are worthy and able* to take on stewardship of their neighbourhoods, communities, and collective interests. For residents, it can be daunting to get engaged; it's necessary to overcome the inertia that is generated by the average resident's feeling of ignorance about the seemingly complicated workings of civic systems. This inertia can be overcome because, as David Crombie famously said, "you don't need training to be a citizen." Something as simple as the story of our lived experience *is* our power, and sharing it is in itself an act of engagement.

So, how can residents ensure that each and every resident of the city leverages their immense power (and right) to influence civic outcomes?

The first part should be obvious: ensure that those who build the city represent the city. Torontonians want to look to their civic officials and see themselves, what they represent, how they carry themselves in the world. This involves more than the current head-counts of women and people of colour. Torontonians need to see their own unique diversity — their own unique civic intersectionality — represented in the city's institutions. This civic intersectionality could include being a person of colour, a Muslim, and a woman. It could also include having leaders who are renters, who live in multi-generational households, who are gender non-conforming, who perhaps don't have a post-secondary education but boast lived experience as their strongest credential.

So, the city and its population as a whole are complex, but so are the residents who make up that whole. In striving for fair representation, we need to regularly remind ourselves that all of our civic intersectionalities may have inherent contradictions in them: there are cycling advocates who own cars, renters who want to be homeowners, and urbanists who feel the need to "flee" the city on weekends. These contradictions are impossible to avoid, and they are okay. We need permission to be human.

What do we do with all of this? It should be clear that a simplified, generic form of fair representation is not enough. We need more stories, and more sophisticated stories, of what success can look like for those living in a city. Take housing, for example: we know that while there is momentum around alternative housing models such as co-housing, most people still see homeownership as a sign of social and economic achievement. A recent study showed that a majority of Canadian millennials still dream of owning the single-family home, and view renting as something to accept for a temporary period only, something that is more of a "holding pattern." This idea has been institutionalized in Toronto's planning and funding, often to the exclusion of other kinds of housing.

These stories we tell ourselves about success are what author Chimamanda Adichie calls "single stories" — incomplete tales generated by mainstream culture. While homeownership may be a hallmark of success, the story isn't that simple, *the story is incomplete*. A story about housing that focuses on homeownership omits so much: renters, those who live in co-ops, those who live in shared accommodation. The challenge to city builders — residents and government officials — is to find ways to create economic stability and emotional satisfaction for those who choose (or are forced because of economic necessity) to co-house, to live in co-ops, or to rent. New prototypes, pilots, and programs are needed, but in creating them we need to ensure that our attitudes, behaviours, and beliefs of what success looks like when we live in big cities accommodate all. This requires spending time with people, avoiding assumptions, and co-designing alongside residents from start to finish, to ensure what is created speaks to the wants, wishes, and needs of the whole community.

We need to accept Rosabeth Moss Kanter's law: "everything looks like failure in the middle … and it's that middle where the hard work happens." City building is a multi-generational exercise, and we, as residents, are partners in creating a work in progress. The acts of creation are varied. We need to celebrate and recognize that city building comes in gestures large and small — it's using piles of leaves and chalk lines to slow traffic at a residential intersection, and it's working with officials in our institutions to fight for fair and non-discriminatory policing policies for racialized individuals. We can't always see progress happening when we're in the middle of it — change can't always be measured against a plan — so, although it's important for the city to support major projects and programs, it's crucial that residents lend their energy and talent to creating and sustaining their own contributions to the city. Toronto benefits from a kaleidoscopic mix of city-building efforts; as a result, the city is able to tackle problems at the grassroots and the institutional levels simultaneously. It is an ongoing process, and the learning is bi-directional. There are big wins and brilliant, punctuated moments — the product of institutional planning — but most of the significant change is unplanned; it results from the amalgam of several "small" efforts that come together to create new norms. Evolution and, sometimes, revolution.

As Toronto continues its efforts to improve — by providing better public transit, for example — it is just beginning the process of addressing many other issues, and making efforts to narrow some of these deep urban divides. *Toronto Reborn* provides the necessary context for residents to meaningfully engage with this progress; it explains how a city that better fulfills the needs and lifestyles of its residents is within reach if residents commit to consistency, courage, and creativity. Throughout his career, Ken Greenberg has committed himself to working with others to create better cities — in Toronto and elsewhere — and in *Toronto Reborn* he gives city builders and residents a history of what has been achieved and a vision of what can be. He reminds us that the creation of a successful city happens when diverse groups of collaborators are unwavering in their commitment to fair and bold change. The story Ken shares with us is a hopeful one. It's a story of potential: what happens when our rich social and creative capital is matched and elevated by a built environment worthy of the incredible residents we have here.

If Toronto is getting all of this attention, if it really is at a precipice moment — a time of "rebirth" — with a global spotlight on it, Torontonians need to do right by their city and their fellow residents. Let's start listening. Let's make space for all. As Larry Keeley says, let's not only invent the new, but elegantly integrate and build on what exists. Let's be the most diverse in our thinking, our representation, in our approaches to progress, and let's be proud of our contribution to the multi-generational exercise.

Torontonians, and Canadians generally, have been extremely good followers, quick in adopting best practices. *Toronto Reborn* reminds us that, in recreating our cities, we have a real opportunity to be leaders, to create the best practice.

Zahra Ebrahim, 2019
Principal and founder of design think-tank archiTEXT

Acknowledgements

I want to thank all of those who have made it possible for me to conceive and write *Toronto Reborn*. My wife, Eti, has been my constant supporter and sounding board, sharing this journey with me at every step of the way. I feel an enormous debt to David Crombie and Zahra Ebrahim, who have so generously offered to write the foreword and afterword that bookend *Toronto Reborn*. Always in my ear, although deeply missed, has been Jane Jacobs, my friend, colleague, and mentor, whose wisdom about how cities really work has been my guiding light throughout. Judy and Wil Matthews, whose generosity in creating the Bentway and tenacity in making it a success, have been a constant source of inspiration to me; that story is really at the genesis of the impulse to tell this story of city rebirth. I am grateful to my editor at Dundurn, Dominic Farrell, and freelance editor Heather Bean, whose many insightful suggestions have helped me to tell this in ways that I hope are clear and understandable.

Along the way I have benefitted from the generous readers whose encouragement and suggestions for parts of this story have been of enormous help. The advice of my esteemed colleagues Anne Golden and Cherise Burda at the Ryerson City Building Institute has been invaluable. David Harvey from Park People, Julian Sleath from the Bentway, Scott James from the Wellington Place Neighbourhood Association, Councillor John

Filion from Willowdale, and Carolyn Woodland from the Toronto and Region Conservation Authority provided assistance by checking my facts for portions of the text that refer to places they know well. I want to also thank the City of Toronto Archives and many others for their help in locating appropriate before and after images to illustrate the text.

I could not have written about any of the transformative places in this book without the passion and dedication of the many talented Torontonians who played critical roles in making them happen. They are far too numerous to name, but in particular I want to acknowledge my valued colleagues Marc Ryan and Adam Nicklin at Public Work; Jake Tobin Garrett, who brilliantly managed the Public Space Incubator at Park People; Ilana Altman at the Bentway; Mitchell Cohen at Regent Park; Dean Richard Sommer at the Daniels Faculty; the many dedicated staff at the City of Toronto and Waterfront Toronto; and the crew at Sidewalk Labs who have embraced Toronto.

I have been privileged to work for and with many dedicated politicians who have played critical roles in guiding the city over the previous decades when the places I describe have come to life, including mayors David Crombie, John Sewell, Art Eggleton, David Miller, and Barbara Hall, and I want to in particular acknowledge city councillors Joe Cressy, Mike Layton, Kristyn Wong-Tam, and former city councillor and current Member of Parliament Adam Vaughan for their commitment to city building.

Finally, I am forever grateful for and humbled by the many thousands of Torontonians in all their myriad guises: citizens, entrepreneurs, designers, developers, volunteers, neighbourhood activists, and members of the city's remarkable array of civil society organizations. Their care and love for the city have contributed to making Toronto truly special.

Image Credits

Toronto Archives: 95 (top; Arthur Goss, photographer), 108 (top), 120 (top), 210 (top), 216 (top), insert page 4, insert page 6

Toronto Region Conservation Authority: 186 (top and bottom), insert page 5

Waterfront Toronto: 120 (bottom), insert page 7

Index

Book Credits

Acquiring Editor: Scott Fraser
Developmental Editor: Dominic Farrell
Project Editor: Jenny McWha
Copy Editor: Heather Bean
Proofreader: Ashley Hisson
Indexer: Sergey Lobachev

Designer: Laura Boyle
Cover Designer: Sophie Paas-Lang

Publicist: Elham Ali

dundurn.com   dundurnpress
@dundurnpress   dundurnpress
dundurnpress   info@dundurn.com

FIND US ON NETGALLEY & GOODREADS TOO!

 DUNDURN